date
city
publisher

WOMEN AND PRIESTHOOD:

Future Directions

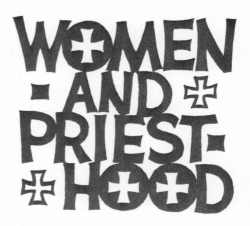

FUTURE DIRECTIONS

A Call to Dialogue
from the Faculty of
The Catholic Theological
Union at Chicago

edited by
Carroll Stuhlmueller, C.P.

foreword by
Carol Francis Jegen, B.V.M.

THE LITURGICAL PRESS
Collegeville, Minnesota

FOREWORD

The *Declaration on the Question of the Admission of Women to the Ministerial Priesthood*, published by the Sacred Congregation for the Doctrine of the Faith on October 15, 1976, has already elicited widespread reaction. This volume, by way of response to the *Declaration*, is a major contribution to the on-going discussion demanded by the viewpoints set forth in that document. Each essay presented here treats the question of woman and priesthood with admirable scholarship, carefully attuned to the multifaceted pastoral situations of today and tomorrow. At the same time, the historical roots of Catholic priesthood are examined afresh, including its Hebraic heritage with its genius for cultural interaction.

The faculty of Catholic Theological Union in Chicago who have authored this text are to be commended for their wisdom in probing the question of priesthood from such a variety of perspectives. The multidisciplinary approach of this study gives strong witness to the necessity of scholarship in breadth and in depth whenever the Church faces questions of such serious ministerial implications. This research into the mystery of Christian priesthood cannot help but be instrumental in freeing the Church from some of the ignorance and prejudice which has tragically marked her history with respect to women.

Here is a book courageously speaking the truth in love, in love for the whole Church in her searchings to make the joys and hopes, the griefs and anxieties of today her own. A spirit of honesty and compassion permeates these writings. May that same spirit permeate the reflection and the dialog this volume will engender.

Carol Frances Jegen, BVM
Mundelein College Chicago

CONTENTS

WOMEN AND PRIESTHOOD:

Future Directions

PART ONE

PRIESTHOOD, UNITY

AND

THE ORDINATION OF WOMEN

1

THE CALL TO DIALOG
WITHIN THE CHURCH

by

Carroll Stuhlmueller, C.P.

Under a mandate of Pope Paul VI, the Sacred Congregation for the Doctrine of the Faith squarely faced the issue of ordination of women.[1] They did so, moreover, in a style that called for further dialog with theologians and pastoral leaders. In the first section of this chapter we listen more closely to that call. We then discuss the authority or force of the *Declaration* and indicate how theological faculties and the local church can interact with it and thus seriously aid the unity and growth of the Church. A final section points out how a strong, integrated church is able to champion liberation movements like that for women and grant them a place within the priesthood.

This overview locates the chapters of this book within the pastoral ministry and religious leadership of the Church today. By means of vigorous, honest and loyal dialog, such as this book achieves, the ministry of the Church will reach out to areas most in need of support. The Church will then manifest an ever stronger credibility. Ministry and leadership together will both communicate a message of hope that is believable and attractive; this word will go out particularly to church members, responsive to injustice and pain, gifted with vision and articulate speech, impatient to do something.

Jesus agonized with these people, potential leaders straining at the leash to run with the message:

> I have come to light a fire on the earth. How I wish the blaze were ignited! I have a baptism to receive. What anguish I feel till it is over! Do you think that I have come to establish peace on the earth? (Luke 12:49-51a)

Fire is the prophet Jeremiah's word for the divine summons within his conscience.

> I say to myself, I will not mention him,
>   I will speak in his name no more.
> But then it becomes like fire burning in my heart,
>   imprisoned in my bones;
> I grow weary holding it in,
>   I cannot endure it. (Jer 20:9)

Fire inspires the prophets, Jeremiah and Jesus. As they run across the mountains, their footprints are beautiful to behold and the sound of their voice resounds across the earth:

> How beautiful. . . !
> Announcing peace, bearing good news,
>   announcing salvation, and saying to Zion,
> "Your God is King!" (Isaiah 52:7)

Fire also becomes a warning and a message of doom. The transition from hope to doom cannot be determined ahead of time. Such at least was the conviction of the prophet Malachi. We must listen to him, the last of the "twelve" whose voice speaks again in John the Baptist, the last of all the prophets before Jesus:

> And *suddenly* there will come to the temple
>   the Lord whom you seek, . . .
> But who will endure the day of his coming?
>   And who can stand when he appears?
> For he is like the refiner's fire,
>   or like the fuller's lye. (Mal 3:1-2)

This messenger of fire, according to Matthew's gospel, is John the Baptist, from whose "time until now the kingdom of God has suffered violence, and the violent take it by force" (Matt 11:12). In Luke's gospel John the Baptist passes the torch to Jesus, who (John declares) "will baptize you in the Holy Spirit and in fire. His winnowing-fan is in his hand to clear the threshing floor and gather the wheat into his granary; but the chaff he will burn in unquenchable fire" (Luke 3:16-17).

Lest the fiery hopes within many pure hearts erupt with anger and doom, we write this book.

I

The Declaration on the Question of the Admission of Women to the Ministerial Priesthood — such is the full title of the Roman document — not only calls for theological and pastoral dialog, but it was also prepared by scholars who had read widely on the subject and seriously interacted with this mass of material. Earlier publications, therefore, usually undertaken on the private initiative of theologians, contributed significantly to the document, directly or indirectly, positively or negatively. The *Declaration* states in its introductory section that "the various arguments capable of clarifying this important problem have been submitted to a critical examination." Furthermore, in its own *Commentary* the Sacred Congregation refers to "doctoral theses, articles in reviews, even pamphlets, propounding or refuting in turn the biblical, historical and canonical data and appealing to the human sciences of sociology, psychology and the history of institutions and customs."[2] Without this unofficial and at times undesired inquiry by biblical or systematic theologians, by Church historians and canon lawyers, this official document could not have been written. What was issued from Rome, furthermore, seems to reach out for further dialog.

By means of an unofficial *Commentary*, which was released in the United States along with the official *Declaration*, the Sacred Congregation has carried the discussion forward into the *theological* arena.[3] Rome, furthermore, extended the conversation to *popular* circles by printing responses to the *Declaration* in *L'Osservatore Romano* (English edition).[4]

Admittedly the popular articles in *L'Osservatore Romano* as well as the more scholarly discussion in the *Commentary* support the *Declaration* and respond only in a laudatory way. Nonetheless, they did enlarge the discussion beyond the Roman *Declaration* and therefore invite further response on both the scholarly and the popular, pastoral levels. This book continues the dialog, not just with the *Declaration*, but with the vast and complicated topic of priesthood in its evolving forms through the ages and in its new directions into the future.

As Alcuin Coyle points out in the concluding chapter, the question of ordaining women involves the relationship of lay ministers with others in liturgical and sacramental offices. It evokes problems and seeks clarification across all the sacred sciences: Bible and the early Fathers of the Church, History, Systematic and Pastoral Theology, Church Law and Liturgy. It looks for help in later Jewish tradition and psychodynamic research. Because the question of women priests has generated the strongest interest in the United States, we are faced with the whole range of interactions between local cultures and secular forms of leadership on the one hand and Church life and its sacred orders on the other. Ordination of women, then, forces a reassessment of priesthood across the whole drawing board.

No doubt, the question has stirred extraordinary interest. When the *Declaration* was first released in early 1977, an impromptu meeting was called at The Divinity School of the University of Chicago, and spontaneously there gathered — to everyone's surprise — a group of prominent professors and graduate students. In volunteering to cooperate on this book, faculty members of the Catholic Theological Union at Chicago realized that top priority was due to this topic. Here would be one, certain way to establish priesthood on a sound and credible base for the apostolate of this century. Training for priesthood would interact vigorously with theology, culture and prophetic issues today.

The faculty of the Catholic Theological Union closely examine the *Declaration* from the Sacred Congregation for the Doctrine of the Faith. At times they challenge its reasons or its conclusions. They do so loyally and zealously within the Roman Catholic Church. They take the *Declaration* and the authority of the Church that seriously. They seek to keep open a hot-line between the hierarchical magisterium on the one hand and the theological-pastoral magisterium on the other. Then on all levels of the Church everyone can find a fair hearing, a careful assessment and a solid base for their community of faith. Whether there be cries against injustice or a longing for effective leadership, these godly expectations will be heard with a full and credible response. The fire within the heart will send forth messengers of hope, not doom.

By replying in the negative, the Sacred Congregation certainly slowed down the movement for the admission of women to the ministerial priesthood. As Dismas Bonner explains in chapter five of this book, this *Declaration* stops short the evolution of any custom contrary to law. Yet, in one of the most tightly reasoned presentations of the book, Gilbert Ostdiek concludes that "change and adaptation are a normative part of a normative tradition." Only then can "the Church . . . remain faithful to the will of the Lord and his Spirit in a major new socio-cultural situation." With three important examples Ostdiek shows that "such a course of action is not without precedent in the history of the Church." Such change can generate tension and even conflict. Yet, these troublesome or at least non-harmonious encounters, according to Sebastian MacDonald in chapter nine, are normally the occasion to purify and enrich, to slough off and to advance, and thus to mediate a new revelation of the Lord's will in our contemporary age.

Even if the *Declaration* has put the brakes upon the movement for women priests — at least, canonical breaks — it has focused the discussion very clearly. It should also be noted that by employing a somewhat low profile in the range of Roman authority and by immediately calling for further theological debate through the issuance of a *Commentary*, the Sacred Congregation for the Doctrine of the Faith has encouraged and strengthened the discussion. We will now look more closely at the authority of this document, so as to determine the proper attitude expected of Catholics. By seeing this issue more clearly, non-Catholics will also be aided in the ecumenical dialog.

II

The Holy See issues statements according to a scale of authority and decisiveness, all the way up to that extremely rare infallible pronouncement, made personally by the Pope or collegially by an ecumenical council. The Vatican's reply on the ordination of women was invested with a rather low degree of authority. From the careful canonical study of Dismas Bonner in chapter five of this book, we learn that technically a "declaration" is defined as " 'an interpretation of existing law or facts, or a reply to a contested point of law.' . . . There is no question of a new law. . . . [nor] should it be seen as the final word which . . . closes off all further discussion." In chapter six Gilbert Ostdiek investigates the authority of the *Declaration* in relation to the development of Church tradition. He establishes the need of tradition to adapt in order to survive.

Right now, however, we turn attention to another side of this document's authority, that gleaned from what I consider its *internal indecisiveness* as well as from a comparison with the earlier decrees of the Pontifical Biblical Commission.

The internal indecisiveness is manifested, first of all, by the honest admission that "we are dealing with a debate which classical theology scarcely touched upon." In its *Commentary* the Congregation openly concedes that "the question has been complicated by the fact that . . . arguments adduced in the past in favour of the traditional teaching are scarcely defensible today." Again, according to the *Declaration*, "Scholastic doctors . . . often present arguments on this point that modern thought would have difficulty in admitting or would even rightly reject" (section I). The Sacred Congregation acknowledges that its own reasons "will become apparent in the long run," thereby implying that the advocates of the opposite position (that women can be ordained priests) even with intellectual sincerity will not see at once the cogency and clinching value of the *Declaration*'s position.

The *Declaration* concludes that the biblical argument requires more study. It admits that "a purely historical exegesis of the texts cannot suffice." Bible texts, taken individually are inconclusive. Again in the words of the *Declaration* we arrive through Scripture only at "a number of convergent indications" (section III). Yet, the Sacred Congregation bases its case primarily upon the "Permanent Value of the Attitude of Jesus and the Apostles" (the title to section IV),[5] an attitude which can be known only through Scripture.

Perhaps, the Sacred Congregation realized the weakness of the biblical argument. It ends the investigation of Tradition[6] and Bible by stating:

In the final analysis it is the Church, through the voice of her Magisterium, that, in these various domains, decides what can change and what remain immutable. When she judges that she cannot accept certain changes, it is because she knows that she is bound by Christ's manner of action. (section IV)

Because the Scriptures are not clear on this point, the document is dealing with an elusive intuition of the Church. Even though "Christ's manner of acting" is not all that clear, still the Church "knows that she is bound by" it. Intuitions such as this produce saints and mystics; they induce exceptionally fine, courageous perceptions. Geniuses are born of such conditions. Intuitions can also be confused with prejudice and lead to irrational and destructive postures. In chapter four Carolyn Osiek analyzes some of the untested intuitions of the Fathers; in chapter six Gilbert Ostdiek investigates Church traditions across a larger sweep of history. In each case there were definite instances where the *sensus ecclesiae* had to be challenged, purified, adapted and even at times radically changed. As we saw a few paragraphs earlier in this chapter, the Sacred Congregation itself stated "that modern thought would have difficulty in admitting or would even rightly reject" arguments from the Church Fathers and Scholastic doctors "on this point."

Along with the unsettled or inconclusive state of the biblical and patristic arguments — what the *Declaration* identifies as "the Church's norm and the basis thereof" (section V) — the Roman document manifests its internal weakness in still another way. It seems to echo, shall we say, the voice of a strong minority position within its own ranks. At key places in its presentation, the document inserts weak or qualifying phrases, not normally found in papal documents. We quote a few of these with italics added:

> The Sacred Congregation . . . does not *consider* herself authorized to admit women to priestly ordination.'' (introduction)[7] The Sacred Congregation deems it *opportune at the present juncture* to explain the position . . . (Introduction)[8]
> The Catholic Church has never *felt* . . . (section I)[9]
> The Magisterium has not *felt* . . . (section I)[10]
> It is true that these facts do *not* make the matter *immediately obvious* . . . (section II)[11]
> attitude of Jesus and of the Apostles, which has been *considered* as normative . . . (section IV)[12]
> This norm . . . is *considered* to conform to God's plan for his Church. (end of section IV)[13]
> It is *not* a question here of bringing forward a *demonstrative* argument, but of *clarifying* this teaching by the analogy of faith. (section V)[14]

Someone secure in their position normally employs a direct demonstrative style, not these qualifying, and in my judgment diluting modifications. The door is left a bit open so that in the future it can swing in the other direction. For instance: "In 1977 the Church did not *consider* herself authorized, but now she does!" Moreover, in any language, words like "feel" and "opportune" and "not immediately obvious" do not cut as clean a message as the unequivocal statement of fact. The phrases occur too often to be accidental or insignificant. They are found, moreover, almost exclusively in the Introduction plus sections one to four, where "the Church's norm and the basis thereof" are established. I conclude to an obvious hesitancy on the part of the Sacred Congregation to put itself definitively on the line.

We are reminded of an important qualification introduced into a statement of Pope Pius XII on polygenism (more than one set of parents at the origin of the human race). In the encyclical letter, *Humani Generis* (12 August 1950), he concluded that "in no way is it apparent how this position can be harmonized with what is proposed in the fonts of revealed truth and with the positions of the Church's magisterium."[16] It has been pointed out that Pius XII left open the possibility that it could later become apparent how polygenism could be compatible with revelation.[17]

We can be further assisted in forming our response to the *Declaration* of the Sacred Congregation for the Doctrine of the Faith about women ordination by turning our attention to the earlier decrees of the Pontifical Biblical Commission, particularly to those issued under Pope St. Pius X. These decrees possessed the same authority as that of a *motu proprio*, *i.e.*, a change of legislation introduced by the Pope's own initiative.[18]

The decrees about the Mosaic authorship of the Pentateuch are a good example. Although one decree allows the use of sources, it was Moses who selected what was to be incorporated into the written work. If secretaries took dictation, still "the work thus produced [was] approved by Moses as the principal and inspired author, [and] was made public under his name." Furthermore, the Mosaic authenticity must be maintained, because of

> the very many evidences . . . contained in both Testaments, taken collectively, the persistent agreement of the Jewish people, the constant tradition of the Church, and internal arguments derived from the text itself . . .

For these reasons the Biblical Commission would not permit that "these books . . . have been composed from sources for the part posterior to the time of Moses."[19]

These decrees are no longer enforced, but it was a long difficult path from the stringent demands of Pius X to the recognition of calm scholarly pursuits under Pius XII[20] and Paul VI.[21] Because of the repressive measures between 1907 and 1943, Catholic biblical studies produced very little solid work, except for the achievements of the more distant Ecole Biblique et Archéologique Française de Jérusalem. This writer still remembers a remark of Cardinal Augustin Bea, spoken while he was still a professor at the Pontifical Biblical Institute, Rome (1951–52). He regretted the excessively stern and at times arbitrary measures taken against biblical scholars in the preceding decades, at that very time when scriptural studies were advancing by leaps and bounds outside the Catholic Church, due among other reasons to extraordinary archeological discoveries in the ancient Near East.

Pope Pius XII released the *Divino Afflante Spiritu* on October 30, 1943. Almost at once Catholic biblical studies began to roll across the world like a stunning avalanche. Another twenty to thirty years were required to absorb and integrate these scholarly conclusions within the pastoral ministry of the Church. Within these years, however, the catechetical work was frequently in disarray and other people with their priests and teachers were shocked, dismayed, disillusioned and even neutralized in their faith.

This book seeks to keep the lines of dialog open between Church authorities, the scholarly world and the pastoral ministry on the question of women ordination and on the reform of seminary training. Otherwise, all sides will withdraw to separate, fortified quarters, attack one another because neither side adequately understands the other and at best remains suspicious of the other group. We must not repeat the tragedy of 1907 to 1943 in biblical studies. For this reason we must applaud the courageous statement of Bishop Joseph H. Hogan of Rochester, New York.[22]

III

The dialog is not simply one between the hierarchical magisterium and that of the theologians. The pastoral scene must be kept ever in mind, particularly on the question of priesthood. This dimension involves the local church and its contribution to the Church universal. The *Declaration* on the ordination of women and its accompanying *Commentary* seem to have the American pastoral scene particularly in mind, if one is to judge from the allusions and footnotes. Undoubtedly, the issue of women ordination has evolved most rapidly in the USA. That fact, however, should not reduce it to a local issue, as the entire world is awakening to the minority plight of women and to the injustice inflicted upon them.

Other theological issues as religious liberty evolved most vigorously in the USA. The theology and pastoral stance of the Church has benefited immensely throughout the world from the American debate on conscience and liberty. That point is scored very effectively by Gilbert Ostdiek in chapter six, section IV, of this book.

The relation of women to local cultures and politics varies greatly from country to country, even at times in the USA from state to state. The question of women ordination is integrally affected by these variations. The pastoral implementation, therefore, will vary greatly from place to place. Even were the theological question settled, the degree of woman's participation in ministry and ordination will range across the dial from full and intense as far down as minimal and preparatory.

The authors of this book are privileged to share in the rich resources of the mission program of the Catholic Theological Union. Almost one-fourth of the students are slated for apostolic work outside of U.S.A. and fourteen different nationalities are studying or teaching at the school. We single out particularly the important contribution made to the faculty and to this book by Rev. Dr. Claude Marie Barbour, Assistant Professor of World Mission, an ordained minister in the United Presbyterian Church, U.S.A., and formerly a missionary in Africa. We can thus appreciate better how diversified and multi-faceted is this question across the world and among all Christian Churches.

This book carefully scans biblical and church history and shows how religious leadership from century to century manifested an exceptional sensitivity to local culture. In chapter two the close interaction between secular and sacred forms of government is traced in the Old Testament period.[23] Throughout chapter three Robert J. Karris brings to light the fluctuating and highly developmental stages of religious office in New Testament times.[24] Carolyn Osiek, in chapter four, points out the serious regression of women from sacred office and religious ministries during the patristic period. Other chapters by Dismas Bonner and Gilbert Ostdiek disentangle the confusing threads of tradition within Church law and tradition. This same delicate interaction with history is clearly proposed by Rabbi Hayim Goren Perelmuter who describes the religious leadership by women in the three principal forms of Judaism — Orthodox, Conservative and Reform. As a result of these historical studies, we detect a continuous line of tradition, but this line becomes sharper or more dull. It collapses and it rises at different moments and in various places. It follows the geography and chronology of human life, as it extends today across our world.

"Our present age," as the *Declaration* states in its opening sentence, is characterized by "the part that women are now taking in public life." These words are a direct quotation from good Pope John XXIII in his encyclical letter, *Pacem in Terris*, of April 11, 1963. What impact this contemporary development will have upon the theology of priesthood is the task to which this book is dedicated. This investigation answers the call to dialog from the Sacred Congregation for the Doctrine of the Faith and engages theological disciplines and pastoral works.

The task reaches into our seminaries and theological schools as well as into the apostolic teams of parishes, hospitals, schools and all church activities. Alcuin Coyle clarifies these lines of work and competence in the final chapter of this book. He points out how the role of lay leaders needs to be sharpened and intensified, their theological education pursued, their status more clearly defined. In this way many secular activities, absorbed within priesthood, will be reclaimed by lay people. We will then be able to distinguish where women and men most properly belong in Church responsibility and ordained priesthood.

All the while women are following graduate courses in theology, which lead to the degrees of Master of Divinity (M.Div.) or Master of Theological Studies (M.T.S.). Both programs are pastoral in scope and in training. How these women feel and where they want to go — into apostolic work or also into ordained priesthood — these are some of the questions put to them by Dennis J. Geaney in preparing chapter eleven of this book.

All this educational and pastoral activity, by men and women, ordained and non-ordained, singly and in teams, is going on within the Church, particularly in USA and Canada. The situation hums with high voltage potential. It can explode in frustration, it can move quickly in false directions, it can blossom into a new Pentecost of apostolic zeal and vocational enthusiasm. It could be the second spring for religious communities of women. Only by respecting it, championing it, dialoging with it, theologizing about it, taking the risk of new forms of education and ministry in serious academic settings as well as in lively and creative pastoral centers — only thus will the prophetic fire announce hope and salvation rather than explode under pressure with doom! The call to dialog, heard within prophetic times like our own, summons us to excitement within our Church.

IV

Priesthood means nothing if it does not call us to serve within the Church. Roman Catholic priesthood makes the most stringent demands of working and dialoging with close, loyal ties to Church structure, tradition and ministry, because of the primary role given to Eucharistic piety and the sacrament of reconciliation. Eucharist symbolizes unity and charity. Reconciliation, in the new Sacramentary, offers "the forgiveness of sins through the ministry of the Church." Frankly, therefore, it makes no sense to extend the priesthood at the cost of Church unity. We must now pursue this question of Church unity, lest the call to dialog degenerate violently into schism or passively into a menial bond of yes-people, unworthy of Jesus' disciples.

Eucharistic churches have always borne the mark of unity. Mainline Christian denominations like Roman Catholicism, the Orthodox Church, the Anglican or Episcopal Church, the Lutheran Church, the Calvinist Church particularly of Switzerland and France, to the extent that they give a high priory to eucharistic piety, also manifest a rather conspicuous unity. In fact, this mark is notably evident in Roman Catholicism where the Blessed Sacrament commanded a central place on the main altar and by reason of this fact had to be integrated into all forms of liturgical and popular piety.[25] It is interesting to note that the dislocation of the Blessed Sacrament from the main altar is also accompanied with increased disunity in the Church.

Bible churches, on the contrary, which manifest little or no Eucharistic devotion and structure their services around the prayerful study of the Bible, tend to divide and sub-divide and to begin anew all over again. At first, it would seem that the centrifugal tendency to flee from the center and break apart would not characterize Bible churches. It should be so obvious what the Bible means and how everyone can agree. Yet, once a body like the Lutheran Church, Missouri Synod, moved attention away from its liturgical or eucharistic assembly and sought its center of unity in biblical interpretation, it was racked with divisive agony.

Eucharistic churches maintain their unity in ways less obvious than the evident sense of a biblical passage. For their part they remain in close accord with a religion of faith, where

> We do not fix our gaze on what is seen but on what is unseen. What is seen is transitory; what is unseen lasts forever. (2 Cor 4:18)

"What is unseen" must be approached and communicated symbolically. As will be explained in chapter two, section III of this book, symbols are more important for what they conceal than for what they manifest. Like the tip of an iceberg, symbols announce a hidden depth of strength, far more mammoth and meaningful than what appears on the surface. Submerged beneath the visible form of eucharistic symbol is the whole, multiple, yet finely honed complex of the Body of the Lord (*cf.*, Eph 4:16; 1 Cor 12). This is the Christ, symbolized and actualized by the priest who offers the Eucharist according to the explanation of Ralph Keifer in chapter seven of this call to dialog. The eucharistic symbol summons us to contemplate at once, in unity, Christ the Church and Christ the Priest, the full reality of the baptized community of Gal 3:18. Robert J. Karris, in chapter two, correctly orientates this text of St. Paul within the baptism ritual of the very early church.

This one body of Christ, symbolized by the one food and one cup of the Eucharist, is *"all of you, . . .* baptized into Christ, . . . clothed . . . with him . . . [no longer] male or female" (Gal 3:18). This combined presence of the masculine and feminine in Jesus, in each of us individually as well as in all of us together, the mystical Christ, is explored in its psychodynamic dimensions by Thomas More Newbold, chapter ten.

The nature of masculine and feminine forces in individual personalities as well as in society as a whole has evolved slowly, delicately yet surely and dramatically over the centuries. Sometimes it seems that each day has packed into itself the developments of a century, so surprising can be the series of changes in certain ages like our own. Thomas More Newbold has unraveled some of these complex developments in his study of masculine and feminine symbolism. All of this life, mysterious in its natural, not to say its supernatural dynamism, is absorbed into Christ, in whom and through whom all stand created and continue in existence (Col 1:15-20).

Such is the risen Christ in the outreach of his personal love and attention, his sympathy and support, his understanding and inspiring direction. *Such too is the Christ, the Church.* As "the whole body grows, and with the proper functioning of the members joined firmly together by each supporting ligament, [it] *builds itself up* in love" (Eph 4:16). The form of the Greek verb here projects the action into the living "body," the Church which continues to "build up" and mature through the centuries.[26]

Such too ought to be Christ the priest, symbolizing this continuous life of the Church, his body as it dies and rises, as it develops and grows, as it faces conflict and masters it by charity. This priestly life of the entire body of Christ reaches its supreme moment symbolically in the Eucharist, realistically in the death and martyrdom of its members. All of these details drawn from the mystery of Christ call for a symbol of union in Eucharist and in priesthood which transcends physical sexuality and combines the masculine and feminine forces in each of us. Just as the symbol of bread and wine is free of sexual connotations and so is able to embrace the wide family of men and women around one table, so should the symbolic representation of Christ the priest reach out to include men and women.

Under the guidance of the Spirit, the Church in solemn assembly arrived at a decision, seemingly simple and direct yet complex and overwhelming in its consequences. Vatican II decided to unite closely priest and congregation in liturgical celebration by permitting the vernacular language and by turning the altar around. At once the human qualities of the priest were accentuated more than ever before, not as someone of the male sex, but as a person capable of leading prayer, preaching the gospel and centering devotion through ritual acts. In this setting it became clear almost at once that what the priest says or does can be accomplished as well, sometimes much better, by a lay person, a married person, whether male or female. In order to unite the congregation, the priest must have refined the human qualities necessary for prayer and sacrament. It would be highly improper if the sexual differentiation of the priest became a focal point of concern.

The movement of the congregation towards the sanctuary and sometimes into it as lectors, singers and distributors of Holy Communion is not an attempt to dislodge the parish priest. The ordination of women need not follow the simplistic path of taking over the position of the priest, donning his vestments and following the rubrics of his sacramentary. To demand or request entrance in this way implies that women can perform as well as men or better, and that they have as much a right to it as men. The validity of these reasons is not our concern. Rather, we ask if there is not a better way to see women in the future directions of priesthood.

In accord with the accepted Catholic position that one must be called to priesthood by the Church through its leaders,[27] women should be considered for priesthood: 1) when they have proven themselves successful and acceptable in the pastoral ministry; and 2) when the power of anointing, absolving and celebrating the Eucharist would evidently make their ministry all the more effective. These two conditions would prevent schism or outrage, for it would restrict the priestly role of women to places and ministries where they have already been affirmed and appreciated. This suggestion is not removing other offices, even that of bishop and pope, theologically out of bounds for women; rather, it is offered on the solid principle that people *be called* to priesthood to further the unity and holiness of the Church.

There is another serious reason for going this route, again in the name of Roman Catholic tradition. All pastoral offices should be closely associated with the Eucharist. If not, then a style of piety less Eucharistic and even more Protestant in tone and emphasis, will become prominent in the Catholic Church. In no way denigrating Protestant spirituality, still the entire Christian community of churches will suffer if Eucharistic piety and its concomitant charism of unity are eclipsed.

Stated as bluntly as possible, the Catholic Church may have to choose between the tradition of an exclusively male priesthood *or* the tradition of a strong Eucharistic-centered piety. As the pastoral ministry is being undertaken ever more fully by women, then to refuse priesthood will necessarily induce non-Eucharistic styles of prayer service, non-priestly forms of reconciliation and anointing.

V

The prominence which women have acquired in pastoral ministry — in the hospital and rest home, on the university and college campus, in the prison and detention center, in adult education and in the office of peace and justice, to name a few — shows a transition frequently enough found in the Bible and for that reason in life generally. This development carries an inner rhythm towards liturgical celebration and for us in the Catholic Church towards Eucharist and priesthood.

The stages can be marked: *first*, *from* neglect or destitution *to* a form of liberation; *second*, *from* new experimental styles *to* proven ways of performing; and *third*, *from* the set and acceptable styles *to* their "ordination" or fixed role within the community or church. The first of these stages is almost always characterized by conflict and pain; the second, by celebration and experimentation; the third, by peace and security. The first stage can be compared with youth and adolescence; the second, with early adult life; the third, with middle age. When we answer the call to dialog about women in the future directions of priesthood, we seek to know if the pastoral work of women has been proven in many experimental areas and has been received with genuine celebration by the community, so that it can proceed to the third stage of "ordination" into a peaceful, secure ministry.

Many biblical examples come forward to exemplify this three-prong development *from* liberation, *to* celebration, *to* canonical status.

Israel's exodus out of Egypt began as a desperate and courageous act to free Hebrew slaves from Egyptian oppression. Faith pulsed at the heart of this liberation and signaled its success. Liturgy kept the wonder alive and summoned later generations to faith.

As the rabbis tell the story, Moses had led the people to the bank of the Red Sea and ordered them to proceed into it! The waters, Moses assured them, would open up before them. The people froze on the spot, trapped, they thought, between the churning sea and Pharaoh's chariots roaring down on them from the distant hills. Then one person broke rank, plunged into the sea and immediately the waters divided, as Moses promised. All the people followed and marched to freedom. Stage One of Liberation was completed. Once they arrived on the east bank and the Red Sea closed the path between them and Pharaoh's chariots, the people forgot the wonder and began to complain about the heat, the brackish water and all their problems. At that moment, Moses' sister Miriam stood up and intoned a hymn of praise (Exod 15:20-21). All the people joined to celebrate, and Stage Two was underway. Soon not only the song of Miriam but the entire episode became a standard part of Hebrew liturgy and the Bible, to finalize Stage Three.

Another example from the New Testament evokes the memory of this first exodus. In fact, the passion and death of Jesus is called his "exodus" in Luke 9:31, "Moses and Elijah . . . appeared in glory and spoke of his passage [in Greek, *exodus*], which he was about to fulfill in Jerusalem." This tragic destruction of Jesus' life turned into a passage to glory through his resurrection. Stage Two begins at once as the disciples of Jesus explain what happened, justify it from the Scriptures, celebrate it with song and ceremony, and compose oral and written accounts. In the Third Stage the four evangelists draw from all these experiences and narratives, liturgies and instructions to compose their gospels.[28] The Passion of Jesus now becomes a canonical source of faith and inspiration, of liturgy and prayer.

Before applying this model of liberation-celebration-canonical status to the ordination of women priests, we want to associate it with the Eucharist. The New Testament offers three major symbols or settings for the Eucharist, each in some way associated with Jesus' death and resurrection. The first series of texts place the Eucharist in the wilderness where Jesus multiplies bread and fish, liberating the people from hunger so that they can continue on their way "home" (John 6; Luke 9:10-17). Particularly in John's gospel, the episode includes a rejection of Jesus by the people and a harbinger of his death. Another set of passages situates the Eucharist in private homes where a small group of poor, isolated and even persecuted Christians gather to break bread (Acts 2:42-47; 4:32-37). What they celebrate had not yet been fully standardized. Finally, a third cycle of texts associates the Eucharist with a large community of believers (1 Cor 11:17-24), in a church or purified temple (John 2:13-25), separated from Judaism (Epistle to the Hebrews), with extended sermons (John ch 13-17).

These Eucharistic models can be further enriched if each is contemplated in its Old Testament background: exodus, Jerusalem temple and prophetic purification; of Jerusalem destroyed, rebuilt and seen in glorious vision; of each major tradition of law, prophets and wisdom, converging in the mystical banquet (Exod ch 24; Is 25:6; Ps 22; Prov ch 9).

The call for women to participate in the future directions of Roman Catholic priesthood is heard within these transitional steps of biblical people. Women, in the conscience of this writer, have not yet been fully liberated in society at large or in the church; too many of them, in some instances all of them, are still in Egypt! At the same time women have passed into the second stage of experimentation and celebration. Like Moses' sister Miriam they are summoning the community to sing and praise God, through the many effective forms of the apostolate enumerated at the beginning of this fifth section.

Many hospitals, universities, adult groups, prisons and now more and more parishes would either be inadequately staffed or be without any Catholic minister, were women to withdraw from the service. In these and other instances women are no longer experimenting and learning; they are teaching priests and seminarians! The time has come, according to many biblical examples, for the Church to "ordain" this ministry fully and equally with priesthood. Otherwise, the woman's voice and experience can go only so far and no further, and from then on it is subject to an independent judgment of the male Magisterium. At this latter point woman's voice remains only consultative and outside the decision-making process. Furthermore, to refuse ordination can result in a growing form of Protestant, non-Eucharistic piety within Catholicism.

Another danger, too serious to leave unmentioned, lurks around the corner. When liturgy directly or indirectly sanctions injustice against women and the privileged status of men, the temple will be cleansed by the prophetic anger of Jesus, by the tongue-lash of Micah and Jeremiah. God twice destroyed the sacred temple to save the people.

God, through women, may be calling us back to the wilderness celebration of the Eucharist, where the homeless and hungry gather for strength to continue living. Women, in their inconspicuous and unadorned forms of the apostolate, in the simplicity and directness of their approach to the poor, the sick and the imprisoned, may be God's instrument, showing us the footprints of Jesus, "beautiful on the mountains"!

Is now the moment to grant "canonical status" and to ordain what has proven itself and been celebrated gratefully within the Church? Is tomorrow too late to save Jerusalem?

Conclusions

The question of the ordination of women calls us to dialog about the future directions of priesthood.

The Sacred Congregation for the Doctrine of the Faith requests dialog, not only by presenting its reply with a rather low profile of papal authority, but also by the internal indecisiveness of its language. Any statement from a Vatican congregation deserves serious, loyal attention, which this book certainly manifests. For this reason the *Declaration* is printed towards the end of the book along with the unofficial report of the Pontifical Biblical commission.

If the writers within this interdisciplinary study interact vigorously and even negatively at times with the *Declaration*, they seek to preserve a hot-line of communication between Church authority, theologians and pastoral workers. Only thus will the hierarchical Magisterium retain credibility on the world scene.

We hope to have learned a lesson from the regrettable effects of the decrees of the Pontifical Biblical Commission between 1905 and 1943. Not only are they embarrassing, but their stern implementation erased almost all Catholic biblical research for some forty, crucial years. Only with the magna carta of the *Divino Afflante Spiritu* (October 30, 1943) did Catholic scholarship surface again and then it shook the pastoral scene with surprise, pain and amazement. Too quickly was it necessary to catch up with too much in Bible research.

The ordination of women opens up a dialog across the whole spectrum of lay and sacramental leadership, of theological training and pastoral response. This book, in fact, is organized in such a way that its text is easily readable by anyone seriously interested in the question of women priests. The footnotes are relegated to the end, so as not to overtax and discourage the general reader. These notes are intended to foster dialog with scholars.

Most of all, we must ponder the effects upon the Catholic Church if women continue to advance and expand their ministry, without access to the priestly power of reconciling sinners, anointing the sick and celebrating the Eucharist. The Catholic Church runs the grave risk of becoming more Protestant in its piety. While such non-Eucharistic forms of devotion produce saintliness within Protestantism, it will still be a serious loss to a rich ecumenical reunion and a critical blow to Catholic fervor, were this tendency to continue.

Women, already accepted in the Church's pastoral ministry, are asking the Church to consider whether or not their apostolate will be even more effective through priestly service from their hands.

The ordination of women enlarges a dialog across the entire Church, male and female, and forces us to re-examine the nature and force of symbol within the sacramental system of the Catholic Church.

Dialog such as this unites rather than divides. It enriches and so makes the bond within the Church more worthy of Jesus' death and resurrection. This book presents no final answers; these are the prerogatives of the Pope and bishops. The authors, however, call all of us to dialog with honesty and dignity, with openness in the pastoral and scholarly forum, that the future directions of priesthood reflect the guidance of the Holy Spirit in our midst.

PART TWO

ORIGINS AND EARLY EVOLUTION

OF PRIESTHOOD

2

CULTURE, LEADERSHIP AND SYMBOLISM
IN THE OLD TESTAMENT

by

Carroll Stuhlmueller, C.P.

The Old Testament is the inspired word of God, yet a continuous debate questions its force for deciding religious issues today.[1] Particularly
with controversial topics the Hebrew Bible lacks the decisive strength of
the New Testament. In discussing that most unsettled topic of women
priests, writers tend to bypass those very scriptures[2] which Jesus and
His first disciples relied upon very heavily.[3] Moreover, during the early
patristic age, the Old Testament style of priesthood sharpened or even
imposed some very clear lines upon the Christian image of priest.[4]
This chapter avoids the simple route of transferring the qualities of
Old Testament priesthood to our own priestly leadership. Nor will we
delay over the religious role of women in the centuries before Christ, in
order to discover Biblical models for women priests today.[5] In fact, a
gap so deep and extensive separates the Old Testament from our late
twentieth century,[6] that quick, thoughtless leaps from ancient biblical
times to our own can be disastrous. For that matter, neither is it wise for
us to copy slavishly the religious forms of New Testament times,[7] nor to
condemn our ways if they do not literally conform to biblical details.[8]
Roman Catholic theology and practise have always emphasized the
necessity to read the Scriptures within the life setting and pastoral needs
of the Church of each new age.[9] Change does not come easily to this
Church, but change it does, even as dramatically as at Vatican II. Within
the twenty centuries of its evolution the Catholic Church has kept its
roots imbedded in the Scriptures — maybe at times too tenuously, but
firmly since 1943[10] — yet its foliage and seasonal changes are adapted to
the environment and geography of later centuries. The question before

us now is simply this: is the ordination of women to full priesthood one of these adaptations, imperative for a strong, pastoral ministry today?[11]

All the chapters of this book study the priesthood *as it evolved* in its theology and ideals, practise and regulations. The eighteen hundred or more years of Old Testament history provide the ideal setting for investigating the evolution of religion with its slow progress and quick transitions, its confrontation and overreactions, its challenges and responses, its set-backs and collapses, its continual renewal and basic continuity. In the first and somewhat lengthy section of this chapter we present some general but very important data about the origin and development of religious forms in ancient Israel, crucial for theological development of any age and certainly applicable to the question of women priests. The second part of this chapter traces in broad outline the origin and principal stages of Old Testament priesthood under internal and external pressures. Finally, we inquire into the impact of biblical symbolism upon priesthood today.[12]

I

In Old Testament times styles of leadership were never revealed directly and immediately by God.[13] Every form of exercising authority, be it religious or civil, that is represented in the Hebrew Bible, can also be found in extra-biblical sources where it antedates Abraham (1850 B.C.) and Moses (1240 B.C.). We conclude then that God did not dictate the institutions of judge or king, prophet or elder, priest or sage. Yet, God was directing the process by which Israel was formed into a nation with lines of authority, and led forward in her history. The record of the legislation and history is called the inspired word of God, the Holy Bible. After giving a number of examples how Israel absorbed culture and forms of leadership from her neighbors, we will look into the way such "pagan" material became the word of God.

This interaction of religion and culture in Old Testament times can direct the Church today. Many important movements, like women's liberation, originates and develops outside the Church, at least outside the Catholic priesthood and episcopacy. As the Church begins to adopt these non-religious movements, we can turn to the Old Testament for guidance and peace. In such a multiple relationship of conflict, challenge and assimilation, the Old Testament indicates how God's will is learned and implemented.

Israel's institutions, we say, originated in surrounding polytheistic cultures. At times the Bible openly admits this fact. Several examples will aid our discussion.

One of the first historical manifestations of priesthood occurs in Genesis 14:

> Melchizedek, king of Salem, brought out bread and wine, and being a
> priest of God Most High, he blessed Abram. (Gen 14:18)

While this chapter has many difficulties, its significance cannot be overlooked.[14] Centuries before Moses had formally established the levitical
priesthood, a priest from Canaanite stock blessed Moses' ancestor,
Abraham. Later, one of the royal Davidic titles granted to the crown
prince on the occasion of his coronation was "priest forever according
to the order of Melchizedek" (Ps 110:4).[15] This title, originally of a
pagan king, absorbed more and more of Israel's messianic hopes, especially at Qumran[16] and later in the Epistle to the Hebrews.[17] In each of
these cases politics, even at times on an international scale, provided the
setting and catalyst for a vigorous religious development of the Melchizedek title. In fact, chapter 14 of Genesis, where the title first appears, opens with a military invasion. Therefore, when priesthood is first
introduced, it was already a fully developed institution, worthy of Israel's chosen ancestors and influential in the long political-religious
struggle of God's people.

   Another institution which became a carrier of great messianic expectations was the Davidic dynasty. Royalty, however, was not anticipated
by Moses, and the first movement towards monarchy admitted its
foreign origin.

> All the elders came in a body to Samuel at Ramah and said to him,
> "Now that you are old, and your sons do not follow your example,
> appoint a king over us, *as other nations have*, to judge us." (1 Sam
> 8:4-5)

Even though Samuel opposed the monarchy, nonetheless, he accepted
the action of the elders as indicative of the Lord's will and arranged a
compromise and anointed Saul and later David as a prince or *nagid*.[18]
David later assumed the title of king or *melek*. Through another prophet,
Nathan, God blessed David with extraordinary promises: "Your throne
and your kingdom shall endure forever before me; your throne shall
stand firm forever" (2 Sam 7:16).[19] A dynasty, born of political expediency and furthered by military might and charming diplomacy, eventually collapsed under the fierce Babylonian invasion. After August 587
B.C., no king ruled from Jerusalem. The divine promises had to be
spiritualized and redirected in a way never anticipated by earlier traditions.[20] Divinely sanctioned institutions could disappear in their original
form and surface again in styles never foreseen in their first endorsement.[21]

   Two other, very important developments — prophecy and wisdom —
were also absorbed into Israelite life from foreign sources. The first extended discourse about a prophet occurs when the Moabite king Balak

ben Zippor summoned Balaam ben Beor from Pethor on the Euphrates (Numbers ch 20–24). The origins of wisdom from outside Israeliate religious tradition is disclosed, not only in its almost exclusively secular interests (1 Kings 5:9-14; Prov 10–31) but also in the geographical origin of many of its great patrons: "Agur ben Jakeh the *Massaite*" (Prov 30:1); "Eliphaz the *Temanite*" (Job 4:1); "Bildad the *Shukite*" (Job 8:1); "Zophar the *Naamathite*" (Job 11:1).[22]

All of these major movements of the Old Testament were so thoroughly integrated within Israel's religious life and traditions that they will appear elsewhere in the Bible as the object of a direct revelation. In other words, the foreign origin was later forgotten and the whole movement was attributed solely to God. The Scriptures, in fact, make quite a habit of overlooking secondary causes and of attributing everything directly to God.[23]

A good example of such a development is present in the highly esteemed order of "elders." In the Sinai desert the older tribal system of government by the "head of the family"[24] was breaking down. Moses' father-in-law, Jethro, a Midianite priest, bluntly told Moses that "you are not acting wisely." "Moses followed the advice of his father-in-law and did all that he suggested. He picked out able men" and appointed them judges or elders (Ex 18:13-27).

The traditions in the Book of Numbers, however, much later and more religiously imbued, leave the impression of a direct revelation from God:

> Then the Lord said to Moses, "Assemble for me seventy of the elders of Israel, men you know for true elders and authorities among the people, and bring them to the meeting tent. When they are in place beside you, I will come down and speak with you there. I will also take some of the spirit that is on you and will bestow it on them, that they may share the burden of the people with you. You will then not have to bear it by yourself. (Num 11:16-17)[25]

This order of "elders" continues in the Bible down to the *presbyteros* of the New Testament[26] and into later Christian usage which adapted this word for its "priests." While divine wisdom "reaches from end to end mightly and governs all things well" (Wis 8:1), still the immediate occasion lay in the pagan priest Jethro and his common sense advice to a young and over-zealous son-in-law.

These examples hopefully will suffice to point out a pattern in the "revelation" of civil and religious leadership, important for our theme of women priests. God expected his people: first, to learn from the experience and sound advice of their surrounding culture, even if it was idolatrous; second, to allow for cultural and even unexpected developments within each institution; third, to see His holy will operative in the political and economic factors responsible for the developments.[27] These same principles functioned in the early apostolic church and throughout church history. They offer a model for a development of ordained priesthood today which would open *all* offices of service to capable women as is being done in secular society.

Today when there is an insufficient number of male, celibate priests, another "Jethro" is appearing from outside the religious community and telling church leaders with equal bluntness:

> You are not acting wisely . . . . You will surely wear yourself out, and not only yourself but also these people with you. The task is too heavy for you; you cannot do it alone. Now listen to me, and I will give you advice that God may be with you. (Ex 18:17-19)

Jethro continues: "Choose able and God-fearing" women, "trustworthy" women, "who hate dishonest gain. . . . Let these render decisions" and lead in prayer — an adaptation of Ex 18:21-22.

Transitions such as this, motivated by secular movements, need not disturb the church, as throughout biblical times styles of religious authority originated and developed under impetus from outside Israel or outside her priesthood. In fact, the Bible goes so far as to warn the Church that she has no competency to create structures and institutions *ex nihilo* (out of nothing) — 2 Macc 7:28; she can only learn and adapt them from the surrounding world. The Bible moreover witnesses to an extraordinary development of institutions, once accepted within the religious organization. These models of biblical life offer clear directives for an evolution of priesthood today which would break its long tradition of male-only ordination and open the ranks to women. When women outside the church can rise to the highest posts of authority and can exert strong, beneficial leadership, biblical precedent would not only permit but urge the church to absorb such a movement within her own lines of authority.

The many cultural transitions of Old Testament times took place within a country of only six thousand square miles with no more space than the state of New Jersey and much less arable soil. The church today occupies the globe which may be one world and yet manifests an extraordinary variety of cultures. A world wide church must adapt itself to each situation so that its *emphases* in doctrine and morals as well as its *styles* of leadership and its prophetic stance for the oppressed will vary greatly. If women have acquired more respectable and productive roles of leadership in some areas of the world than they have in others, then the Church is expected to absorb the progress of women according to each country or district where she is present. The Church today has to live at once the many styles of organization spread over a longer period of time in the Old Testament period.

There is another principle or norm (besides relieving the burdens of the overworked priest!!) which the Old Testament offers in the controversial question of women ordination. This position will be more acceptable to the mood and ethics of our contemporary world. In the Bible priesthood underwent an extraordinary development through the impact of the prophets, who championed the rights of the poor and the unprotected "minority." The women movement today is itself the voice of a minority group. By ordaining women the prophet's voice would add a new tone and quality to the words of the priest. The Church's teaching and liturgy would then more effectively sharpen the conscience of all Catholics to the suffering of neglected or persecuted people.

A quick historical survey of Israel's religion will enable us first to appreciate the role of the "classical prophets" in biblical times and then to recognize their image today in the movement of women for religious leadership and for priesthood.

Around 1200 B.C. Moses organized the disspirited and enervated slaves of Pharaoh into a unified people with tradition, laws and government. Authority tended to be vested in gifted individuals, like Moses and Joshua, who were not necessarily succeeded by their own sons or relatives. Moses, nonetheless, did set up an institution of elders for civil matters (Ex 18:13-27) and he chose his own tribe of Levi for religious instruction and worship.

After Moses' death and the settlement of the Promised Land, a complementary and sometimes rival form of religious leadership appeared in the charismatic bands or communities, simply called "prophets" in the Bible. These are to be distinguished from the "classical" prophets, individuals like Amos or Jeremiah with books to their name, who at first denied the name "prophet" and were not associated with any band or community.[28] The charismatic groups first show up in 1 Sam 10:5-6, clearly distinguishable in lifestyle and work. Later in 1 Kings 17 to 2 Kings 6 the characteristics of their organization become still more evident. They shared many qualities with the Canaanite prophets; the two groups, nonetheless, opposed one another, even violently (1 Sam 19:22-24; 1 Kings 18). These "charismatic prophets" became ever more popular and powerful. They acquired the right to anoint or depose kings (2 Kings 9) and stood next to the royal throne as advisors directing the wave of the future (2 Sam 7).

Because many abuses surfaced among the charismatic prophets, a change was necessary. God summoned a whole new series of prophets; we give them the name "classical prophets."[29] The first of them, Amos, was determined not to be associated even by name with the other group. He even denied to be a prophet or a member of any prophetic band (Am 7:10-15). Such was his non-conformity that king and high priest banished him, prodded into action by the ladies and gentlemen whom Amos lashed with his bitter, sarcastic tongue (cf., Amos 4:1-3; 6:1-8).

Although rejected by the institution, Amos developed his preaching within the larger context of Israel's traditions. At first in angrily championing of the rights of the poor (Amos 4:1; 5:7-15), he seemed to be profaning sacred places and people (4:4-5; 7:16-17) as well as denying sacred traditions (3:2, 12; 5:18; 9:7). Actually, Amos was making the "heart of the matter" more visible as a reforming power in people's lives and in the institutional forms of religion.[30] To be a chosen people, he insisted, did not consist simply in biological birth from Abraham's stock (Amos 3:2): one must also manifest Abraham's justice, humility and kindness, as another prophet Micah declared (Mic 6:8). The promised "Day of the Lord" can turn into darkness if that be the only way to sweep away pride and oppression (Amos 5:18).

If Amos had simply repeated traditional theology by rote, then he would have been, according to a recent work of James A. Sanders, among "false prophets [who] invoked an otherwise decently good theology but at the wrong time, supporting leaders and people when they needed a challenge."[31] Amos' challenge was remembered. Who could ever forget his sentences, at once brilliant, sarcastic, devastating and crude? They were gathered together into convenient blocks or sermonettes, producing one of the most orderly books of the Bible.[32] The prophet, "excommunicated" by the priest Amaziah, is incorporated within the Bible by postexilic priests at Jerusalem!

Prophecy and priesthood merge in still another way than by priestly editing and accepting of prophet's words. During the Babylonian exile and particularly in the early postexilic period, between 539 and 400 B.C., the prophets Ezekiel, Haggai, Zechariah and Joel turned out to be quite different from their predecessors.[33] Some were priests, others preoccupied with priestly matters. The book of this late period closest in form and spirit to pre-exilic prophecy is that of Malachi, yet here again the prerogatives of the levitical priesthood are seriously defended (Mal 2:1-9) and the site of messianic fulfillment, where the prophet Elijah will suddenly appear, is *the temple* (Mal 3:1).

Looking back on this development, we see that organizational leadership will always need its "Amos." At first it will usually oppose such spontaneous unconventional leaders, but if the prophet perseveres, remaining in the council of the Lord (Jer 23:18, 22) and within the community of Israel, even through agony and destruction as did Jeremiah (Ch 39–40), then their ministry will be absorbed within the structure of traditional leadership.[34] Charismatic authority will be institutionalized, while more ancient structures will be radically transformed.

The example of Old Testament prophecy, as studied here, has provided us with one example among many how a priestly institution can be challenged and eventually enriched by loyal, prophetic opposition. The steps in biblical times consisted in prophet, disciples, remembered words, accepted tradition, book of prophecy. The movement which began as a bitter challenge and even a condemnation of priesthood eventually produced a prophetic priesthood. For today the steps might be summarized thus: the women movement in society at large; its prophetic challenge to church authority; a growing number of disciples within the movement; articles and books which document the movement and direct its progress; hesitancy, rejection, re-study and gradual acceptance by church authority; incorporation within Church law with an enriched form of priesthood.

Such a new prophetic priesthood does not simply reproduce the former manner of priestly life and activity, but manifests new models within the traditional structures. Women aspiring to ordained priesthood do not want to take over the position of the male priests, robe themselves in the same vestments and function in the same way.[35] Rather, they look towards an enlarged, diversified priesthood, with a particular outreach to minorities.

Up till now we have remained almost exclusively on the *historical* plane in discussing the interaction of Old Testament religion with surrounding cultures. We now turn the coin to its *theological* side and seek the religious principle by which Israel discerned what and how to accept from the culture of her neighbors. An intuition about God's personal love, breathed by divine initiative into Israel, enabled her to choose what was fitting, to purify and even transform it and then to turn it into something quite different from its expression outside of her own community.[36]

Before Israel could react to God's goodness on her own initiative, she had to be called into existence. It was this part of the Lord's personal love which gave birth to a people uniquely His own, distinct from all other nations. This idea of a chosen people is expressed with tender eloquence:

> Tell the Israelites: You have seen for yourselves how I treated the Egyptians and how I bore you up on eagle wings and brought you here to myself. Therefore, if you hearken to my voice and keep my covenant, you shall be my special possession, dearer to me than all other people, though all the earth is mine. You shall be to me a kingdom of priests, a holy nation. That is what you must tell the Israelites. (Ex 19:4-6)

First, we notice that in His goodness God intervened and called Israel *in the midst of her history*. She was already a part of the ancient Near Eastern fertile crescent, manifesting the cultural strengths and weaknesses of its inhabitants. Deuteronomy ch 26 expressed it this way in a very early credal statement: "My father was a wandering Aramean who went down to Egypt. . . ," while another *credo* in Joshua ch 24 admits: "In times past your fathers, down to Terah, father of Abraham and Nahor, dwelt beyond the river and served other gods." With loving concern God then accepted the people *as they were* not only at the starting point of salvation history, but also at each new transition along the way.

Israel, as a result, was always conscious of a forward movement in her theology. No matter where she was, God would be there, living among His people, beckoning them onward. Naturally, she looked backward to great moments of salvation, yet the past was not considered the golden model which every subsequent age must reconstruct.[37] Rather, the past was being relived with new and greater possibilities. In historical continuity with her past, Israel was able to fulfill ancient hopes with dramatic leaps forward (cf., Is 43:18-19; 48:3, 6b-8, 11-12).[38]

At the roots of her origin and major developments, Israel was radically different from her neighbors. All other peoples traced their origin to the founding of their city and especially of their temple. Here on great feast-days, especially New Years, they celebrated the act of creation, primeval paradise and first innocence.[39] Israel, instead, commemorated her freedom from sin, slavery and oppression and awaited a new creation in the future. With the non-Israelites the gods came to be regarded as omnipotent powers, following the seasons of the year, yet like weather capable of erratic change and uncontrollable violence. Seldom if ever do these gods sustain a prolonged personal interest in the people, and in these cases the object of their divine concern must be of noble, if not of royal blood.

Religion outside the Bible did manifest a limited forward vision, that winter shall be followed by a new spring or that victory shall crown a military expedition. Yet, no surge of life nor any triumph in battle could ever equal first creation with its explosive energy, its titanic struggle of the gods, and its idyllic first paradise. Non-Israelite religions then sought balance and fertility in nature, victory in war, protection against evil spirits, wisdom to anticipate and control life's fortunes and misfortunes. Basically, non-Israelite religion attempted to placate divine powers and so to recover as much as was *humanly* possible of primeval paradise. Israel's religion, on the contrary, provided the liturgical and moral opportunities to respond to God's personal love and to await a *new* paradise *beyond* human possibilities.

The essential difference between Israel's religion and that of her neighbors helps to explain Israel's determination that her future must be far superior to anything experienced in the past and that this mysterious development is to be instilled, furthered and finally accomplished by the

Lord's very personal love for His people. Israel's normal evolution, therefore, was bound to spring many surprises which *only afterwards* would be perceived in continuity with the country's previous history!

At important transitions Israel was often shocked into the reality of what God can do: destroy Jerusalem and wipe out the Davidic dynasty, bring an end to such noble institutions as judgeship and prophecy, build a new people out of the catastrophe of the exile and grant unrivaled authority to priests (Neh 8-13; Zech 6:11) and later to the Maccabean-Hasmoneans, a non-Davidic and non-Zadokite family (1 Mac 10:21). Furthermore, all of Israel's institutions were seen as absorbed into the mystery of God, the Davidic dynasty acquired such honorific titles as "Wonder-Counselor, God-Hero, Father-Forever, Prince of Peace" (Is 9:5). Wisdom was the Lord's "firstborn, . . . poured forth at the first, before the earth" (Prov 8:22-23). Prophecy was present, standing "in the council of the Lord" (Jer 23:18).

This basic attitude of the devout Israelite — continuity with overwhelming surprise, leading to a future golden age — meant that all institutions, once taken over from their pagan neighbors, were no longer controlled by a past model *ab initio* but were open to surprising developments. As we saw earlier, these developments happened within the societal, military and political interlocking of Israel's life; yet they were interpreted as the *mirabilia Dei*, God's wondrous works. Israel, consequently, was able to survive cataclysmic disasters and still trust God.

Her prophet thus enunciated God's oracle:

> See, I am doing something *new*!
> *Now* it springs forth, do you not perceive it? (Is 43:19)

A disciple of this prophet wrote still more excitedly:

> Oh, that you would rend the heavens and come down, . . .
> While you wrought awesome deeds we could not hope for,
>   such as they had not heard of from of old.
> No ear has ever heard, no eye ever seen, any God but you
>   doing such deeds for those who wait for Him. (Is 63:19; 64:2-3)

Lines such as these ought not to be interpreted simply of Jesus' incarnation, but rather of what is to happen consistently in Israel's future which is also ours.

These wonders are not ostentatious impersonal deeds. They center upon the Lord's intimate presence among a hungry, discouraged people. This concern of the Lord for the needy is very evident in the larger context of Is 63:7-64:11, just quoted.

If we apply this Old Testament model to the question of Catholic priesthood and the ordination of women, the following conclusions emerge for our serious consideration.

First, the church today like Israel in Old Testament times consists of a people on a journey.[40] True, a very important difference separates church and synagogue, in that the fulness of hopes is manifest in Jesus. "He is the pledge of our inheritance, the first payment against the full redemption of a people God has made His own" (Eph 1:14). Yet, the full details and the perfect blueprint of church structure were not revealed in Jesus' lifetime nor during the apostolic era. This fact is apparent in Paul's struggles for the acceptance of Gentile converts and for church unity (cf., Gal; 1-2 Cor). The same openness to future re-structuring becomes evident in the significant transition to a more monarchical form immediately *after* the close of New Testament writings. The Catholic Church, moreover, has modified the functions of sacred orders, has totally dropped such an important New Testament order as "prophet," and has granted extraordinary power to non-biblical offices like patriarch and cardinal. Again, the evolutionary journey of ordained priesthood to include women would follow this theology of a migrant church.

Second, throughout the Bible as in any world culture continuity provides a most valuable ingredient for survival and development. Yet, within Israel's continuity, dramatic transitions occurred, so overpowering that at their first announcement by the prophets, not even the major religious authorities understood and accepted the message (Jer 7:26) and the prophets themselves were baffled (Jer 12:1-5) and terrified (Jer 4:19-21). Such threatening oracles and fearful experiences turned out to be the only way continuity was possible, at least continuity worthy of God's ideals.

Today the Church needs to consider how to enrich her tradition by new movements as the ordination of women. True, many members of the Church will respond negatively, as though sacred traditions were being violated and cultural patterns upset. Their reactions must be taken into consideration on the very principle being discussed here of God's loving concern for each of His people. Nonetheless, traumatic upset in one part of the Church is not necessarily a proof of God's displeasure. Furthermore, one of the qualities of intimate love is to take the loved one by surprise! Religiously to live by faith means an availability to God's secret wonders. "Those who wait upon the Lord renew their strength" (Is 40:31). At this hour when women have proven their effective leadership in many parts of the secular sphere, the Church is obliged by biblical precedent to open leadership roles to them and to await the wonder and the surprise of such a move.

Third, we saw that God directed the development of biblical tradition through a prophetic concern for the poor and oppressed "minorities." Most of Israel's spectacular changes were announced as a necessary response to oppression: Moses' leading the Israelite slaves out of Egypt;

the prophetic oracles leveled against Jerusalem because the "orphan" and the "widow" were mistreated (Is 1:16). Today "women" constitute one of the oppressed minorities. If the Church cannot move to visible leadership in furthering the full and equal rights of women in all areas of church authority, other prophets will raise the alarm and summon the invader (Jer 4:5ff).

Finally, if the church combines a strong piety towards the person of Jesus with her prophetic rage to defend the oppressed, then she will be able to direct and purify any new developments like women ordination. In fact, the church's experience will provide respectability to the prophetic movement; her traditions will modify excesses and best of all her continuous concern for *all* the oppressed will prevent this movement from hurting anyone within the church.

II

Our study now turns to the history of Old Testament priesthood.[41] Not much is gained for our purposes here from presenting ancient facts within their ancient setting, but it will be beneficial to observe how divine revelations about priesthood were seriously modified in later periods. The church may find a model here in the Old Testament for authorizing important changes in what was considered up till now a divine order to restrict priesthood to the male sex.

In the Old Testament the differences between one age to another in revealed doctrine could be very pronounced. An unguarded reader might even charge the Bible guilty of error or at least of contradicting itself, if he or she did not appreciate the close relation of biblical revelation with world culture and its adaptation to new cultural situations. Even when earlier inspired texts seemed to have closed the case and ended theological development — *i.e.*, that the Davidic dynasty would reign always from Jerusalem (2 Sam 7:16) — still new changes were sanctioned by the authority of God's word. These alterations were eventually absorbed within tradition and seen in continuity with the past. One of the stylistic ways to regroup under tradition was the genealogical tablet.[42]

These tablets of names[43] served a much wider purpose than to follow biological origins. They could substantiate some major political or sociological changes, as when the Kenizzites, originally non-Israelites from the line of Esau (Gen 36:11, 15) were absorbed within the tribe of Judah, son of Esau's twin brother, Jacob, and given full rights.[44] The table of nations in Gen 10 served a political and religious purpose: the fulfillment of God's promise to Noah and his sons, "be fertile and multiply and fill the earth" (Gen 9:1), viewed Israel's salvation "exclusively within the realm of history,''[45] a history reflecting the crucial political period ''between the end of the eighth and the end of the seventh centuries.''[46]

Historical events, then, as described in the Bible, become carriers of a profound pastoral theology closely linked with peoples' needs and hopes. We propose to look at the complicated history of Old Testament priesthood in order to clarify the theology and to draw parallels for theological development within Catholic priesthood today.

As mentioned already, Moses presided over the formation of civil and religious institutions. He bestowed special privileges upon his own tribe of *Levi*, up till then under a curse for its violence and betrayal of trust (cf., Gen 49:5-7); Levi was to be principally responsible for teaching and for conducting liturgical ceremonies (cf., Deut 33:8-11).[47] After Moses' death, these ''Mushite'' Levites,[48] as scholars refer to them in distinction from others who were later admitted to the ranks of Levi, were in charge of the sanctuary at Shiloh in central Palestine and cared for the Ark of the Covenant (Judg 20:27-28; 1 Sam 1-4).

It was more normal for religious duties to be confided to the Levites, but non-Levites could and did function as priests (Judg 17:5; 1 Sam 7:1; 2 Sam 8:18). It was due to politics and military might that David's sons performed priestly acts (2 Sam 9:18), that David and his successors after the conquest of Jerusalem assumed the title of the former Jebusite king of that city, ''Priest forever according to the order of Melichizedek,'' that Solomon sacrificed at the most renowned high place of Gibeon (1 Kings 3:4). In fact, throughout the books of 2 Samuel and 1-2 Kings, the kings were superior to the levites installed by Moses and could take their place on very special occasions.[49]

David named two high priests: Abiathar, representing the Mushite Levites who were direct heirs of the Mosaic traditions and the Ark; and Zadok, formerly a Jebusite priest who converted to the worship of Yahweh and was representative of the southern group (2 Sam 8:17; 20:25).[50] David similarly installed two commanders-in-chief, Joab in charge of the northern troops with closer ties to Moses, and Benaiah in charge of the Cherethites and Pelethites, people with fragile ties to Moses. Upon his accession to the throne, Solomon removed the northerners Joab and Abiathar, who unfortunately had sided with the losing contender, Adonijah. At Solomon's orders, Adonijah and Joab were executed and the priest Abiathar was exiled from the Jerusalem court and sent to live at Anathoth (1 Kings 1:5-8, 38-39; 2:24-25, 26-27, 33-35; *cf.*, Jer 1:1).

From the death of Solomon in 922 B.C. till the destruction of Samaria in 721 B.C., the tribes were divided into two kingdoms, with the Zadokite priests (originally non-Israelites) in charge of religious functions in the southern Kingdom of Judah, and with Mushite and non-Mushite Levites functioning in various sanctuaries of the northern kingdom of Israel. After 721 B.C., all religious and civil life was concentrated around Jerusalem. During the reform of King Josiah (640–609 B.C.) the northern or Mushite Levites regained some power at Jerusalem, but the reform and the Levites' respectability collapsed at the king's tragic death.

During the Babylonian exile (587–539 B.C.) remnants of the two rival priesthoods each drew up plans for Israel's return to the Holy Land and the revival of their own religious institutions. One of these documents is located in the final draft or redaction of Deuteronomy; the other is found in what is called the "Priestly" or "P" tradition.

Deuteronomy very explicitly defends the equal rights of *all* levites to lead religious services:

> When a levite goes from one of your communities anywhere in Israel in which he ordinarily resides, to visit, as his heart may desire, the place which the Lord chooses, he may minister there in the name of the Lord, his God, like all his fellow Levites who are in attendance there before the Lord. He shall then receive the same portions to eat as the rest, along with his monetary offerings and heirlooms. (Deut 18:6-8).

Not only is the part-time levite granted full liturgical privileges at the sanctuary, but he may also support his family from the "stipends," portions of the animal and grain sacrifices and other monetary gifts.

Ezekiel, on the other hand, sided with the Zadokite priests; in fact, he himself as a priest belonged to their ranks (Ez 1:1). As a venerable leader around whom the elders gathered (Ez 10:1; 14:1), he threw all his weight into the statement: "These are the Zadokites, *the only Levites* who may come near to minister to the Lord" (Ez 40:46; cf., 43:19). Then he laid down the law which reversed the position in Deuteronomy and reduced the other levites to menial roles of "minor orders":

> But as for the Levites who departed from me when Israel strayed from me to pursue their idols, they shall bear the consequences of their sin. They shall serve in my sanctuary as gate keepers and temple servants; they shall slaughter the holocausts and the sacrifices for the people, and they shall stand before the people to minister for them. . . . They shall no longer draw near me to serve as my priests, nor shall they touch any of my sacred things. (Ez 44:10-11, 13)

The final words of this passage deprived these other levites even of their "stipend." To clear the records, the Zadokite priests were equally guilty of idolatry, as Ezekiel admitted in ch 8–10.

Though the development is complex, the main lines ought to be clear. Zadokites, once not even followers of Moses, became co-equal in the priestly office with the other levites. Under the strong influence of Ezekiel, they became Levites with a capital "L" and all the others were reduced to a small "l" as levites!

Many conclusions emerge not only about the interaction of priestly leadership with world forces and internal politics, but also about the process of divine revelation.

First, history witnesses to a distinct but complicated evolution, at times of revolutionary force (David's conquest of Jerusalem, and the establishment of his dynasty, the adoption of the Zadokites as levitical priests and the construction of the temple), yet in retrospect these actions were recognized in a line of continuity with Moses. Notice David's concern to house the Ark at Jerusalem (1 Sam 6). *Conflict* constituted a major ingredient of theological development.[51]

Second, out of the convoluted interaction of religion and politics, of world culture and biblical faith, of good and bad motives, God's word was born and revelation recorded.

Third, a wide variety of priestly styles are noticeable. Levites were preferred to lead religious functions, but non-Levites would be chosen, at times temporarily for the task, particularly if they were gifted for liturgical ceremonies and for teaching. Levites in the northern Kingdom often had secular jobs and exercised priesthood only on special occasions when they went up to the sanctuary "as their heart may desire" (Deut 18:6). Evidently levites were not automatically chosen but had to prove themselves.

Fourth, while none of the levites possessed landed property,[52] those at Jerusalem were much more securely ensconced under the king's good pleasure and vigilance.

Fifth, Israel's priesthood reacted sensitively to cultural changes and political conflicts ending up with a decision interpreted as "divine revelation."

Just as the patristic age of the church drew rules and expectations from Old Testament priesthood, especially as it functioned in the late postexilic age, and applied these qualities to the Catholic priest, we, too, in this our age of the church can find support and guidance from the same Old Testament in our search for God's will in the pastoral development of priesthood. The absorption of Zadokites and other non-levites into levitical priesthood would undergird a development towards women-priests and certainly countenance a much larger ministerial role to women. This new change would provide an opportunity to reconsider other options, such as part-time priests with secular jobs, occasional functions in priestly work, a more democratic form of exercising priestly and episcopal authority. This suggestion asks that priesthood be modeled less upon the authoritarian Zadokites of postexilic Jerusalem (where the patristic age garnered ideas) and more upon the levites of the preexilic northern kingdom (where the New Testament disciples of Jesus turned).[53]

These new visions of priesthood would correspond to the determination of most women, who in their call to priesthood, want to create new models and life styles rather than duplicate what is being done now by men priests.

III

Priesthood in both Old and New Testament times functioned within a world of symbolism. The entire sacramental system of the Church, as mentioned already, unites the assembly with God through symbols like bread and wine, water and oil. This focal position of symbol is recognized by the Roman *Declaration* in its study on women ordination. Its strongest argument — at least in the mind of its authors — and certainly its most extensive discussion is based on sacramental symbolism. "Sacramental signs," here it is quoting from St. Thomas, "represent what they signify by natural resemblance." The document immediately concludes that "this 'natural resemblance' which must exist between Christ and his minister" would be violated "if the role of Christ were not taken by a man: in such a case it would be difficult to see in the minister the image of Christ. For Christ himself was and remains a man" (sec. v).

Because of its importance the question of symbol is discussed from many angles in this book. Here we inquire into the Old Testament and test the position of the *Declaration* on "natural resemblance" against the style of symbolism in the Holy Scriptures before Christ. In the Old Testament symbols were formed from the elements of earth and human life. They emerged from decisive events like the exodus out of Egypt, the journey through the desert and the crossing of the Jordan River. Symbols included the world of people like Moses, David and Solomon. Stories like Noah's flood and Jonah's voyage in the belly of the whale take on the status of a continuing symbol, like the Shakespearean character Macbeth. Every symbol began with something or someone so real and so impressive, that people began to see in them all sorts of meaning and power. In some cases, like Noah's flood, the reality is difficult to recover from all the stories that have been told about it in the ancient Near East.

For people, events and things to develop into symbols, they must be contemplated in the depth of their existence and then that hidden meaning be expressed in a striking way, charged with emotion. This expression, now become symbol, may take its "parent" by surprise. Symbols are thus born out of the past but project mysterious signals of the future. They exemplify parts of our discussion in section two of this chapter. As many people together contemplate the exodus or the bread and wine, new depths of meaning are perceived, inner union achieved, challenges given, decisions made. These conclusions may be very subconscious, intertwined with will, emotions, memory and desires; as a result deep contemplative responses are evoked.[54]

The Old Testament adds another important quality to its symbols, which will be considerably important in our treatment of women priests. In the Hebrew Bible it is possible that one set of symbols abound with items which clash with one another. Especially in the apocalyptic books like Zechariah and Daniel ch 7–12, but also in an incipient way with Ezekiel ch 1, the composite symbol becomes so weird that we cannot possibly imagine it, all at one time. Each item must be taken separately for what it is worth: eyes = visions; wheels = mobility; wings = swift flight; bull = strength; lion = royal power. Clothing, color, numbers, celestial bodies and bodily limbs, each has a distinct communication. Yet, they can be meshed together in one cacophonous conflict of parts to symbolize the mystery of God beyond human language and even beyond human symbols!

At times the clash of symbols may so disturb us, that like the prophet Ezekiel we fall exhausted upon our face (Ez 2:1). At other times the dissonance is more subtle, as in the prophecy of Hosea. In ch 2–3 the prophet focuses attention upon a sexual symbol which portrayed the Lord Yahweh as Israel's spouse. The New Testament follows with the example of Jesus who compared himself to a bridegroom in his loving and joyful presence with his disciples (Matt 9:15). This image of Christ as spouse of the church is developed in 2 Cor 11:2; Eph 5:22-33; Rev 21:9; 22:17. The *Declaration* refers to this symbol in order to explain the exclusion of the female sex from priesthood. It insists, as we saw at the beginning of this section III, upon the "natural resemblance" of all priests to Jesus' male sexuality, for they act *in persona Christi*.[55]

Hosea's symbol was drawn from the experience of his marriage, in particular from the infidelity of his wife. Chapters 1–3 develop this image at length, with emotional eruptions, profound dejection, vaulting hopes, poignant tragedy. So acutely did Hosea experience the violent swings of emotional response, that we almost lose sight of the symbolic value and think only of his personal tragedy. Chapter two introduces the religious application, sometimes very quickly as in v 15 ("and she forgot *me*, says *the Lord*"), at other times explicitly as in the mention of Egypt, the valley of Achor and the covenant (v 17, 20-22).

From this heartbreaking matrimonial context there was born that rich symbol of Yahweh, Spouse of Israel. Israel is the adulterous wife, again and again violating the Lord's love, yet always received back again. Israel then is cast in a female image. In the use of this image, however, the prophet directs his complaint against the priests and here comes the clash of images — from female harlot to male priest. "With you is my grievance, O priests." "They sin against me, exchanging their glory for shame. They feed on the sin of my people." This account reminds us of prostitution where money is made off of sex. Hosea declares God's verdict, again with sexual allusions:

> I will punish them for their ways . . . .
> They shall eat and not be satisfied,
>   they shall play the harlot but not increase.
> Because they have abandoned the Lord to practise harlotry.

Hosea saw the image or symbol of his harlot wife fulfilled in the male priests. There is no question here of homosexuality nor of any sexual offense. Hosea listed other crimes in ch 4. The priests are "adulterous wives" because of their excessive wealth, their reliance upon clout, their lax religious spirit, their routine liturgies. Several times in ch 4 and 5 Hosea moved from female to male without explanation or transition. Images in the Old Testament can clash that way.

Other, important examples of such turbulent transfers of images can be seen in the Old Testament. For instance, "tabernacle" can signify the "home" or protection which God provided for Israel in the desert or in the agricultural land of Canaan (Deut 16:13-17). Later it signified the home which Israel made for God, the temple at Jerusalem (1 Kings 8). Subsequently, the Jerusalem temple began to symbolize the messianic home which Israel offers to all the peoples of the earth (Is 2:1-4; Zech 14). In the New Testament tabernacle means the human body of Jesus (John 2:21), the church (Luke 24:50-53), or heaven (Rev 21:2).[56] This enduring and significant symbol never preserved "a natural resemblance" to its original form of a desert tent. Even the principal agents change roles, so that sometimes God, at other times human beings raise up the tabernacle.

This biblical background to symbol cuts against the position in the *Declaration* about "natural resemblance." The symbolic representation of Jesus, spouse of the Church, must preserve and communicate not only the intimate union of life and the fertile reproduction of life, but it must as well manifest that aura of mystery and conflict involved in such intimacy. It seems that if the necessity of "natural resemblance" is pushed to its extreme, then the symbol of Hosea's marriage would require that Jesus himself and all priests not only be married but also be victimized by unfaithful wives! The same ultimate need of "natural resemblance" would exclude the saints from the church (which is the adulterous spouse), implicitly deny Mary's Immaculate Conception, and correspond best with that false theological system which emphasizes the corrupt nature of all flesh.

Furthermore, an over-emphasis upon "natural resemblance" distorts other basic qualities inherent in good symbolism. Symbols almost always transcend their origin and take their parents by surprise. They are born from the past but point to the future. If priesthood must remain the prerogative of the male sex because of a natural resemblance to Jesus' male sexuality as spouse of the church, then priesthood may fail to point in a striking way to the future where there will "not exist among you Jew or Greek, slave or freeman, male or female" (Gal 3:28).

In heaven each of the elect will certainly maintain a line of continuity with their earthly personality, grounded in male or female sexuality. Yet, heavenly sexuality will be such that "they neither marry nor are given in marriage but live like angels in heaven" (Matt 22:30). They will express their intimate love for one another in a way infinitely more ecstatic than ever on earth. These heavenly realities of love can be glimpsed not only in the symbolic banquet of the Eucharist which exceeds any family dinner on earth (cf., Is 25:6; 54:1-2; Ps 22:72) but also in the priesthood which should transcend the bounds of earthly sexuality.[57]

Biblical symbolism then not only supports an extension of priesthood to women but even seems to encourage it.

Conclusions

The two main areas of Old Testament religion, priesthood and symbolism, discussed in the second and third sections of this chapter ought to be considered integrally together, so that one is not applied to priesthood independently of the other. Secondly, each had its own history or evolution, as did the entire ancient Near East and individual countries within it like Israel.

Within Israel's long, complicated history, various symbols rose in importance, then declined, each at a different rate in various parts of the country. The symbols of exodus and desert tabernacle were eclipsed by the symbols of the city Jerusalem and its temple in the south at Jerusalem. Biblical symbolism, moreover, not only sustained but even delighted in a clash of images. A major symbol might seem to explode, as one image is heaped upon another, yet the awesomeness of God's way of salvation, its overwhelming and uncontrollable mystery are being communicated. Priesthood, too, must not be tied to any excessive "natural resemblance" but in its unity and variety it must stir contemplative wonder over the mystery of God's transcendent intimacy with his people. Extending the priesthood to women would follow these biblical norms and accentuate the *mysterious* presence of Jesus, *wondrous* spouse of the Church.

The rise, fall and revival of symbols depended upon the political and economic fortunes of Israel and Judah. This close interaction of religious institutions with historical events was also apparent in Part Two of this chapter. The institution of priesthood did not follow a single line of biological descent from the levites and the family of Aaron. Pagan priests like the Zadokites of pre-Davidic Jerusalem were absorbed within the ranks of the levites and eventually became the Levites with capital "L". Catholic priesthood must also evolve and gather new forms of leadership within its ranks. Women are just now emerging with strong leadership qualities and for this reason should be included in priesthood.

While the second and third sections of this chapter carried the main burden or more specific aspects of the Old Testament focus on women ordination, the first section provided basic orientation. Here the crucial point was discussed that neither in the Bible nor in the Church does divine revelation dictate distinctive styles of leadership. It is not the competence of Bible or Church to create forms of authority; and therefore, it is not godly for either Bible or Church to differ too radically from secular culture in the *general* lines or styles of leadership. The Church risks repudiating the cultural advance of women in many areas of the world, if she refuses them the right to aspire to the supreme area of leadership, which resides in the priesthood in its various orders. Not to open priesthood to women may imply that their social, political and economic advances elsewhere are ungodly and evil. This serious charge stems from a quality of biblical history where *all good* forms of leadership and culture were tried and absorbed within the life of Israel.[58]

Israel discerned what forms were good and what forms were bad by the intuition of Yahweh's personal, compassionate love. This revelation purified and enhanced whatever was accepted within the chosen people. It exercised its influence most vigorously in the preaching of prophets who championed the rights of the poor, the neglected, the "minorities." Today women constitute such an oppressed minority. In the secular world, prophets are sounding the alarm! Their voice must be heard as well in the ranks of the church. If not, then the Old Testament prophets will cry out again that Jerusalem be destroyed, so that a renewed Holy City rise from the ruins. If the warning is heard and God's voice obeyed, again something new will evolve without the ordeal of Jerusalem under fire. Prophets do not repeat the past, however good and orthodox that may have been. They challenge it to be better, purer and more reflective of God's personal love for the poor. Ordination of women might exercise such a profound prophetical impact upon priesthood and church.

Finally, in the prophetic evolution of symbols and institutions, continuity with tradition is maintained yet a fresh and vigorous form is most of all in evidence. Women priests would not simply imitate what the men are doing. They would introduce the priesthood and Eucharistic piety into new areas of ministry, with new styles of action, within neglected and non-evangelized neighborhoods. Women priests will call forth a prophetic spirit within priesthood. They will diversify and enrich its ranks. With a new enthusiasm, they will inspire a wide variety of capable people to join the various types of priesthood, be they religious orders or diocesan groups, male or female.

This Old Testament hope must be tested against the fuller revelation of the light of Christ and the long tradition of the church. This we proceed to do in the following chapters of this book.

3

THE ROLE OF WOMEN ACCORDING TO JESUS AND THE EARLY CHURCH

by

Robert J. Karris, O.F.M.

As a transition from the Old Testament into the New, let me invite the reader to engage in a brief exercise in imagination. Suppose that the New Testament (NT) texts on women are a landscape. That landscape is varied, with valleys and hills, rough and smooth terrain, myriads of lush trees and plants. Imagine yourself viewing that landscape through two different pairs of colored glasses.

The first pair of glasses reveals the landscape in this light:

> Jesus Christ did not call any woman to become part of the Twelve. If He acted in this way, it was not in order to conform to the customs of His time, for His attitude towards women was quite different from that of His milieu, and He deliberately and courageously broke with it.[1]
>
> The apostolic community remained faithful to the attitude of Jesus towards women. . . . They (the Twelve and Paul) could therefore have envisaged conferring ordination on women, if they had not been convinced of their duty of fidelity to the Lord on this point.[2]

The second pair of glasses enables the viewer to spy the landscape in this wise:

> It (the Jesus movement in Palestine) rejected the priestly laws of Jewish religion and attracted the outcast of its society. Jesus' followers were not the righteous, pious or powerful of the time, but tax collectors, sinners and — women, all those who were cultically unclean and did not belong to the religious establishment or the pious associations of the day.[3]

> The self-understanding of the Christian community eliminated all distinctions of religion, race, class and caste, and thereby allowed not only gentiles and slaves to assume full leadership in the Christian community but also women. Women were not marginal figures in this movement but exercised leadership as apostles, prophets, evangelists, missionaries, offices similar to that of Barnabas, Apollos or Paul.[4]

This scanning of the landscape raises the immediate question: Why do the colored glasses show up the landscape in such vastly different lights? I would suggest that the answer is partly to be found in the examination of contemporary NT criticism and in a survey of the recent discussion on what the NT says about the ordination of women.[5] Most people reading this chapter are more familiar with the first set of glasses, provided by the *Declaration* of the Sacred Congregation for the Doctrine of the Faith. People normally do not view women's ordination through the second set, provided by Dr. Elizabeth Schüssler Fiorenza. For this reason I will proceed in this chapter by showing the place the *Declaration*'s views occupy in contemporary NT criticism and in the recent discussions about what the NT says about the ordination of women. In organizing the data, I adapt the very handy schema of Reginald H. Fuller: 1) Old Testament; 2) Jesus; 3) The Earliest Church; 4) St. Paul; 5) Early Catholicism.[6]

I

The *Declaration* follows the lead of most recent discussions of the biblical data and eliminates as irrelevant any discussion of the Old Testament concept of priesthood. John Reumann clearly stated the 1973 consensus on this point: ". . . it is by and large agreed that the New Testament ministry is no continuation of the Old Testament priesthood. Israel provides no answer on the ordination of women to the ministry of the church of Jesus Christ."[7] Yet Reumann himself[8] and Carroll Stuhlmueller in chapter two of this volume provide keys for opening up the Old Testament for further exploration in this area.

II

The *Declaration* is at one with the best of contemporary Gospel scholarship when it generalizes: "As we have seen, an examination of the Gospels shows on the contrary that Jesus broke with the prejudices of his time, by widely contravening the discriminations practiced with regard to women."[9] We still smart at the cacophony of this discrimination when we hear the synagogue prayer: "R. Judah says: Three blessings one must say daily: Blessed (art thou), who did not make me a gentile; Blessed (art thou), who did not make me a woman; Blessed (art thou), who did not make me a boor."[10] There may have been synagogue voices more favorably disposed to women, but R. Judah's is the dominant voice.

But the *Declaration* is not at one with contemporary Gospel scholarship when it attempts to fathom the attitude of Jesus and thus arrive at the Lord's example as normative for all time. The *Declaration* draws the inference from Jesus' radical stance toward women: "But it must be recognized that we have here a number of convergent indications that make all the more remarkable the fact that Jesus did not entrust the apostolic charge to women."[11] The authors of the *Declaration* are apparently so intent on pursuing their argument, based on Jesus' example, that they shortcircuit one of the most signal scholarly accomplishments of recent memory, *scil.*, the recognition and approbation of the methodologies by which the Gospels are seen to be the results of three stages of formation. This three-fold approach was endorsed by an *Instruction* of the Pontifical Biblical Commission, approved by Pope Paul VI in the first year of his pontificate (April 21, 1964), later incorporated into the Constitution on *Divine Revelation*, Ch. V, of Vatican II (Nov. 18, 1965) and summarized here in the following paragraph.[12]

While based on what the Twelve remembered of Jesus' words and deeds (first stage), the Gospels contain the added insights of faith, granted to the Twelve and to the churches through Jesus' resurrection and the gift of the Spirit (second stage). These insights, as developed and used by the early church in its various ministries, provided the base for the evangelists who selected what they deemed necessary to create a literary work which would meet the faith needs of their people (third stage). Put in less technical terms and from a different angle, the Gospels do not provide us with transcripts or tape-recordings of what Jesus was about. They are documents of faith. It is not a simple undertaking to attain to what the *Declaration* calls "the attitude of Jesus towards women."[13]

But focusing more directly on the topic at hand, I make the following observations. First, it is almost certain that Jesus of Nazareth established the Twelve. They are symbolic of the unity of Israel imaged by the twelve tribes of Israel which are governed by males, i.e., the twelve patriarchs. It is not clear that Jesus of Nazareth called apostles. Thus the Twelve and apostles cannot be facilely equated nor can the Twelve and apostolic charge be easily identified.[14] Thus, the *Declaration* has not arrived at the attitude of Jesus of Nazareth when it equates the calling of the Twelve with the apostolic charge[15] and thus eliminates women from the priesthood.[16]

Secondly, ". . . NT criticism makes it very unlikely that we can picture the historical Jesus as omniscient, foreseeing the future of the

Church in detail.''[17] Put in another medium, we can say that contemporary Gospel criticism does not support a bible blueprint ecclesiology, which in the words of Raymond E. Brown ''is usually based on the Gospels and Acts as evidence that God's intentions were vocalized by an omniscient Jesus who foresaw the future. . . . In such a blueprint ecclesiology based on the Bible, it is clear that if Jesus wanted women priests, he would not have ordained only men.''[18] Jesus of Nazareth, on the contrary, had limited knowledge of the future. From the Gospel data it is a most perilous task to probe serenely and confidently into what he thought of the future and determined as absolutely normative for priesthood.

In sum, if one applies the scholarly and ecclesiastically approved methodologies which stand behind the insight that the Gospels were gradually formed, then it is incontrovertible that Jesus of Nazareth broke with the prejudices of his time and widely contravened the discriminations practiced with regard to women. This is Jesus' attitude. This is the example which is normative for the rest of the NT churches and for contemporary churches. The Church must be faithful to this example and not to the putative example of a Jesus who called only men to ministry.[19] In this regard Reumann makes a most telling point when he observes: ''indeed, we may say historically with more confidence that Jesus gave women a role in his ministering than we can claim Jesus, prior to Easter, instituted a Ministry with a capital M.''[20]

III

Our discussion proceeds from the lifetime of Jesus to the earliest days of the church.

On three different occasions the *Declaration* is stride for stride with the best NT scholarship in highlighting the significance of Galatians 3:28 for the question of the ordination of women.[21] While calling this text ''one of the most vigorous texts in the New Testament on the fundamental equality of men and women, as children of God, in Christ,''[22] it cautions that ''this passage does not concern ministries: it only affirms the universal calling to divine filiation, which is the same for all.''[23]

By placing Gal 3:28 under the rubric of ''The Earliest Church,'' I call attention to a factor which the *Declaration* has not mentioned. Namely, Gal 3:28 is a baptismal formula which accords well with Jesus' attitude toward women and probably dates from the second decade of the Christian movement. Furthermore, although Paul approved the formula by quoting it, he did not create it.[24] This baptismal formula was used by the Hellenistic churches, to which Paul was heir, to describe what the experience of the gift of the Spirit meant to them. As Fiorenza puts it:

The theological self-understanding of this early Christian movement is best expressed in the baptismal formula Gal 3:27-29. In reciting this formula the newly initiated Christians proclaimed their vision of an inclusive community. Over and against the cultural-religious pattern shared by Hellenists and Jews alike, the Christians affirmed that all social, political and religious differences were abolished in Jesus Christ.[25]

The Christians who fashioned this baptismal formula were surely faithful to Jesus' radical attitude toward women. Although Gal 3:28 does not say anything directly about ministry, it has vast implications for ministry because its vision does not limit any aspect of Christian life to either of the sexes.[26]

IV

Paul's letters[27] emerged out of the problems and needs of the early church. They were intended to correct, clarify, and direct the communal faith in Jesus.

The *Declaration*'s use of St. Paul's letters is difficult to chart within contemporary NT criticism and the recent NT discussions on the ordination of women. We will orientate some of its views within current NT criticism.

The *Declaration* apparently subscribes to the view that Paul authored all the letters ascribed to him.[28] This view is not favored by many within the contemporary discussion of the Pauline data.[29] Also, the *Declaration* capitalizes on three points which are hardly present in the genuine Pauline letters nor found in the vast majority of the scholarly discussions on the subject.

The first point is "ordination."[30] "Ordination" is our contemporary term, and it is not helpful to introduce it into a discussion of texts which do not use it. As Reumann so aptly says: " 'Ordination,' it is well to remember, does not appear, fullblown and in our sense of the term, in the Scriptures."[31]

Secondly, the *Declaration* seems to limit ministry/priesthood to the "official and public proclamation of the message."[32] According to the arguments proposed by the *Declaration* on the basis of this point, women did not engage in such proclamation because their femaleness prevented the apostles from ordaining them. To arrive at such a conclusion is not only to misread the data in the genuine Pauline epistles which abound with references to women in ministry, but also to commit the methodological sin of imposing upon the varied riches of ministry in Paul and in the NT a unilateral concept of what ministry should be.[33]

Finally, the *Declaration* makes a distinction between "my fellow workers" and "God's fellow workers" in Paul: "but he [Paul] reserves

167670

the title 'God's fellow workers' (1 Cor 3:9; *cf.*, 1 Thess 3:1) to Apollos, Timothy and himself, thus designated because they are directly set apart for the apostolic ministry and the preaching of the Word of God."[34] As Reumann has convincingly shown, this is a ephemeral distinction.[35] How can one say that "Greet Prisca and Aquila, my fellow workers *in Christ Jesus*" (Rom 16:3) is not equivalent to "*God's* fellow workers"? Moreover, the reading "God's fellow workers" is textually suspect in 1 Thess 3:1. In the *one* passage in which "God's fellow workers" does occur, 1 Cor 3:9, it is called forth by the rhetoric of the composition: "For we are *God's* fellow workers; you are *God's* field, *God's* building." In brief, no ephemeral distinction can annihilate the fact that it is of major theological significance that Paul calls women "his fellow workers."[36]

We now turn and examine more directly the place of the *Declaration* in the recent discussion on what Paul has to say about the ordination of women. These discussions concentrate primarily on Gal 3:28 and the fact that Paul had female fellow workers. Since I have already dealt with Gal 3:28 in sufficient detail above, suffice it to say that the Declaration is au courant with the contemporary discussions by emphasizing the collaboration that Paul asks of women in his apostolate.[37] But as we have just seen above, the *Declaration* interprets this data in a strained way. Rather than introduce artificial points like ordination, official and public proclamation of the message, and the distinction between "my fellow workers" and "God's fellow workers," it seems much sounder to follow Paul and say that Paul, in discerning the Spirit's workings in his communities clearly recognized that the Spirit called both women and men to ministry. For example, Paul recognized the gifts of prophecy and prayer given by the Spirit to women (1 Cor 11:5) and put his stamp of approval on them. There were no barriers of discrimination to prevent women from assuming leadership positions within the Pauline communities and mission.

Yet the authors of the *Declaration* and I are sagacious enough to realize that most readers of Paul skim over Gal 3:28 and the Pauline texts on the roles women played in ministry and pounce on the troublesome 1 Cor 11:2-16 and 1 Cor 14:34-35.[38] Within the confines of this chapter a few remarks on each passage must suffice.

Paul's main point in 1 Cor 11:2-16 is not to subordinate women. We call attention to the mutuality of men and women emphasized in 1 Cor 11:11-12:

> Nevertheless, in the Lord woman is not independent of man nor man of woman; for as woman was made from man, so man is now born of woman. And all things are from God.

Rather, in 1 Cor 11:2-16 Paul wanted to correct an abuse which arose in the community at Corinth because of an exaggerated understanding of the implications of Gal 3:28. Carried along by the intoxicating newness of this understanding, men and women tried to abolish their sexual differences as symbolized by such things as hair style and head covering.[39] Paul strains to correct this abuse, but, as the *Declaration* so rightly notes,[40] he does not forbid these women from performing the ministries of praying and prophesying in the public assembly (1 Cor 11:5).

In commenting on 1 Cor 14:33b-36, I will resume arguments which I have developed elsewhere at greater length.[41] But first let's quote this troublesome text in the Revised Standard Version:

> As in all the churches of the saints, (34) the women should keep silence in the churches. For they are not permitted *to speak* (*lalein*), but should be subordinate, as even the law says. (35) If there is anything they desire to know, let them ask their husbands at home. For it is shameful for a woman *to speak* (*lalein*) in church. (36) What! Did the word of God originate with you, or are you the only ones it has reached?

If we view the unqualified verb "to speak" (*lalein* in Greek) of 1 Cor 14:34-35 in its context of a discussion of charismatic speech (see 1 Cor 14:2,4,5,6,9,13,18,19,21,23,27,39), then we cannot agree with the *Declaration* that "to speak" in 1 Cor 14:34-35 refers to "the official function of teaching in the Christian assembly."[42] Nor is 1 Tim 2:12, "I permit no woman *to teach* (*didaskein*) or to have authority over men; she is to keep silent," a legitimate interpretive parallel to the meaning of "to speak" in 1 Cor 14:34-35 as the *Declaration* intimates. For the verb "to teach" (*didaskein* in Greek) in 1 Tim 2:12 is not the same verb as "to speak" (*lalein*) in 1 Cor 14:34-35 nor are the historical contexts of the two passages identical. I find persuasive Wayne Meeks' view on this difficult passage: "In his concern for order in the cultic assembly, Paul adds an afterthought which is expressed unfortunately in too absolute a fashion, obscuring the fact that the *lalein* of these women who want to enter into a discussion to 'learn' cannot be the charismatic *lalein* of the context."[43] Most simply put, "to speak" in 1 Cor 14:34-35 means "to ask a question." Paul is not forbidding women from teaching in the public assembly.

Obviously, I have barely scratched the surface of Paul's teaching about women. Much more could be said. In summary, Paul's prime principle is the one he inherited and expressed in Gal 3:28. From this principle he drew insight and strength to warmly endorse those women whom Jesus called to ministry through the gifts of his Spirit. Members of Paul's community at Corinth misunderstood the implications of Gal 3:28 and initiated abuses like the teaching that marriage is wrong (see 1 Cor 7) and that all differences between male and female are to be abrogated (see 1 Cor 11:2-16). Paul struggled mightily to oppose these abuses and to assimilate the teaching that "there is neither Jew nor Greek, there is neither slave nor free, there is neither male nor female; for you are all one in Christ Jesus" (Gal 3:28).[44] On this reading of the data of the genuine Pauline letters, Paul has been most faithful to Jesus' radically new and liberating attitude toward women.[45]

V

"Early Catholicism," to which we now turn our attention, may be a somewhat new and strange term to many readers. A few introductory remarks on this phenomenon, therefore, may be helpful. For our purposes Early Catholicism refers to the following NT writings: Luke-Acts, Colossians, Ephesians,[46] 1-2 Timothy, Titus, 1-2 Peter, and Jude. These NT books, written in the last decades of the first century or early decades of the second, are early Catholic because they

> show traces of, or tendencies in the direction of, the following: the organization of the Church according to hierarchical in contrast to charismatic ministry; the development of the monarchical episcopate; an objectification of the proclamation and an emphasis upon a strictly formulated rule of faith; a stress upon 'orthodoxy' or 'sound doctrine' in opposition to false teaching. . . . a concern for ecclesiastical unity and consolidation; and an interest in the collecting of the apostolic writings.[47]

It might be said that the motto of early catholic writings is "law and order."

Except in passing,[48] the *Declaration* does not deal with NT writings which are reputedly early catholic.[49] Thus it does not treat passages like Colossians 3:18: "Wives, be subject to your husbands, as is fitting in the Lord"; like Ephesians 5:22: "Wives, be subject to your husbands, as to the Lord"; like 1 Timothy 2:11-12: "Let a woman learn in silence with all submissiveness. I permit no woman to teach or to have authority over men; she is to keep silent"; like Titus 2:3-5: "Bid the older women likewise to be reverent in behavior, not to be slanderers or slaves to drink; they are to teach what is good, and so train the young women to love their husbands and children, to be sensible, chaste, domestic, kind, and submissive to their husbands, that the word of God may not be discredited."

If these statements are Paul's, what has happened to the Paul who quoted with solemn approval the early baptismal formula in Gal 3:28? What has happened to the Paul who worked side by side with women in the ministry of proclaiming the Gospel? What has happened to the Paul who seemed so very faithful to the attitude of Jesus toward women? Many scholars answer these questions by saying that the writings which contain these harsh, anti-feminine statements do not stem from Paul, but are written by later followers in his name.[50] But whether written by Paul or not, these texts and their vision of the role of women in the Church must be addressed.

Two answers have been given to the question which the very existence of these harsh texts trumpets. The first answer proposes that, after Paul's death, gnostic heretics won over many Christians, especially women, to their views of super-realized salvation: since they were completely resurrected (see 2 Tim 2:18), why should they observe the order of creation, *i.e.*, marriage, the value and beauty of sexual intercourse, the distinctions between the sexes? To counter these abuses the authors behind these early catholic writings emphasize the order of creation. Fuller expresses this solution quite neatly: "What then happened to Paul's eschatological woman? She was sacrificed to the needs of consolidation, of accommodation to the mores of contemporary society, to the threat of gnosticism. The answer to our question is that Paul's eschatological woman had probably become a gnostic!"[51]

The second answer is that the dominant patriarchal model of the surrounding culture won out over the vision of Jesus and Paul with regard to women. Perhaps, John Reumann expresses this viewpoint clearest of all:

> Thus Paul, building on what Jesus did and the theology and practice of the church he knew, emerges not as a chauvinist but a rare champion of the place of women as equals of men, in Christ, in the church. But the vision succumbed to the heritage of centuries in the Jewish and Greek worlds, swallowed up in the watchwords of submissiveness, silence, and subordination for women as the will of God for them. The line of development which ran through the pre-Pauline and Pauline church was submerged by the stronger, older patriarchal trajectory and the 'reactions of the mainstream church.'[52]

As the astute reader has no doubt noticed, the two answers are not mutually exclusive: part of the ammunition the Church used in its battle against the gnostics was the adaptation of the observance of the patriarchal household codes. I, therefore, agree with the view of Scroggs who combines the best points of the two answers.[53]

In sum, it seems that the Pauline communities after Paul had even more trouble than Paul himself — remember 1 Corinthians — in living up to the implications of and warding off misinterpretations of the baptismal reunification formula of Gal 3:28. A considerable number of Christian women took this formula to mean that the created order was to be denied.[54] The Church restored "law and order" by introducing the traditional household codes and by forbidding heresy-prone women from continuing in or assuming leadership functions in the Church. Perhaps, Meeks is absolutely correct when he concludes his brilliant article on how the powerful myth of the reunification of the opposites, male and female, pulsates through Gal 3:28 by observing:

> Thus an extraordinary symbolization of the Christian sense of God's eschatological action in Christ proved too dangerously ambivalent for the emerging church. After a few meteoric attempts to appropriate its power, the declaration that in Christ there is no more male and female faded into innocuous metaphor, perhaps to await the coming of its proper moment.[55]

Conclusions

From the rapid tour I have conducted of the landscape of the NT texts on women, it is clear that the colored glasses of the *Declaration* are not the only pair available.

What other conclusions can be drawn from our tour? For me one of the conclusions of the Pontifical Biblical Commission is too minimalistic: "It does not seem that the New Testament by itself alone will permit us to settle in a clear way and once and for all the problem of the possible accession of women to the presbyterate."[56]

More in accord with the data we have surveyed is the view of twelve of the seventeen members of the same Commission, who do not agree with their five colleagues that in the scriptures there are sufficient indications to exclude the possibility of the accession of women to the presbyterate.[57] On the contrary, these twelve think that the "church hierarchy, entrusted with the sacramental economy, would be able to entrust the ministries of eucharist and reconciliation to women in light of circumstances, without going against Christ's original intentions."[58] In support of their position I would say that the NT texts about ministry bequeath to us the principle of adaptation to historical circumstances.

In fidelity to the example of Jesus, Paul promoted the equality of women and sanctioned the Spirit's gifts of ministry to them. After his death, members of his school found that they had to adapt his teaching to new circumstances lest gnostic women overrun the church and lest the reputation of the church be ruined because women conducted themselves unsubmissively and thus acted against the mores of their culture.[59] This principle of adaptation is articulated very well by Maly: "One thing stands out from any careful study of New Testament texts relating to ministries in the Church and it is that the Church itself felt, from the very beginning, competent to establish and denominate these offices."[60]

In sum, Jesus had limited knowledge and did not engage in the dangerous art of biblical blueprint ecclesiology. His Spirit guided the Church to adapt itself to changed circumstances. The varied ministries of men and women, evidenced within the NT, are proof of the rich guidance given by the Spirit to the Church as it adapted to diverse circumstances. This principle of adaptation is surely valid today in the changed circumstances of the United States.

The other studies in this volume will be able to give additional answers to the question I posed originally: Why do the colored glasses show up the landscape in such vastly different lights?

4

THE MINISTRY
AND ORDINATION OF WOMEN
ACCORDING TO
THE EARLY CHURCH FATHERS

by

Carolyn Osiek, R.S.C.J.

Throughout the Old Testament into New Testament times biblical religion was responding to new circumstances and absorbing new forms of leadership. Older religious structures, as we saw in the previous two chapters of this book, evolved, most often in a gentle way, at times with dramatic leaps. These developments were gradually introduced into the written tradition of the Bible.

With the dawn of the Patristic Age, the Bible became a closed book. Nonetheless, its interpretation remained open to new and more developed forms of liturgy and sacred orders. We continue our search for the line of continuity within the early Patristic Period, a line which led to new adaptations within liturgical leadership. Can we spot signals which will permit such an evolution today, so as to open the priestly order to women?

Several early Church Fathers have left us brief comments scattered among their writings concerning the exercise of some form of official Church ministry by women. These remarks are often cited as part of a "continuous" and "authoritative" tradition forbidding women access to the ordained ministry.

When each of the texts, however, is examined within its own literary and social context, it becomes clear that their witness is by no means unanimous; there is no common agreement on the content of such forbidden ministry. Moreover, as we shall see, their reasons for prohibiting the exercise of the presbyteral function of women are untenable from the viewpoint of contemporary theology. Those ways in which women did exercise ministry were progressive adaptations to circumstances.

I

There is a problem of historical and theological perspective that must be kept in mind from the beginning. We know from a variety of ancient sources that many Christian communities of the first four centuries allowed extended leadership roles to women, including the ordained ministry in many cases. These groups for the most part represented strains of early Christianity which did not become contributors to the formation of the Christian tradition which we have inherited.

Rather, they were considered "heretical" by the "orthodox" tradition which eventually became the only legitimate Christianity; they are known to us as Gnostics, Montanists, Marcionites, and others. Whatever the theological factors involved, it is important to understand that what has survived is basically one theological tradition, the "orthodox" one, represented by the writers known to us as the Church Fathers, whose bias against "heretical" Christianity is obvious.

Tertullian was a fiery North African theologian of the late second century whose own spiritual journey led him eventually into the Montanist Church. Yet he provides two of the most direct and comprehensive statements opposing the participation of women in church ministry. It would be well to begin there.

In his treatise *On Prescription Against Heretics*, Tertullian very cleverly employs his gift for satire to present practices and teachings of Christian groups that he considered heretical in such a way as to make their adherents look ridiculous. One of these practices is the part played by women in the leadership and ministry of their communities. In chap. 41.5 he exclaims: "These heretical women, how bold they are! They dare to teach, to dispute, to perform exorcisms, to promise healing, perhaps even to baptize."[1]

There is a yet more specific statement prohibiting Church ministry to women which comes, strangely enough, from Tertullian in his Montanist days. In the treatise, *On the Veiling of Virgins*, he says plainly: "It is not permitted for a woman to speak in church, nor to teach, baptize, offer [eucharist], nor to take upon herself any male function, least of all the priestly office."[2]

Before going on to examine other texts, it is worth pausing to point out several important features of the two given above. First, Tertullian is one of the earliest Christian writers to speak of episcopal and presbyteral functions as "priestly" (*sacerdotalis*) though he is ordinarily using the term metaphorically. Second, it is not to be assumed that all the activities enumerated in the two passages are considered by Tertullian to be the work of the ordained minister alone. Elsewhere he indicates that both exorcism and baptism can be performed by laymen,[3] but apparently from the above two texts, if he is being consistent, not by women.

The two important actions are teaching and the offering of the eucharist. As for the latter, we shall see that only two other writers, Firmilian and Epiphanius, voice concern over women celebrating eucharist.[4] The objection to women teaching deserves more attention, for it is a key factor in later texts. Tertullian indicates the basis for his statement by partially quoting the text, "It is not permitted for a woman to speak in church" from 1 Cor 14:34-35: "Let women keep silence in the churches, for it is not permitted them to speak, but let them submit, even as the Law says. If they wish to learn anything, let them ask their own husbands at home; for it is shameful for a woman to speak in church."

This text is frequently cited and always thought of by early Christian writers in connection with 1 Tim 2:11-12: "Let women learn in silence in all subjection; for I do not permit a woman to teach nor to have authority over a man, but to be in silence."[5]

The passage goes on to attribute the need for woman's submissiveness to the fact that Eve was created after Adam but sinned before him. This of course immediately evokes both the second creation account and the story of the first sin from Gen 2 and 3, climaxing for our purposes at 3:16 where the woman is punished by the pain of childbearing (see 1 Tim 2:15) and consignment to the authority of the man. This triad of biblical passages, 1 Cor 14:34-35; 1 Tim 2:11-15; Gen 3:16, is the key to understanding the position of the early Church regarding ministry for women. Though Tertullian quotes only the first in *Virg. vel.* 9.1, he is aware of all three.

The treatise *On Baptism*, written earlier in Tertullian's career, was composed against just such a woman teacher as he condemns in general terms in the passages cited above. She was a Gnostic of the obscure Cainite sect which rejected baptism, and she was exercising her teaching career in Carthage where Tertullian lived. He criticized her for taking upon herself the right to teach at all.

At the same time he attempted to squelch any other woman's claim to the right to teach or baptize after the example of St. Thecla, who both taught others and baptized herself in the *Acts of Paul and Thecla*. Tertullian declared that the *Acts* had been written very recently by a presbyter of Asia Minor who was deposed for his efforts, and could therefore command no authority. Besides, he concluded, the same Paul who wrote 1 Cor 14:34-35 could never have authorized a woman to teach, as Paul does to Thecla in the *Acts*.[6]

Tertullian's esteem for prophecy kept him from denying to women that spiritual gift, and he was able to cite Pauline authority equally for this position.[7] He in fact knew of female prophets and visionaries from his own experience but tried rather unconvincingly to distinguish the exercise of prophecy by women from their speaking for the sake of their own instruction or imparting it to others — all apparently based on the attempt to hold literally to Pauline precepts on the subject.[8]

II

Another early Church writer who attempted to reconcile with one another the Pauline precepts on prophecy and public speaking by women was the third century Alexandrian, Origen. In his *Commentary on 1 Corinthians*[9] he directs his comments regarding 1 Cor 14:34-35 against the Montanist female prophets Priscilla and Maximilla. In order to discredit their prophecy, he invokes the Pauline injunction "Let women keep silence in the churches" to the effect that no authentic woman prophet spoke in the public assembly, neither the four daughters of Philip (Acts 21:9) nor Deborah (Jdg 4:4), nor Miriam (Exod 15:20-21), nor Hulda (2 Kings 22:14-20), nor Anna (Luke 2:36).

Origen uses arguments from silence, as in the case of the daughters of Philip, and sometimes simply distortion of the evidence, as in the case of Deborah, to whom people came for judgment (Jdg 4:5). He then goes on to quote Titus 2:3-4 to show that women may indeed teach, but only other women, and that when Paul in 1 Cor 14:35 sends women home to find out what they wish to know from their husbands (literally, "men"), the injunction concerns not only married women, but also widows and virgins, so that "men" must here be understood generically to include a brother, a relative, or even a son.

The clear implication is that any man is more capable of teaching the faith than any woman, even a son his mother! "For men should not sit and listen to women, as if men capable of being responsible for the Word of God were entirely lacking. . . . A woman speaking publicly is a shameful situation which reflects judgment on the whole Church."[10]

It is important to note several things about this passage. Like Tertullian's *Praes*. 41.5 it is a polemical statement, aimed against a particular group of opponents, the Montanists. In spite of its citation by the Vatican *Declaration* on the Ordination of Women as evidence of the Church Fathers' opposition to women in priesthood,[11] the passage is really not concerned with any presbyteral or sacerdotal function except that of teaching as public speaking in church, *i.e.*, as a sign of authority exercised over men as well as women.

On this point Origen holds literally to 1 Cor 14:34-35 and 1 Tim 2:11-12. If the authors of the Vatican *Declaration* consider this text relevant to a contemporary discussion about women in the ordained ministry, it can only be because they understand the authority to teach the Christian faith as essential to the priestly office.

If women are still today considered incapable of teaching the faith to men as well as to women, then the educational work of several generations of Religion teachers in official Church schools, colleges, and adult education programs is in a precarious position. If a fine distinction is to be made between communicating the faith in a classroom and to the same people from the pulpit, we are entering into legalism. If the validity of women's participation in Christian education is not to be questioned, then the association of this passage from Origen with the priestly ministry of women is irrelevant.

III

Though Origen's dealing with the Montanists in the above passage focuses on their women's activity as prophets and teachers, there is other evidence of sacramental functions performed by women apart from passages already cited. A letter of Firmilian of Caesarea in Cappadocia to Cyprian, bishop of Carthage, in the middle of the third century recounts the story of a woman whom the author knew of personally. About 20 years previously she had begun not only exercising gifts of prophecy in the neighborhood but also baptizing and celebrating the eucharist for her followers according to accepted orthodox rites.[12] While leveling against her the usual accusations of madness, diabolic possession, and moral turpitude, Firmilian assumes that of course her sacramental ministry was not valid, anymore than that of heretics and schismatics, about whom the discussion is really concerned.

The interesting thing about the story is that Firmilian does not connect her with any recognized heretical group. She seems to have exercised her ministry on the fringes of an orthodox community and in an orthodox manner. Unfortunately, we do not know whether she had been ordained by someone whose ministry Firmilian would have accepted. He does not say. Lacking that information, it is impossible to say whether he considered her sacramental ministry invalid because her ordination (or lack of it) was also invalid, or simply because as a woman she could not perform such ministry.

It is especially to Epiphanius that we must turn for more specific information on sacramental ministry by women, as well as for more

specific rejection of it. The fourth century bishop of Salamis says that
the Marcionites allowed women to baptize [13] and that the Montanists

> attribute a special grace to Eve because she first ate of the tree of
> knowledge. They acknowledge the sister of Moses as a prophetess as
> support for their practice of appointing women to the clergy. Also, they
> say, Philip had four daughters who prophesied. . . . Women among
> them are bishops, presbyters, and the rest, as if there were no dif-
> ference of nature. 'For in Christ Jesus there is neither male nor female
> . . .' (Gal 3:28)
>   Even if women among them are ordained to the episcopacy and pres-
> byterate because of Eve, they hear the Lord saying: 'Your orientation
> will be toward your husband and he will rule over you.' The apostolic
> saying escaped their notice, namely that: 'I do not allow a woman to
> speak or have authority over a man.' And again: 'Man is not from
> woman but woman from man;' and 'Adam was not deceived, but Eve
> was first deceived into transgression.' Oh, the multifaceted error of this
> world! [14]

The exegetical approach of the orthodox Fathers is typified by the end of
this passage. While the more free-form group quotes Gal 3:28, the orthodox theologian replies with Gen 3:16, 1 Cor 14:34-35, 1 Tim 2:12-14
and 1 Cor 11:8 thrown in for good measure. There is no doubt that sheer
quantity of quotable material is in his favor, and that he readily uses it to
support his position.

Epiphanius' longest discussions about women and priesthood occur in
two passages concerning a group about which it would be very helpful to
have more information. From the data we have it is quite justifiable to
call them a feminist religious society. They are a group of women in
Arabia (though the organization came originally from Thrace) who assemble together in honor of the Virgin Mary with a special kind of prepared cake called a *kollyris*, whence they are called "Collyridians" by
Epiphanius. They have what is assumedly a eucharistic liturgy: in the
name of Mary they assemble *hierourgein dia gynaikōn* — literally, to
function as priests for women. [15]

The author launches into a long treatment of the absence of women
priests throughout history, beginning with Eve who performed no sacrifices while Cain, Abel, Abraham, Jacob, Moses, Aaron and the levitical priesthood after him did; [16] and so on into the New Testament. At
this point Epiphanius brings in an argument that has since become
classic, but which occurs for the first time only a short while before in
the third century Syrian Church Order known as the *Didascalia Apostolorum*: the exemplary will of Christ. If Christ had wished that women
baptize, he argues, then surely he would have been baptized by his
mother instead of by John, and he would have named women among
those commissioned to spread the gospel. Instead, the twelve, Paul,
Barnabas, and James were sent out to baptize, to "perform the priest-

hood of the gospel,'' and to be ''leaders of the mysteries.'' There were no women appointed among them.[17]

Thus 250 to 300 years after the death of Jesus his positive will begins to be interpreted with regard to women in the ordained ministry, which by this time has acquired a clear image of consecration as setting apart for the performance of holy rites as well as for the service of the community.

IV

In the churches of the *Didascalia*, the *Apostolic Constitutions*, and Epiphanius, however, there were recognized official functions performed by women. From the earliest years of Christian community organization there had been a special place for widows. They were recipients of charity in return for their responsibility of prayer and fasting for the Church, hospitality, and instruction of younger women.[18]

In Tertullian's Carthage widows were clearly an official order (*ordo*) in the Church[19] and even formed part of the ecclesiastical tribunal along with bishop, presbyters, and deacons.[20] In early third century Rome widows were also officially designated as persons to be honored but not ordained.[21] This latter situation perdured in third and fourth century Syria as witnessed by the *Didascalia* and *Apostolic Constitutions*, but not in the fifth century Syrian document known as the *Testamentum Domini Nostri Jesus Christi*, where the same language regarding ordination is used of widows as of the rest of the clergy.[22] Widows held positions of honor and service in many times and places in the early Church, but only in the late second century Carthaginian Church of Tertullian and the fifth century Syrian Church of the *Testamentum Domini* is there good indication that they were considered members of the clergy.

It was in Syria that another group of ministerial women came into prominence: the deaconesses.[23] The *Didascalia* and *Apostolic Constitutions* speak often of them[24] and Epiphanius echoes the same information about their role in the Church:[25] they assist at the baptism of women (by immersion) and visit sick women at home, both cases when it would not be suitable for a male cleric to be the principal ministrant. In other passages deaconesses instruct female catechumens and newly-baptized women, and preside over the good order of women during liturgical gatherings.

Were deaconesses ordained? In the eighth book of the *Apostolic Constitutions* (for which there is no parallel in the *Didascalia*), the formulae for ordination and establishment of those in major and minor orders and specially designated groups are given in descending order of importance: presbyter (chap. 16), deacon (chaps. 17–18), deaconess (chaps. 19–20), subdeacon (chap. 21), lector (chap. 22), confessor (chap. 23), virgin (chap. 24), widow (chap. 25), and exorcist (chap. 26).[26]

The characteristic term *cheirotonia*, or its related verb, meaning ordination into the ranks of the clergy, is used for presbyter and deacon. Then when describing the ritual for deaconesses, the text does not use *cheirotonia* but rather substitutes an alternate expression meaning "having placed hands on her. . ." Next, the ritual for the subdeacon uses *both* the present participle of the verb *cheirotonein and* the alternate expression used for the deaconess.

After this, the ritual for the appointment of a lector uses the same expression as that used for the deaconess: "having placed hands on him . . ." followed by the actual prayer to be recited. Then of the following four groups, confessors, virgins, widows, and exorcists, it is specifically said for each that they are not ordained (*ou cheirotoneitai*) and there is no prayer of blessing prescribed for them, even though they are recognized groups in the community.

There is no clear conclusion to attain in regard to the ordination of deaconesses in the *Apostolic Constitutions* because the evidence presented above can be interpreted in two ways. The fact that the important word *cheirotonein* does not appear in the directives for either deaconess or lector can be seen as a deliberate omission indicating that they did not actually receive ordination in spite of the fact that the subdeacon whose ritual is placed between them did.

On the other hand, the fact that it is specifically said of all groups following the lector that they are *not* ordained may imply that those mentioned above *are*, in which case the absence of the term *cheirotonia* in the case of the deaconess and lector may simply be a change in wording for the sake of variety; the verb *cheirotonein*, upon which we are placing considerable importance did after all originally mean simply "to lay hands on," or "to appoint."

In support of the second interpretation, i.e., that deaconesses did receive an actual ordination, are three additional pieces of evidence. First, they appear with other members of the clergy, for example in the distribution of leftover gifts from the offerings of the faithful; even though they are mentioned last, they are the only group of women included in a list that stops with lector or cantor.[27] Second, a later *Epitome* or summary of this part of the *Apostolic Constitutions* entitles the two sections on deaconesses (*Ap. Const.* 8.19-20) "About the Ordination (*Cheirotonia*) of a Deaconess" and "Prayer for the Ordination (*Cheirotonia*) of a Deaconess."[28] Third, Canon 15 of the Council of Chalcedon (A.D. 451) directs that a woman shall not receive the ordination (*cheirontonia*) of a deaconess until she is at least 40 years of age, and she must remain unmarried.[29] Here in an independent source from approximately the same period the ordination of deaconesses is taken for granted.

There is good indication that the office of deaconess was widespread in the East for at least several hundred years, beginning in the third century. In the West, evidence is far more scarce and exists mostly in the form of later synodal decrees witnessing negatively to the institution, that is, attempting to prevent or suppress its development.[30]

The reasons for this geographical disparity become clearer when one looks more closely at the actual role of the deaconess. In all the texts at our disposal, her pastoral activity was restricted to the care of women, and for the most part to those kinds of care that could not be given by men. This work, moreover, was further circumscribed by the norms of society in which respectable women were inhibited in their social movement and access to the outside world. Chief among these kinds of pastoral care were assistance at the unclothing required for baptism by immersion, and the visting and nursing of sick women at home, which sometimes included bringing the eucharist to them. Other activities that made the deaconess a focal point for the religious life of female Christians also developed: supervision of women in the assembly (seated separately from the men) and religious instruction of women and younger children.

It is important to recognize that, although it may have been different in the first Christian generation, the vast majority of the evidence indicates that in the orthodox tradition during the patristic period the ministry of women was directed almost exclusively to women. Within some of the alternative Christian traditions, this was not so.

To accept the witness of pastoral practice in those churches requires, as was stated at the beginning of this chapter, a significant shift of historical perspective which should not be expected to overtake us in the immediate future. Only when the horizon of Christian consciousness has broadened beyond its present denominational limits will we be able to respect the diverse traditions in early Christianity as we are learning to respect religious diversity today.

Conclusions

The question remains, whether women were ordained in the early Church. It is the judgment of this author that only in light of the above observations can that question be intelligently discussed. It would seem that women *were* ordained in some times and places and that this ordination was respected *within the limits of its function in each particular community*. A church observing the statutes of the *Apostolic Constitutions* may have had women serving as deaconesses, while down the street in the same city the local Marcionite church may have had women composing half its assembly of presbyters. Any ordination to the ministry is ordination to a specific role of service that varies according to time and place. It was no different with the ministry of women.

What was — hopefully — different then than now is the attitude of men toward women in the Christian community. Tertullian could call women "the devil's gateway";[31] Origen could declare shameful whatever a woman said in the assembly, "even if it be marvelous and holy, it still comes from the mouth of a woman;"[32] Epiphanius could say that "the female sex is easily mistaken, fallible, and poor in intelligence."[33] Much of the pastoral practice of the early Church incorporated and reflected similar views.

It has often been pointed out that the blatantly misogynist statements of the Church Fathers are sometimes balanced by other more appreciative reflections about women.[34] Be that as it may, belief in the natural inferiority of women was an assumption that went largely unquestioned in antiquity and lies behind most of the repressive restrictions against women in early Christianity. The Vatican Declaration's assertion that "the undeniable influence of prejudices unfavorable to women" found in the writings of the Church Fathers "had hardly any influence on their pastoral activity, and still less on their spiritual direction"[35] is at best naive.

It is, however, useless to blame past generations for what to us appears as short-sightedness because it was based on limited awareness. We can only blame ourselves and our own generation if we do not change and act on our own expanded awareness just as faithfully as past generations did on theirs.

Future directions for women in ministry cannot be founded solely on past practice for several reasons: the evidence is too disparate, the social role of women in general was entirely different then than it is now, and most importantly, because Tradition cannot be interpreted in this manner. To understand Tradition as that which dictates limits for present and future Christian life is to make of it our plaything and our instrument to try to control the Spirit. Rather, Tradition is that solid base upon which the living experience of Christians builds.[36] The way in which Tradition becomes normative and yet develops and unfolds new ways of understanding is precisely what is at issue in this book, and is expanded in other chapters.[37]

Believers of every age are called upon to adapt fundamental Christian insights to their own new situations. This is what the apostolic generation, as well as every generation since then, has had to do. Christian history and tradition can show how those before us have dealt with diversity and change by creating and adapting structure and practices according to the circumstances in which they found themselves while yet remaining loyal to the faith given them in Jesus Christ. We are not observers of that history. We are part of it.

PART THREE

LAW, TRADITION AND LITURGY

5

CHURCH LAW AND
THE PROHIBITION TO ORDAIN WOMEN

by

Dismas Bonner, O.F.M.

"Only a person of the male sex who has been baptized can validly receive sacred ordination."[1] In these few words, canon 968 χ 1 of the *Code of Canon Law* effectively rules out the possibility of ordaining women to the priesthood in the Roman Catholic Church. It is this long standing discipline that is sustained as apostolic tradition by the Sacred Congregation for the Doctrine of the Faith in its *Declaration on the Question of the Admission of Women to the Ministerial Priesthood*.[2] And it is this same discipline that many scripture scholars, theologians, canonists and other deeply concerned members of the contemporary Church question seriously in the face of urgent pastoral needs and social developments which have given new status and recognition to women.

What indeed is the basis of the norm contained in canon 968 χ 1? Is it the current expression of some unchangeable apostolic tradition manifesting the divine law, or is there ultimately a question of ecclesiastical tradition and law which need to change in order to respond adequately to the contemporary situation?

I

Evidently, the *Declaration* is not primarily a canonical document. In fact, neither in the text itself, nor in the Commentary or the notes is there any explicit reference to canon 968 χ 1. However, at the close of Part 4, which treats the "Permanent Value of the Attitude of Jesus and

71

the Apostles,'' there occurs a paragraph that has significant canonical implications:

> This practice of the Church, therefore, has a normative character: in the fact of conferring priestly ordination only on men, it is a question of an unbroken tradition throughout the history of the Church, universal in the East and in the West, and alert to repress abuses immediately. This norm, based on Christ's example, has been and is still observed because it is considered to conform to God's plan for his church.[3]

This statement places the matter squarely in the arena of legal custom, which Gratian defines as ''the kind of law that is established by usages which have been in observance for a long time, and which is accepted as law where there is no law.''[4] Thus many juridical institutes and structures in the Church, including for example some matrimonial impediments and even clerical celibacy, were introduced by custom before they were ever the subjects of written legislation.[5] It has long been recognized that custom can obtain in the Church the same normative and obligatory force as written law.

According to canon law, the key element for the establishment of custom is the consent of competent authority. This constitutes a departure from Roman Law, which situated the force of custom in the consent of the people.[6] Once legitimately established, the law of the Church does not regard the force of lawful custom lightly. Thus in a text that is cited as one of the sources of the *Code of Canon Law*, Pope Honorius III wrote to the Chapter of Paris:

> Since the authority of custom and long usage is not trifling, and novelties most commonly breed discord, We forbid you by authority of these presents to change, without the consent of your Bishop, the approved constitutions and customs of your Church as also to introduce new ones; declaring void any that you might have made.[7]

The text of the *Declaration* is surely sensitive to the requirements for the validity of ecclesiastical custom in canon law, requirements that grow out of long tradition and are presently enshrined in the *Code of Canon Law*.[8] In order that a custom which lies beyond or outside the written law may have legal force, it must be knowingly observed by the community with the intention of binding itself. It must, moreover, be reasonable,[9] and be lawfully prescribed for forty continuous and complete years, i.e., practiced openly without any complaint of legitimate authority. Thus, to meet the requirement that a custom outside the written law be knowingly observed by a community with the intention of binding itself, the *Declaration* offers the conviction that the practice of ordaining only men ''has been and is still observed because it is considered to conform to God's plan for his Church.''[10]

Moreover, lest any contrary past or present practice be cited as the foundation for a custom contrary to the law, the *Declaration* announces that the Church has always been "alert to repress abuses immediately."[11] Indeed, by its insinuation that the prohibition to ordain women is a matter of divine law, and by its evident and continued opposition to any contrary custom, the *Declaration* insures for some time in the future that an essential requirement of canon 27 for customs against the law will not be fulfilled, since to acquire legal force, such a contrary custom must be in peaceful possession without interruption or protest by lawful authority for at least forty continuous years. Moreover, no contrary custom can in any way prevail over divine law.[12] Thus, the Commentary on the *Declaration* is able to claim:

> It is an undeniable fact . . . that the constant tradition of the Catholic Church has excluded women from the episcopate and the priesthood. So constant has it been that there has been no need for an intervention by a solemn decision of the Magisterium.[13]

In the light of the Church's long standing tradition and custom, the Commentary on the *Declaration* raises the further question: Does the fact that the Church has never ordained women to the priesthood constitute proof that she cannot do so in the future? "Does the negative fact thus noted indicate a norm, or is it to be explained by historical and cultural circumstances? In the present case, is an explanation to be found in the position of women in ancient and mediaeval society and in a certain idea of male superiority stemming from that society's culture?"[14] The answer to these questions involves us in the effort to evaluate not only the *Declaration* itself, but also one of the most cogent and scholarly works to treat this problem in recent years, *The Exclusion of Women from the Priesthood*, by the German scholar Ida Raming.[15]

II

Dr. Raming's research purports to show, by a thorough study and interpretation of the pertinent sources, that the law limiting priestly ordination to baptized males was based on forgeries, mistaken identities and suppressions, as well as on the assumption that women are inferior beings. The core of her argumentation is summed up well in the following paragraph:

> It is clear from the application of this discussion to the problem before us that the *Decretum* had a negative influence on the evaluation and the position of women in the church. The ritual regulations for women, which consist exclusively of prohibitions — including the Pseudo-Isidorian decretals and texts (*Statuta Ecclesiae Antiqua*) falsely attached to an important Council — have established or at least confirmed a status of legal deprivation and inferiority for women in the ecclesiasti-

cal sphere. (Assisting in the process were genuine and non-genuine patristic citations, which were used in the Middle Ages as legal sources,
and the accepted opinions of Magister Gratian.) This status became a
generally accepted and permanent condition, which is still determinative
for the law of the *Codex Iuris Canonici*.[16]

For those who might not be initiated into the intricacies of canonical
lore, it will help to identify the cast of characters. Magister Gratian is
known as the "Father of Canon Law" because of his monumental 12th
century *Decretum* which brought new order and clarity into the confused mass of ecclesiastical legislation. The *Decretum*, completed about
the year 1140, became the most important and widely used source of
canon law, despite the fact that it was never officially commissioned or
approved by ecclesiastical authority. Its influence on future law and
theology was immense, and it is one of the principal sources of the
present law of the Church.

The *Statuta Ecclesiae Antiqua* (*Ancient Laws of the Church*) is a collection of canons taken from certain Greek councils as well as from the
Decretals or laws of certain Popes. In an effort to bolster the authority of
these canons, they were falsely and incorrectly ascribed to the IV Council of Carthage (398 A.D.) or to the Synod of Valentia in Gaul (347 A.D.).
Their most likely place of origin, however, is the city of Arles in the first
part of the 6th century.[17]

Much more influential were the Pseudo-Isidorian Decretals, which
Cicognani labels "a forgery altogether unique, a bold and successful
fraud."[18] Most prominent of a number of collections containing false
texts, these decretals were the result of a tendency to accomplish canonical reform through a process of ascribing recent canon law to authorities
of the past. Their principal thrust was to strengthen the position of the
Roman See, as well as to vindicate the rights of bishops and clergy,
particularly in regard to secular authority. The forgers began with a prior
collection, the *Collectio Hispana*. This collection actually had evolved
over a period of time from the 6th to the 8th centuries. But, because of
the great respect for his authority, the entire collection was already attributed to St. Isidore, bishop and doctor of the Church (died 636). Thus
the collection was also known as the *Isidoriana*.

It was this particular body of laws which, further embellished and falsified as the needs of the time dictated, became the *Pseudo-Isidorian
Decretals*. The work was most likely done by an unknown group of compilers between the years 845 and 852, either in Rheims or Le Mans. Drawing upon Scripture, various canons and decretals, Greek, Roman and
Gallic councils and a host of other sources, the forgers cleverly in-
terspersed genuine and spurious texts, and thus were able to perpetrate a
deception that perdured for centuries. Given the universal and almost

immutable force attributed to pontifical decisions, even though neglected and forgotten for a long time, together with the confused and incomplete state of the science of canon law and its sources, compilers found it relatively easy to fill in the gaps with needed legislation, to invent and fabricate papal decrees, without anyone becoming suspicious. Given this situation, it is not surprising that some of the material of the Pseudo-Isidorian Decrétals managed to find a place in the *Decretum* of Gratian and thus to exert its influence on our present law.[19]

III

Does the reliance of Gratian and later legislation on these false decretals constitute a major reason for the present exclusion of women from ordination to the priesthood? Dr. Raming argues strongly that it does. One of the principal vehicles for the transmission of Pseudo-Isidorian texts contained in the *Decretum* was the *Summa* of Huguccio, a very extensive and important work of the Bologna school where Gratian himself worked. Commenting on the role of Huguccio, Dr. Raming writes:

> The viewpoint represented by Huguccio and his epigones, that male sex is the *conditio sine qua non* for the validity and effectiveness of ordination as well as for the exercise of the functions of clerical office, is based in the first place on a fundamental misunderstanding of ordination. As official commissioning and spiritual preparation for ecclesiastical service, ordination can never have sex as essential presupposition for its validity and operation; it is always directed toward a *human* being. In the second place and especially, Huguccio's viewpoint is based on disrespect for woman, her baptism, and her personal and religious worth, all of which qualify her as well as man for receiving ordination and for the exercise of the functions of clerical office. Therefore it must be emphatically emphasized that the church opposes the ethos of the Christian message in an essential point, as long as it preserves this viewpoint and elevates it to a legal norm.[20]

Indeed, Dr. Raming's argumentation tries to build a strong case for these conclusions. Without a doubt, Huguccio's viewpoint, like that of other canonists, is strongly influenced by a low opinion of women and their status in the Church. But to contend that his doctrine is based on these notions about women without mention of any other possible source is to conclude more than the argumentation will bear. It may possibly be, as the *Declaration* maintains, that there is an apostolic tradition which declares the will of Christ in this matter, quite apart from the inadmissible argument drawn from faulty notions about the dignity of women. It may be that such a tradition, together with their ideas about the low status of women, influenced the work of the canonists.

It is likewise quite true that ordination, as "official commissioning and spiritual preparation for ecclesiastical service . . . is always directed toward a *human* being." What Dr. Raming does not add is that the tradition indicates that ordination is always directed toward a *male* human being. If "ordination can never have sex as essential presupposition for its validity and operation," it is nonetheless true that, from a canonical viewpoint, the presumption stands in favor of the Church's immemorial tradition and practice. Surely her argumentation points to the need to reassess this practice, to look once again at the ancient tradition in the light of the contemporary situation. But to conclude that, in the Church's present discipline, "a fundamental misunderstanding of ordination" is operative, or that "the Church opposes the ethos of the Christian message in an essential point" seems to beg the very question that is at issue.

Perhaps the tendency to derive too much from the texts of Huguccio and other canonists can be explained by a reviewer of Dr. Raming's book, writing in *Library Journal* for Nov. 15, 1976, and cited on the dust jacket of the book itself: "She writes in the style of a militant feminist and the mixture of vast scholarship and barely suppressed rage makes a fine combination." This "barely suppressed rage" at times, as in this and other instances,[21] distracts from the dispassionate objectivity that is necessary in matters of this nature.

Any attempt to evaluate the effects of the Pseudo-Isidorian Decretals must be based on some fundamental notions about their historical credibility. It may be that a document consists entirely of genuine canons and is, moreover, circulated under the name of the true author of the collection. However, canons may also be ascribed to someone who is not really the author of the collection, perhaps to give greater authority to the norms. Such canons are truly valid laws, but the collection is not genuine insofar as it is attributed incorrectly to a certain authority. It is known as a "pseudoepigraph." Finally, a given collection may consist either entirely or partially of falsified or invented canons; these canons are not valid law in themselves, although they may, of course, influence the course of later valid legislation.[22]

One of the first instances of this type of compilation occurs in the case of the Pseudo-Apostolic Collections which were circulated under the names of the Apostles from the late first to the fifth centuries, works like the *Didache*, the *Didascalia*, and the *Constitutiones Apostolorum*. Only later were they discovered to be apostolic in character, but not actually the work of the Apostles themselves. To a modern critical scholar, this may seem like rank forgery; in the eyes of the early Christians it was quite another matter. They simply assigned the works to the Apostles because they contained rules which were considered in all good faith to be legitimate developments of the apostolic tradition.

These works, which profoundly influenced the *Decretum* of Gratian, have great significance for the history of ascetical and moral life in the early Church, and for the liturgy and canon law of that time, presenting a fairly ideal picture of the situation of the early Church, its discipline and law. So, in all truth, if we wish to search out "forgeries" which have deeply influenced the life and structure of the Church to our very day, we must, as Dr. Raming indicates, go back far behind the Pseudo-Isidorian Decretals to discover such formative influence.[23]

Turning now to the Pseudo-Isidorian Decretals themselves, scholars note three areas of influence upon the development of canon law: 1) the Decretals do contain some entirely new material, mostly norms vindicating the rights of the Roman Pontiff and the clergy; 2) the collection served to solidify the weak and corrupted church discipline of its day; 3) it exerted an influence on later collections of law which draw material from it.[24] It should be noted that, in most instances, only the texts of the canons were forged; the rights, institutes and structures they were vindicating were already in existence, even inherent in the structure of the Church. Thus:

> The assertion that many novelties were thus introduced is false. Substantially, all its enactments were already in existence. . . . It is sufficient to note that if novelties had been introduced, the collection would not have been so readily accepted; objections would have arisen, and the fraud would have been easily detected. Our argument is strengthened by the fact that certain new laws contained in this collection were never observed. . .[25]

If the mere fact that a text is a forgery does not in itself vitiate its witness to tradition, there is still, as Dr. Raming correctly observes, the question of its objective historical worth.[26] The fact of the matter is, as she well demonstrates, that a number of key texts have been altered in a manner which is highly prejudicial to women, probably out of motives that were based on a very low regard for them. Thus she points out:

> . . . it is clear that the excerpt from the Pseudo-Isidorian decretal of Soter, which Gratian in dist. 23, c. 25 takes as authority, has no convincing historical basis and therefore cannot be used uncritically, *i.e.*, without considering this fact as a traditional proof for the exclusion of women from liturgical functions.[27]

The particular offending text contained a prohibition that no monk (*nullus monachus*) might touch the altar cloths or incense the church. The author of the later *Liber Pontificalis* altered the text to achieve the same prohibition against nuns (*nulla monacha*) instead of monks. Dr. Raming, in a thorough and expert analysis of the texts of the *Decretum*, indicates similar problems with the treatment of other key areas: reservation to men of handling sacred objects, the prohibition for women to take communion to the sick, the prohibition against teaching and baptizing by women, and the exclusion of so-called *presbyterae* in the Church.[28] It is not at all certain just what this final prohibition meant or what this office of *presbytera* was in the Church, but in any case women as a result were excluded from ecclesiastical roles which they had formerly filled.[29]

There is only one place in the *Decretum* where the opinion of Gratian himself about the possibility of ordaining women is expressed. The *dicta Gratiani* aver that "women can attain neither to the priesthood nor even to the diaconate. . ."[30] This is important to note because, as Dr. Raming observes, his own opinion naturally affected his choice of legal texts and the manner of their arrangement. Finally, she observes that it is not clear whether Gratian regards this prohibition as the result of ecclesiastical law alone, or whether he sees it as divine and unchangeable in nature. A number of indications point to the latter view.[31]

IV

The *Commentary* appended to the *Declaration On the Question of the Admission of Women to the Ministerial Priesthood* assesses some of these canonical factors, directly or indirectly. The *Commentary* is quick to acknowledge that, "because of this transitory cultural element . . . some arguments adduced on this subject in the past are scarcely defensible today."[32] Reference is made to St. Thomas' idea of the state of subjection of women and to a similar idea contained in the *Decretum* of Gratian, tempered by the excuse: ". . . but Gratian, who was quoting the Carolingian Capitularies and the false Decretals, was trying rather to justify with Old Testament prescriptions the prohibition — already formulated by the ancient Church — of women from entering the sanctuary and serving at the altar."[33] The Commentary adverts to recent polemical arguments which have recalled and commented on texts that develop this line of argumentation, but concludes that:

> It would be a serious mistake to think that such considerations provide the only or the most decisive reasons against the ordination of women in the thought of the Fathers, of the mediaeval writers and other theologians of the classical period. In the midst of and going beyond speculation, more and more clear expression was being given to the Church's awareness that in reserving priestly ordination and ministry to men she was obeying a tradition received from Christ and the Apostles and by which she felt herself bound.[34]

This contention is bolstered by reference to significant pseudo-apostolic collections and documents, *scil.*, the *Didascalia Apostolorum*, the *Apostolic Constitutions* and an ancient Egyptian collection of 20 canons.[35]

The Commentary turns to deal with theological and canonical treatment of the sacraments. It notes that writers who discuss the nature and value of the tradition reserving ordination to men base their case on a principle formulated by Innocent III. This principle was contained in a letter written Dec. 11, 1210, to the Bishops of Palencia and Burgos, and was included in the Decretals compiled under the auspices of Gregory IX:

> Although the Blessed Virgin Mary was of higher dignity and excellence than all the Apostles, it was to them, not her, that the Lord entrusted the keys of the Kingdom of Heaven.[36]

The context of this assertion is the condemnation of the practice of certain abbesses who were giving priestly blessings to their nuns, hearing their confessions, reading the Gospel and preaching publicly. The Pope calls these practices intolerable and absurd, "thus showing unmistakably that such practice is thoroughly incompatible with his narrow view of women."[37] In any case, whatever may have been the anti-feminist motivation of ecclesiastical authority, the above theological reasoning was introduced and became a common source for commentators on the question. Since the commentary admits that canonists have based their case on this Mariological principle, it surely merits further scrutiny.

Raming cites H. Van der Meer to emphasize that the question of the priesthood of the Mother of God is far from being solved. Certain theologians do admit to a priesthood of Mary, but not the ministerial priesthood or priesthood of office which, she says, "is mistakenly understood as priesthood in the full sense."[38] These theologians deny that Mary could be a priest in the full sense because she was a woman. Commenting on this, Raming points out:

> This kind of reasoning certainly raises questions and leads to the conclusion that the denigration of the female sex on the one hand, and the over-emphasis on the sacramental priestly office on the other, could have brought about a falsification and distortion of Mariology in this respect. H. Van der Meer rightly points out that the argument — Mary was not a priest because a woman cannot be a priest — can no longer be used as proof for the thesis that a woman may not be a priest. For this unproved thesis is being used as basis for the statement that Mary is not a priest: one cannot at the same time prove the first by the second and the second by the first.[39]

Moreover, Raming cites arguments which indicate that rejection of Mary's priesthood suggests a truncated understanding of her place in salvation history as well as an exaggerated understanding of the priestly office itself, an understanding "which does not conceive ministry in terms of the whole church and its charismatic essence, but rather as isolated from them."[40] She points out that Mary is not only the image and archetype of the believing and receiving Church, but also the image of the Church proclaiming the Gospel and conferring the grace of salvation in sacramental signs. In other words, she is the image of the Church of priestly office, and she is the one who bestows on the world the gift of the eternal Word.

It is not, therefore, in Raming's thinking, legitimate to separate the two aspects of the Church, or to identify one with the laity and the other exclusively with priestly office. If Mary is the model of the Church, her priestliness cannot be taken from her, and the fact that she is not numbered among the twelve apostles and was not given the power of the keys does not necessarily prove that she was not a priest. Like Christ's priesthood, Mary's priesthood did not come about by sacramental ordination or apostolic office, but had its origin in her election and calling by God.[41] On the basis of this argumentation, Raming maintains:

> Considering then the place of Mary in the salvation activity of God, it seems clear that the Mariological argument . . . has little merit. Therefore the prohibition of blessing, hearing confessions, and preaching cannot be justified by reference to Mary and her position. On the contrary it is weakened by such reference.[42]

V

Is the prohibition to ordain women, under sanction of invalidity, a matter of divine law which cannot be changed, or is it, in the final analysis, only a question of changeable ecclesiastical legislation? Gratian seems to have held to a divine origin of the law, and the Commentary on the *Declaration*, citing several theologians and canonists, remarks:

> So it is no surprise that until the modern period the theologians and canonists who dealt with the question have been almost unanimous in considering this exclusion as absolute and having a divine origin. The theological notes they apply to the affirmation vary from "theologically certain" (*theologice certa*) to, at times, "proximate to faith" (*fidei proxima*) or even "doctrine of the faith" (*doctrina fidei*). Apparently, then, until recent decades no theologian or canonist considered that it was a matter of a simple law of the Church.[43]

Thus, for example, a later author like Cappello holds that angels, separated souls, unbaptized men and all women are radically incapable of ordination; should they be illicitly ordained, it would be null and void. He argues that, since the priesthood itself is of divine positive law, so the prohibition and incapacity here in question is also a matter of the divine law.[44] The foundation for this common opinion seems to be the interpretation given by the Fathers to 1 Cor 14:34-35 and 1 Tim 2:11-12, texts which enjoin upon women silence in the assembly. These texts have been understood by canonists like Cappello as requiring the absolute exclusion of women from the ecclesiastical hierarchy and therefore from receiving orders.

Thus too the tendency to brand as heretical the opinion that women can validly receive the priestly office.[45] The notes to the *Commentary* on the *Declaration* support this line of thought, citing Gasparri to the effect that the prohibition to ordain women is under penalty of invalidity. Gasparri bases his doctrine on the fact that tradition and Catholic teaching have interpreted the doctrine of St. Paul in this way and notes that, for this reason, the Fathers have branded as heretical the notion that women can be validly ordained.[46] Evidently there is question here of basing the divine law status of this invalidating prohibition on scripture texts, which, however, bear heavy marks of cultural conditioning.[47] Indeed, it would seem that these texts, taken at face value, would have to rule out not only ordination of women, but also most of the important roles which the *Declaration* itself recognizes for women in the contemporary Church.[48]

VI

Sometimes a great deal of confusion is engendered relative to the status and effects of documents that emanate from Rome. There is a tendency to invest anything that comes from the Vatican with a kind of "creeping infallibility" inculcated with the magic phrases, "Rome says" or "the Pope says." Actually, there exists a variety of ways in which the Pope and the Roman Curia issue official statements. Thus, if a statement comes from the Holy Father himself, it can be anything from a formal solemn dogmatic definition to an address at the weekly papal audience. It may be a solemn Apostolic Constitution, a change of legislation introduced on the Pope's own initiative (*motu proprio*) or merely a homily or allocution.

Moreover, the different Congregations of the Roman Curia utilize various forms of communication and promulgation, such as decrees, instructions and responses. Among these options is the form of the "declaration" — the particular type of document used by the Congregation for the Doctrine of the Faith to express its mind "On the Question of the Admission of Women to the Ministerial Preisthood." A declaration may be defined as "an interpretation of existing law or facts, or a reply to a contested point of law."[49] In the case of the *Declaration* on the ordination of women, there is no question of a new law. Rather it is intended to be an authentic (i.e., official) explanation and interpretation of the current legislation of the Church and the current situation in the Church. It must be understood in this light. In no sense should it be seen as the final word which forbids and closes off all further discussion. Had this been the aim and intent of the Holy See, there were far more solemn forms of pronouncement available than that of a declaration coming from a Congregation of the Roman Curia.

Conclusions

The foregoing discussion makes it abundantly evident that the canonical discipline in regard to the ordination of women has resulted from the interaction of complex cultural and theological trends over many centuries. The prohibition to ordain women to the priesthood rests on long established custom that has been written into the law of the Church. Moreover, the antecedents of the written law lie in spurious texts which were accepted into the *Decretum* by Gratian and thus transmitted to the future, so that even today they exert their influence on the law of the Church. However, the mere fact that a text is spurious does not necessarily serve to vitiate its witness to a long standing tradition. The forgeries were attempts to give greater authority and credibility than was already implied by the established practice of the Church, and must be viewed with an understanding of Christians, who, in good faith, sought to bolster rights and structures that were in many cases already inherent in ecclesial life.

What appears rather plain is the fact that no purely legal reason stands in the way of modifying the present law to admit women to priestly ordination. Customs and written norms, insofar as they are expressions of ecclesiastical law, can give way to contrary customs and norms which are better adapted to the pastoral needs of the day. The only requirement is the intervention of competent authority to promulgate a new discipline that is better suited to the good of the Church and its mission. Assuredly, the form of promulgation chosen by the Congregation for the Doctrine of the Faith for its *Declaration* does not rule out the possibility of such a future change.

The real problem, however, is to get at the root of the custom and tradition which later questionable methods tried to strengthen and embellish. To what extent does that tradition represent cultural conditioning stemming from the low opinion of women that was admittedly current in Roman Law and in the whole cultural milieu of the early Church? To what degree is the present discipline the expression of an apostolic tradition which declares the will of Christ in an area that is essential for the structure of the Church? In this connection, it must be noted that later attempts to bolster the tradition as enshrined in the written law of the Church relied largely on the highly questionable mariological argument of Innocent III. Moreover, it must be granted that the argument for the divine law status of the prohibition to ordain women is based on interpretations of Sacred Scripture that cannot be sustained in current biblical scholarship.

Given this entire context, the fundamental question must be posed: What is the value of the tradition that is being proposed and defended by the magisterium in the *Declaration*? And what is the effect upon that tradition of the formidable arguments brought to bear against it from so many directions? In the last analysis, of course, ecclesiastical law is an ancillary discipline. It can only reflect the status of the tradition as interpreted by the magisterium in dialogue with the community of theologians and scripture scholars, and in the context of contemporary pastoral needs. Thus the following chapter of this work turns its attention to the question: To what extent and in what directions can the tradition grow and develop as the Church fulfills its mission to be the living gospel in the contemporary cultural context with its specific pastoral requirements?

6

THE ORDINATION OF WOMEN
AND THE FORCE OF TRADITION

by

Gilbert Ostdiek, O.F.M.

The publication of the *Declaration on the Question of the Admission of Women to the Ministerial Priesthood* by the Sacred Congregation for the Doctrine of the Faith on October 15, 1976 marked a new phase in the development and current discussion of that question.

Recent years have witnessed a dramatic upsurge of books, articles, conferences, and various forms of public action in the Roman Catholic Church directly addressed to the question of women in ministry, especially the ordained ministry. All too often the participants in this discussion seem to have formed two isolated groups. One camp advocates a firm retention of the traditional exclusion of women from ordination to the ministerial priesthood. Those in the other camp fight for a reconsideration of the binding force of that tradition, and many among them call for a bold new tradition admitting women to ordination. As P. Lakeland has noted, the two camps seldom engage each other directly, content to carry on their separate soliloquies.[1]

This *Declaration* marks the first official Roman intervention in the present discussion. The *Declaration* itself notes that there has been no previous intervention representing a solemn exercise of the extraordinary magisterium: "The Church's tradition in the matter has thus been so firm in the course of centuries that the Magisterium has not felt the need to intervene. . ."[2] In issuing this *Declaration* the teaching authority in the Church has now directly engaged itself in the discussion on a non-solemn or non-infallible level.[3] In so doing it has happily offered a focal point for common discussion which may finally provide the occasion and spur to move the discussion from simultaneous soliloquies and monologues to partnership in a true dialogue.

To be sure, the stated intention of the document, echoing an earlier statement of Pope Paul VI who mandated and approved the *Declaration*, is "to recall that the Church, in fidelity to the example of the Lord Jesus, does not consider herself authorized to admit women to priestly ordination" (par. 5). In alerting the participants in the discussion to the Church's constant tradition and the reasons behind it the Congregation clearly envisions that the tradition in force until now will not be changed. Is that to be taken to mean an official closure of all discussion, so that there will be no new discussion?

As K. Rahner has observed in a finely balanced commentary on the *Declaration*, classical methods of establishing the theological qualifications of a Roman document lead one to conclude that this document is an authentic, i.e. an authoritative but not definitive, intervention of the magisterium. In virtue of the form used, then, the document is reformable and in principle it is possible that it be in error.[4] By choosing to intervene on a less than solemn level the teaching authority has provided the opportunity for further study of the question. Rahner then goes on to draw the implications for theologians debating this question. The *Declaration* calls them to treat the stated traditional position with a respect which is not measured solely by the value of its theological arguments but which is due to it as an official church pronouncement. It also leaves them the freedom and duty to critically study that position and its supporting reasons. The discussion must therefore continue.[5] All partners in the dialogue can share with the Congregation its hope that there will be a "deepening understanding of the respective roles of men and women."[6]

Using the *Declaration* as such a focal point, this chapter will investigate the following areas: 1) the constant tradition; 2) the reasons behind the constant tradition; 3) these reasons revisited; and 4) the normative value of a constant tradition.

I

The exclusion of women from ordination to the priesthood and episcopate within the Roman Catholic Church is an acknowledged fact.[7] This practice has enjoyed long periods of peaceful and uncontested acceptance in our Church and is readily accorded the status of a constant tradition. Although the alternate practice is to be found in christian tradition, it has not been accepted as an "orthodox" part of our received tradition.[8] This constant history of factual exclusion remains the single most dominant and critical factor in the discussion for both sides of the debate. That constant practice is the heart of the "unchanging tradition" cited by those who wish to see the *status quo* maintained. Its significance and unchangingness must be explained by those who advocate the ordination of women. It will be well to begin our consideration there, as does the *Declaration*.

Chapter one of the *Declaration*, entitled "The Church's Constant Tradition" (*Traditio perpetuo ab Ecclesia servata*), begins with the words: "The Catholic Church has never felt that priestly or episcopal ordination can be validly conferred on women."[9] An attentive reading of this and similar phrasings used throughout the document suggests that three aspects are fused together when the phrase "constant tradition" is used. The first of these is the constant practice itself (a traditional *praxis*). The second is the teaching presumably implied in the continuance of this practice (an implicit doctrinal tradition).[10] And finally there is an abiding, generalized awareness in the Church embodying the conviction that this constant practice must be maintained if the Church is to be faithful to the Lord's example. This third aspect seems to be the key factor in the constant tradition in that it grounds the constant practice in the absence of an explicitly articulated doctrinal tradition or principle. I believe the discussion would profit greatly from a more nuanced attention to these three facets of the constant tradition.

In regard to the first aspect, the history of the *praxis* has been sufficiently mapped that startling new data is not to be expected. Re-examination of the known data, however, might well have much to contribute to the discussion. Current understandings of tradition, of the historical character of the Church's existence, and of the appropriate methods of interpretation would have to shape the project.[11] Such a study would also have to take fuller account of the cultural images and status of women in the various periods of the Church's history and the ways in which these influenced the Church's understanding and practice.[12] Such an enterprise is beyond the scope of this chapter. The cultural aspects are treated elsewhere in this volume, particularly in chapters 2 and 3, as well as in chapters 8, 9 and 10.

As to the second aspect, a doctrinal tradition can not be invoked to settle the issue as long as it remains implicit. Whether or not the present discussion will (or should) lead to a more explicitly and solemnly formulated doctrine as its end product and what that doctrine will be remain to be seen. Hopefully the discussion will at least help the Church test its reasoning and clarify the conviction that now roots the constant practice. In as much as chapters two and three of the *Declaration* represent the Congregation's first attempt to formulate theologically the teaching implied in the traditional practice, we will turn to those chapters in the next two sections of this study.

The third aspect may not be immediately evident and merits closer inspection. The *Declaration* flags this third aspect when it habitually prefaces its statement of the constant tradition, saying that the Church "considers . . .", "feels . . .", "intends . . ."[13] If one follows out the analogy from personal experience implied in these phrases, the Congregation's wording suggests that the Church takes its stance with a certain measure of self-consciousness, perhaps even of reserve; yet, at the same time, the Congregation speaks as though in possession of the *Church's* conviction. This combination of diffidence and certainty suggests further that the Church possesses a generalized awareness of a course of action to be taken, but an awareness that has not yet been objectively investigated and clearly stated. This does not mean that the conviction is groundless, a mere subjective persuasion without foundation. The phrases cited above refer variously to the example of the Lord, the type of ministry willed by him, and God's plan for the Church. If the Church continues to exclude women from ordination, it is because the Church is convinced that it must act in this manner to be faithful to the Lord, even if its reasons are not totally clear and compelling.

This dual quality of certainty and reserve which marks the Church's conviction raises the question to be taken up in the final section. Might it not be possible for the Church to change this conviction, the keystone in the constant tradition? That conviction is now facing its stiffest test. The final answers, theological and official, are not yet in on the permanent value and unchangeableness of the tradition. In the meantime, the reasons on which the conviction is based need to be studied more fully.

II

In chapters two and three the *Declaration* sketches the main lines of its argumentation and lays out the reasons behind the constant tradition. Further illustrative arguments are elaborated in chapters five and six.[14] The line of reasoning used is quite similar to the reasoning of those who advocate maintaining the traditional exclusion and can serve well as our illustration of that point of view.

We will summarize the salient points of the *Declaration* as background for our own discussion of the tradition.

The starting point of the argument is the practice of Jesus, who "did not call any woman to become part of the Twelve" or "entrust the apostolic charge to women."[15] His free association with and acceptance of women in other circumstances, contrary to established Jewish customs concerning the role of women, are cited to establish that this withholding of the call was a free choice on his part and not determined by the socio-cultural context. However, "It is true that these facts do not make the matter immediately obvious. . . . In order to reach the ultimate meaning of the mission of Jesus and the ultimate meaning of Scripture, a purely historical exegesis of the texts cannot suffice.''[16] The document therefore cites as a ''convergent indication'' the fact that Jesus did not invest his mother Mary with the apostolic ministry, a traditional argument first elaborated by the Fathers and still favored by many current theologians.

The argument then moves to the practice of the Apostles, stressing that the apostolic community chose a man to replace Judas, that the proclamation of the Gospel was carried out by men (Peter and the Eleven), and that the Apostles and Paul did not confer ordination on women. As above, the Apostles' freedom of action in this matter is established by referring to their willingness to break with Mosaic law and Jewish customs in other matters and to the more favorable climate concerning the role of women found in the non-Jewish cultures into which the young Church spread.

The argumentation is completed by recounting the evidence of the continuing practice in subsequent church history. Special attention is given to the anti-ordination statements of the Fathers occasioned by the ordination of women among the heretical sects and to the reasons offered by medieval theologians for excluding women. This segment of the argumentation had already been developed in chapter one of the *Declaration*.

The conclusion is thus reached that the exclusion of women from ordination is an unbroken and therefore unbreakable tradition which can be traced back to the will of Christ as expressed in his manner of acting and to the Father's will or plan for the Church. The *Declaration* will later note, in chapter four, that the Church is not free to change this dispensation because she has no power over the substance of the sacraments.

Finally, the argument is further illustrated by additional theological reasons in chapters five and six. The first of these reasons is that priests and bishops in exercising ministry, especially in celebrating the Eucharist and presiding over the christian assembly, act ''in persona Christi'' and represent him. Extending the dictum of St. Thomas that ''sacramental signs represent what they signify by natural resemblance''[17] to the person of the minister, the *Declaration* concludes that ''there would not be this 'natural resemblance' which must exist between Christ and his minister if the role of Christ were not taken by a man: in such a case it would be difficult to see in the minister the image of Christ. For Christ himself was and remains a man.''[18] The second illustrative reason is drawn from the mystery of the Church, its distinctiveness from human social structures, and the full and equal baptismal dignity which all share as members of Christ and his priestly people.[19]

This entire line of argumentation had already been subjected to extended discussion and assessment within the ranks of those who promote the admission of women to ordination or call for an open consideration of the question. They too admit the long historical practice in force until now, but question whether it is a binding, unchangeable tradition. They conclude rather that the exclusion may be or actually is a practice historically conditioned by its socio-cultural context and therefore capable of being changed. They are led to this conclusion by a number of reasons.

First, both Jesus' manner of acting towards women and the text of Gal 3:28 seem to offer evidence of an original attitude of total equality and non-exclusion of women on the part of Jesus and the early community.[20] In this reading the adoption of contemporary socio-cultural attitudes towards women was the work of the subsequent community when the forms of ministry were being shaped to meet new community situations.

Further, scholarly study of the historical process by which ordained ministry has taken on its present structure indicates that the process was much more nuanced and culturally conditioned than the Roman document seems to allow.[21] Consequently any *easy* move from the exclusion of women from the Twelve or from apostolic ministry to their exclusion from ordained priesthood and episcopate is suspect.

Further, when seen in the light of such historical study, the roles played by women in the ministry of Jesus and in the apostolic ministry take on a more important significance, as does the later rise of deaconesses.

Finally, to many critics the representation argument seems at best less than persuasive and possibly even theologically faulty.

From considerations such as these, writers in the second camp are increasingly calling for a re-interpretation of the data. Has the long history of exclusion, they are asking, resulted from inescapable socio-cultural influences or from the inner needs of God's plan of redemption. Their conclusions are usually stated in a negative form, to the effect that the data from Scripture, history, and theological tradition do not exclude the possibility of the ordination of women and leave the issue unresolved.[22]

And so the argument returns to its starting point, the accepted fact of the tradition itself and the question as to whether or not there is an adequate rationale for the Church's conviction and its retention.

III

As indicated above, the *Declaration* is not to be interpreted as closing the discussion as far as theology is concerned. Rather, it may have providentially furthered it in providing a common meeting ground for the discussion.[23] The reasons behind the tradition need to be submitted to further critique and development before the issue can be resolved.[24] Toward that end it may be of help to pose some questions and alternate lines of thought in four areas: 1) the intention of Jesus and the apostolic church to exclude women from ordination to priesthood; 2) the case of the Blessed Virgin; 3) the representation argument; and 4) the question which the order of deaconess can raise about the exclusion of women. The arguments on both sides need to be as fully and critically developed as possible and attention ought to be directed to related theological areas which have a bearing on these arguments. As the *Declaration* itself observes, "As we are dealing with a debate which classical theology scarcely touched upon, the current argumentation runs the risk of neglecting essential elements."[25]

First, great care must be exercised in drawing conclusions about the will of the Lord (or of the apostolic church) implied in a certain manner of acting. The fact noted in an earlier chapter in this book, that the argument from the will of Christ did not appear for the first 250–300 years,[26] already hints that it may not have been that clearly perceived or decisive in early church development of ministerial structures. This type of argument is not unlike an argument from silence in the absence of an express declaration of intention. To be fully effective it has to pass muster on a series of steps such as the following. First, Jesus (and the early Church) did not call women to ministry. Second, Jesus deliberately broke with established Jewish customs concerning the status and role of women in other matters, thus establishing the presumption of sufficient awareness and freedom to do so. Third, Jesus ought to have and would have included women in the call to ministry if he could have. Fourth, since Jesus did not, therefore he could not, and therefore women as such are to be excluded from ordination.

The third step is the weak link in the argument. It is not necessarily implied in step two. To establish this third step it is necessary to exclude all other possible explanations; only then can we be sure that Jesus *ought* to have included women in the call to ministry. The possibility of an inescapable socio-cultural influence is precisely the point at issue. It must be disproved if the argument is to be conclusive.[27]

We can only mention in passing another serious problem with the argument. That is the implicit equation of apostolic ministry in the New Testament church with ordained ministry as later found in the three-fold hierarchy of orders: bishop, priest, and deacon. As Robert Karris brought to our attention in chapter 3 of this book, it is questionable whether this equation can stand the test of current biblical and historical research on the structuring of ministry in the early Church.

The reasoning based upon the fact that Jesus and the early apostolic community did not call Mary to a place among the Twelve also seems to contain a number of hidden assumptions. Let me state the case as strongly as I can, well aware that this argument serves a highly symbolic function. One of the favored texts cited in this argument is that of Pope Innocent III: "Although the Blessed Virgin Mary surpassed in dignity and in excellence all the Apostles, nevertheless it was not to her but to them that the Lord entrusted the keys of the Kingdom of Heaven."[28] The argument seems valid only on the assumption that God has graciously and fittingly chosen to bestow all possible dignity and excellence on Mary in an unsurpassed degree, that the absence of priesthood, if priesthood had been possible for her, would have constituted a loss of the dignity and excellence she ought to have possessed, and that therefore it was not possible for her, or any women, to be ordained a priest for no other reason than the precise fact that she was a woman. Hence in Mary all women have been excluded from ordination.

This reasoning seems to contradict a later insistence in the *Declaration* that "The priesthood is not conferred for the honor or advantage of the recipient, but for the service of God and the Church; it is the object of a specific and totally gratuitous vocation."[29] As Pope Innocent intimated, Mary's all-surpassing dignity and excellence had already been established by her vocation to be the Mother of the Savior; her excellence and dignity could have been neither enhanced nor lessened by a calling to priestly ministry and hence the question of dignity is not germane to her exclusion from ministry if, with the *Declaration*, ministry is conceived as service.[30] Mary had already received her unique call to service. Finally, if the service of ministry is the "object of a specific vocation," Mary's case cannot be made a universal statement of exclusion for all women.

Let us turn, thirdly, to the representation argument and focus on the liturgical-sacramental aspect of the argument, leaving aside other promising lines of re-examination in the areas of christology[31] and theological anthropology.[32]

The classical formula used in theological and ecclesiastical documents to describe the relationship between Christ and the ordained priest is that in ministering the priest acts "in persona Christi."[33] The understanding behind this phrase is that the ministering priest represents Christ, taking his place and acting in his name, so that the effective power of the action flows from Christ and not from the priest. The priest's representation of Christ, however, goes beyond the causality and effectiveness of the action. In keeping with the classical theological dictum that sacraments cause by signifying, there is also another dimension to the relationship in the sense that the sacramental action images

Christ's own action and the priest images Christ himself by a "natural resemblance."[34] As the *Declaration* puts it:

> The supreme expression of this representation is found in the altogether special form it assumes in the celebration of the Eucharist, which is the source and center of the Church's unity, the sacrificial meal in which the People of God are associated in the sacrifice of Christ: the priest, who alone has the power to perform it, then acts not only through the effective power conferred on him by Christ, but *in persona Christi*, taking the role of Christ, to the point of being his very image, when he pronounces the words of consecration.[35]

This understanding of the relationship of Christ to the priest in the act of sacramental ministry needs to be re-thought in the light of current sacramental theology and some alternate data from theological tradition. Contemporary sacramental thought is making an ever greater use of the model of symbolic action/interaction found in the experience of human relationships. This model is supplementing and in some ways replacing the aristotelian model of causality in describing the sacraments.

The capital theological point still remains that sacraments are the personal saving actions of Christ in a very real sense.[36] Would it not follow then that the minister of every sacrament truly takes the place of Christ and represents him in a visible fashion within the liturgical assembly? Thus the formula "*in persona Christi*" could be applied to each case of sacramental ministry.[37] If we then keep in mind the theological traditions which admit valid administration of baptism and marriage by women,[38] we have already implicitly admitted that women do and can represent Christ. This also means that we can retain the representational (imaging) character of the ministerial act, and of the person of the minister, without reducing the iconic character or figurative quality of the sacramental symbol to that of an image (icon) or representation taken in a completely literal sense in all its concrete, empirical details. In other words, the maleness of Jesus and the minister would no longer be considered essential to either the act of ministry or the recipient of the sacrament of orders.

A fourth area which might well merit re-examination is that of the nature and implications of the female diaconate. The traditional teaching of the Church holds that diaconate, priesthood, and episcopate together form one sacrament of orders, received in varying degrees of fullness. If it be acknowledged that at least some deaconesses received ordination in a true sense of the word,[39] would it not follow that the admission of women to the diaconate conferred on them the first degree of the sacrament of orders and thus implies the possibility of their admission to the remaining degrees? "Because of the underlying unity of Church office, admission to one office implicitly affirms the theological possibility of admission to any of them."[40]

What is the value of such theological considerations? The classical distinction between the force of an authoritative teaching of the magisterium (now being invoked in the question of women's ordination) and that of its supporting theological arguments lead one to acknowledge that the theological debate alone will not be able to determine the future of the traditional practice. That determination will occur only within the *sensus fidei* of the church under the guidance of the magisterium. However, that debate can serve two more modest purposes. It can successfully establish that the scriptural and theological arguments are inconclusive and unfinished, thereby opening the way for further discussion of the traditional practice. It can also serve to clarify the issues involved in the tradition and thus prepare the way for a more thoughtful determination of future practice.

And so we are brought back once again to the constant tradition of the Church and the Church's conviction that this tradition has a normative value. Let us take up that question in the final section.

IV

The heart of the Congregation's position is found in chapter four of the *Declaration* which takes up the critical question of the binding force of the constant tradition. It begins by asking: "Could the Church today depart from this attitude of Jesus and the Apostles, which has been considered as normative by the whole of tradition up to our own day?"[41] It first answers two arguments against the normative value of the tradition, namely that Jesus and the Apostles acted out of an anti-feminine prejudice under the influence of their milieu and that Paul's prohibition of women from speaking in the assembly was a transitory ordinance inspired by the culture and customs of the times.

Next the document turns to the question of the Church's power to change the sacraments. The *Declaration* recalls the teachings of Trent, Pius XII, and Paul VI that the power of the Church over the sacraments is limited and does not extend to the substance of the sacraments.[42] It then states that the Church's decisions concerning what can or can not be changed are made in the light of her knowledge that she is bound by Christ's manner of acting. It concludes in answer to the opening question:

> This practice of the Church therefore has a normative character: in the fact of conferring priestly ordination only on men, it is a question of an unbroken tradition throughout the history of the Church, universal in the East and in the West, and alert to repress abuses immediately. This norm, based on Christ's example, has been and is still observed because it is considered to conform to God's plan for his Church.[43]

The fundamental issue is thus made clear: an unbroken practice which goes back to the Lord's manner of acting has normative value and can not be changed because it reflects his will and that of the Father for the Church.

The *normative value* of tradition, it seems to me, is determined by one's *concept of tradition*. In the remaining pages I draw attention to the differing approaches to tradition[44] and what normativeness means for each. By way of illustration there will be a brief development of three cases from tradition which can serve as useful analogies for the case of the ordination of women.

In the first of these approaches, the one which seems to underlie the *Declaration*, tradition is understood to be the Spirit-guided transmission of the deposit of revelation (the "faith"). Revelation is pictured primarily in the model of word/teaching/message which was completed with Christ and closed after the apostolic church's final recording of the message in the Scriptures. This message of revelation, consisting of all that Jesus taught explicitly or implicitly in his words and manner of acting, has been entrusted to the Church's teaching authority as a deposit which the Church is to preserve and faithfully hand on under the guidance of the Spirit. It is this Spirit which enables the entire Church, believers and magisterium, to grow in their understanding of all that was implied in the original deposit through a process of explicitation.

This classical approach to tradition is often allied with an "essentialist" attitude toward truth; it also normally presumes an undifferentiated historical consciousness. In that view truth is objective and absolute, free from the vicissitudes of history. The divinely inspired human forms of thought and language in which revelation and tradition are contained have a perennial validity. Thus this approach logically sees the unbroken practice stretching back to Christ as the revelatory expression of his will. The traditional practice is unbreakable and normative for all times and excludes the development of any contrary practice.

The contrasting approach is more insistent on the living, historically-situated character of tradition. The typical starting point would be an understanding of revelation such as that found in Vatican II's *Dei Verbum*. Revelation, which occurs in both word and event, is completed and summed up in the Word Incarnate, who accomplished this "by the *total fact of his presence and self-manifestation* — by words and works, signs and miracles, but above all by his death and glorious resurrection, and finally by sending the Spirit of truth."[45] Thus it is Jesus in his person, as well as his words and works, who is *the revelation* to be received and handed on. Correspondingly, the Church made one with its living Lord through the abiding gift of the Spirit becomes *the living tradition* of the Lord who is revelation. "In this way the Church, in her doctrine, life and worship perpetuates and transmits to every generation all that she is, all that she believes.''[46] The Church is tradition in the concrete sense, whether tradition is conceived actively as the ecclesial process of transmitting or passively as the content transmitted.

Up to this point the second approach does not differ from the other in insisting on the inner role of the Spirit as well as the external elements of tradition.[47] The second approach, however, does differ in shifting emphasis from the verbal model of communication to a model drawn from our experience of interpersonal relationships. In those relationships we express and communicate ourselves not only in word, but also and more importantly in all bodily actions and expressions, in the total fact of personal presence and self-disclosure. In this model communication moves beyond a sharing of knowledge to full self-disclosure and self-offer. It is in this sense that the Church in perpetuating itself is the living tradition (act and content) of the presence of the Lord.[48] This approach, in working from a model of personal presence and self-communication, is also more alert to the dialogical character of revelation and tradition as the living address of God which becomes such only when it is heard in faith by those addressed.

This approach is also increasingly allied with a differentiated historical consciousness. It recognizes that all human life and forms of expression are inescapably conditioned by their historical setting. These forms, taken from and always bound to human culture in all its historical particularity and changeableness, are the only forms in which the Church can express and realize itself under the guidance of the Spirit. This approach logically concludes that living adaptation and change are both expected and necessary in changing life-contexts. In major new socio-cultural situations, whether personal or societal, the change has to be major if continuity and authenticity of life are to be maintained.[49] Conversely, to preserve past forms literally in such a new situation could prove to be infidelity and discontinuity.[50] In this view, then, change and adaptation are a normative part of a normative tradition.[51]

The question would then be, is it not possible that the Church may have to change its unbroken practice to remain faithful to the will of the Lord and his Spirit in a major new socio-cultural situation? Such a course of action is not without precedent in the history of the Church.

By way of analogy, allow me to briefly sketch three parallel cases to illustrate how new socio-cultural situations have occasioned notable changes in official church teachings and positions.

The first of these examples concerns the ruling conception of christian marriage in recent catholic tradition and practice. The chief, though not the only understanding of marriage in recent catholic theology stressed the exchange of consent, often described in terms of contract. That consent concerns rights proper to the married state and the three ends or blessings of marriage: offspring, conjugal fidelity, and indissolubility. This framework of reference has determined much of the canonical and ethical norms and practices in our recent tradition.

Starting in the 1940's a gradual shift occurred in the vocabulary used by the magisterium. That development culminated at Vatican II. There the language of community, covenant, and a conjugal love that is eminently human, i.e., bodily-spiritual, came into official prominence alongside that of contract and ends. This fresh conciliar perspective takes on added significance when seen in its context. The Council elaborated its teaching on marriage in part two of *Gaudium et Spes*, only after it had ''set forth the dignity of the human person'' in part one.[52]

In effect, a more biblical and personalist anthropology was called into service to meet the new needs of married christians facing a socio-cultural situation where marriage had been cut free, sometimes violently, from all the supports and secondary definitions of its previously assumed place in the structure of society. As a result of this elimination of all other secondary relationships, the primary reality of marriage was clearly disclosed to be that of a marital love-relation between man and woman.[53] Norms and theoretical traditions, in some cases representing radical departures from previous tradition, are being gradually built up in both jurisprudence and ethics on the basis of this fresh understanding of the Council. The change taking place in our tradition thus flows from a new understanding of person and the personal nature of the marital relationship.

In parallel fashion, a new understanding of the full personhood of woman is also being forged in our culture. It, too, will require modifications and changes in our traditional practices.

A second analogy can be worked out from the development of our tradition concerning slavery. The text of Gal 3:28 so prominent in the discussion of the ordination of women also taught the full equality of slaves and free persons who had been baptized. Despite this firm profession of the religious liberation and equality of slaves, the sociological practice of slavery was accepted during the biblical period and remained a constant practice well into modern times. One finds only occasional and seemingly ineffective reprobation of the practice by the magisterium of the Church in the last four centuries. Yet a little more than a century after the violent struggle that led to the abolition of the practice in U.S. civil law, Vatican II in a matter-of-fact manner describes slavery as an ''offense against human dignity'' and unhesitatingly includes it among its list of crimes against that love of neighbor which is commanded by Christ.[54]

The key factor in this example also is the full development, *spurred by changes in the sociological structures*, of an understanding of the personal dignity and freedom due to every person and of the sociological consequences that necessarily flow from such an understanding.[55] It is an instructive parallel to the ordination of women not only because of the text of Galatians and patristic texts comparing the status of women to that of slaves, but especially because of its witness to a long coexistence in the Church of a principle and a contrary unbroken practice. This same dichotomy between religious principle and sociological practice seems to many to be the heart of the matter in the ordination question.

A third analogy can be drawn from the recent development of our tradition on religious liberty. These few paragraphs will only attempt to highlight some of the aspects that make it a pertinent analogy.[56]

The condemnation of religious freedom and freedom of worship, promulgated by Gregory XVI in his *Mirari Vos* (1832) and by Pius IX in his *Quanta Cura* and the accompanying *Syllabus of Errors* (1864), are well known data of modern Catholic church history. On the face of it how different that nineteenth century position is from the one officially adopted by Vatican II!

> The Vatican Council declares that the human person has a right to religious freedom. Freedom of this kind means that all men should be immune from coercion on the part of individuals, social groups and every human power so that, within due limits, nobody is forced to act against his convictions in religious matters in private or in public, alone or in association with others.[57]

The history of this changing practice is an intriguing study in the development of doctrine.

To our way of thinking the nineteenth century theory and practice seem so inimical to the basic biblical heritage — according to the Scriptures God has a loving regard for each individual, his Word can be accepted only in freedom, and the kingdom of heaven is not a political one — that the origin and meaning of that practice need an explanation.

The context in which this position took shape was influenced by a number of historical factors. In the course of the medieval development of church-state union in the form of the "confessional state," the Church came to accept both the practice and a theory of church-state union which put aside an earlier church insistence on the distinction between the political and religious spheres. The reformation conflict sharpened and confirmed the Catholic Church's conviction that it enjoyed in an unique fashion the certain possession of revealed truth, "objective and absolute, free from the vicissitudes of history." We have already discussed this "classical" or more static idea of tradition earlier in this chapter. The Church, therefore, could not tolerate religious neutrality or indifferentism, since this would be tantamount to acknowledging that one religion is as good as another. This implied that the confessional state ought to be Catholic.

Later in the nineteenth century this ideal was formulated into the thesis that in such a nation the Catholic Church alone ought to be recognized with full right of public worship and propagation, with official state intolerance of all other religions. This was commonly expressed in principles to the effect that truth enjoys primacy over freedom and that only truth, and not error, has the right to exist.[58] This ideal of intolerance was normally softened by the acceptance of a practice of tolerance (the hypothesis) to meet the real situation of religious pluralism in most states.

Additional historical factors behind the condemnation of religious freedom are to be found in the Enlightenment and the movement toward secularization of the European states. The Enlightenment glorified human reason and goodness, often to the detriment of religion and the supernatural. The secularization movement harbored a strong, overt anti-religious bias and strove to separate the state from the church. The attack on established religion easily became an attack on religion itself.

It was in that context that Gregory XVI and Pius IX condemned freedom of conscience and freedom of cult, since these were ideological formulas in which was inherent "the moral judgment that the individual conscience is absolutely autonomous, and the further theological-social judgment that religion is a purely private affair, irrelevant to any of the public concerns of the political community."[59] The proscription of errors in the *Syllabus* thus inculcates a practice of religious intolerance, a practice theologically motivated and politically implemented.[60]

A number of developments had already been set in motion that would soon lead to a complete reversal of this position. John Courtney Murray cites two such nineteenth century movements. First, there was the movement from the sacral concept to the secular concept of society and state. Leo XIII met this development by reviving the ancient christian distinction between the religious and political realms. This distinction was developed to mean not just two separate powers in one state, but two distinct societies, each with their own laws and powers. Second, there was the movement from classicism to historical consciousness.[61] Outside the pale of express church interests, the fact of religious pluralism in most modern states continued to have its impact, particularly in the widespread adoption of civil and constitutional provisions for religious freedom.[62] Finally, the rise of the dictatorial and totalitarian states focused the attention of the Church on the question of the dignity and freedom of the individual human being.[63]

It was the interweaving of these developments which set the stage for

Vatican II's declaration on religious liberty which completed the radical reversal of the official church position of a short century before. The critical factors seem to have been the emergence of a new understanding of freedom and a desire for it in the personal and public realms, in religious as well as in secular matters. Such freedom was seen as the inherent right of all persons in society. In the Church there was a corresponding reflection "on true human dignity," the highly symbolic opening phrase of the Council's declaration,[64] and on the nature and role of the state in that light. H. Schlette describes this process well when he writes:

> From the point of view of the history of ideas, and also from that of intrinsic coherence, religious freedom, like freedom in general, is founded on biblical anthropology, soteriology and eschatology, and on the resulting positive fundamental esteem for the individual as such. But various developments in history and the social order . . . had to take place before the basic religious and theological convictions as to the dignity of the individual, of conscience, of freedom, of equality before God, of love (especially love of enemies), of brotherliness, etc., could have full play. It was only at the end of a long evolution that theologians grasped the full scope of the rights of the individual and of religious groups outside the Church, and hence the civil, political and finally the theological desirability of religious freedom.[65]

This analogy is instructive for the case of the ordination of women from several aspects. The new socio-cultural situation made it necessary for the Church to formulate a new official position. The key element in that change centers on the new understanding of our God-given personal dignity as necessarily involving religious freedom. Each person has the right to exercise that freedom in private and in public. Finally, one needs only to recall the heat of the conciliar debates on this topic to realize that the Council Fathers clearly had to face the question of retaining or radically changing a traditional position that was rather deeply ingrained. That same intensity of feeling seems to mark the ordination question. Hopefully, as in the case of religious liberty, that will not block an open consideration of the newly developing understanding of the personhood of woman and the radical revision of church practices this may entail.

Conclusion

A series of brief statements will serve to summarize this chapter and express my own deep convictions in the matter.

The issue of the ordination of women to the ministerial priesthood remains an open question; the *Declaration* has not resolved it definitively.

One of the most fruitful responses to the *Declaration* will be for proponents of both sides of the question to use the document as the common focus for a true dialogue.

The theological discussion will not of itself be able to resolve the issue. The arguments do merit further critical development so as to provide a fund of supporting, well-refined theological understandings for that final resolution. The debate ought to be carried on with more attention to related questions in other areas of tradition and with a respectful awareness of the "risk of neglecting essential elements" always present in an argumentation that has not yet undergone extensive development.[66]

The critical factor in the whole question is the constant practice of excluding women from ministerial priesthood and the meaning and normative value of such a practice.

The question of the normative value of a tradition is pre-determined by the understanding one has of tradition and of revelation. Accordingly, it is urgent that all who take part in the discussion reflect on the understandings they presuppose. One of the best results of the *Declaration* may well be to trigger consideration of this neglected point. If we adopt *a priori* the stance that "tradition must change" or that "tradition can't change," then we are once again exiling ourselves back to the fortified camps, viewing one another from a hostile distance.

The understanding of tradition accepted by the writer of this chapter follows the second line of approach described in the last section. Tradition is simply the living Church bound to its crucified and glorified Lord in the abiding gift of the Spirit, just as the Lord Jesus is himself the living revelation. And just as that original Word was authentically Incarnate, so too the Church, the People of God on pilgrimage through history, must find full and authentic embodiment in "the mentality and character of each culture."[67] Major changes in the forms of a culture will then demand major changes in the forms assumed from that culture by tradition, but in that process continuity and fidelity must be preserved. We are not without recent precedents to illustrate such adaptation and major change in long-standing, constant traditions. This does not necessarily militate against continuity and fidelity to the Spirit and the will of the Lord. Tradition is normative; change and adaptation are a normative part of that normative tradition.

In the case at hand the reigning socio-cultural understanding of woman and of the roles suited for her has historically argued against the ordination of women to priesthood. Yet that understanding is undergoing a cultural shift; society is recognizing ever more clearly and forcefully the full personhood of woman and her roles as distinctly woman, not simply as a substitute male. As in the analogous cases cited in this chapter, this cultural shift will be the critical factor. As this revolutionary change is accomplished in society at large, it will demand that the Church rethink and reshape her tradition on ministry and the exclusion of women from the priesthood. Should the Church delay and wait for the new understanding of woman to take final shape in our culture before she rethinks her theology and practice, then many women will be alienated from the Church and that understanding will be deprived of the leaven of the Gospel which the Church is called to witness.

7

THE PRIEST AS "ANOTHER CHRIST" IN LITURGICAL PRAYER

by

Ralph A. Keifer

The question of the ordination of women to the Roman Catholic presbyterate raises a liturgical question: would the ordination of women be
liturgically disruptive? Or, to pose the question another way, would a
decision to ordain women to the presbyterate represent a break with the
basic patterns of liturgical prayer in the Roman rite? In a church which
takes its patterns of liturgical prayer as normative for belief (*lex orandi
legem statuat credendi*), the question has major import. If the ordination
of women were to pose the possibility of a basic disruption of the
church's prayer patterns, it would be *prima facie* evidence that the ordination of women is theologically questionable.

I

It may be useful to indicate what I mean by "disruption" of "basic
patterns". I do not refer to the dismay which might attend the introduction of the practice of women's ordination, or to the difficulties which
some Catholics might experience in accepting women in the role of presiding over sacramental celebration. Change, even major change and innovation may evoke dismay from some. Such change need not, at the
same time, affect the basic patterns of liturgical prayer. For instance, the
introduction of the use of the vernacular into the liturgy was dismaying
to some, but did not affect basic liturgical patterns. By "basic liturgical
patterns" I refer to those aspects of liturgical prayer which express and
signify the fundamental reality of the church. The question which I ad-

dress is: would the fact and presence of female presbyters represent a basic change in those patterns?

It is the belief of this writer that the ordination of women would not represent a basic change in liturgical pattern. The difficulty with proving this is that negative facts are more difficult to prove than positive ones. I can, for instance, prove that I was in Moscow at noon on Tuesday of last week. It would probably be impossible to produce proof that I was never in Moscow. The only way to prove negative facts is to entertain all the possibilities and then rule them out.

With regard to the ordination of women, there are only two critical possibilities that can be entertained: the fact that ordination prayers speak exclusively of male ministers, and the common understanding that the presbyter represents Christ in the role of liturgical presidency. As to ordination prayers, the argument on liturgical grounds is inconclusive. Since women presbyters have been unknown to Roman Catholicism, its prayer formulae cannot be expected to speak of the ministry of women, past or present. That the ordination prayers appeal to paradigms such as the priesthood of Aaron, the priesthood of Christ, the office of the apostles, etc. is also inconclusive. The question is not whether women ever occupied such offices, but whether they can be assimilated to the office of presbyter without betraying the church's tradition on the nature of presbyteral ministry. It is not a question which the prayers answer.

We must turn, then, to the question of the presbyter's role of representing Christ as liturgical president, most notably as presiding at the eucharist. Similar to other chapters in this book, our discussion will center around the *Declaration on the Question of the Admission of Women to the Ministerial Priesthood*, from the Sacred Congregation for the Doctrine of the Faith.

II

To clarify its conclusion that women cannot be ordained, the *Declaration* appeals to the fact that the bishop or priest, in the exercise of his ministry, represents Christ, who acts through him. The supreme expression of this representation is found in eucharistic celebration. The priest acts "*in persona Christi*, taking the role of Christ to the point of being his very image, when he pronounces the words of consecration." [1] The document then explains that since the priest is a sacramental sign of Christ, Christ's role in the eucharist would be obscured if the priest were to be a woman. A "natural resemblance" must exist between Christ and the priest:

> The same natural resemblance is required for persons as for things: when Christ's role in the eucharist is to be expressed sacramentally, there would not be this natural resemblance which must exist between

Christ and his minister if the role of Christ were not taken by a man: in such a case it would be difficult to see in the minister the image of Christ. For Christ himself was and remains a man.[2]

It is easy to counter this line of reasoning with the following objection. In exercising the ministries proper to their offices, the priest or bishop represents the entire church, a body consisting of women as well as men. There is no reason then why such offices might not also be assumed by women. The *Declaration* takes note of this objection, but meets it by asserting that the priest represents the church "precisely because he first represents Christ himself, who is Head and Shepherd of the Church."[3]

The *Declaration*, furthermore, develops the nuptial symbol. It draws upon the Old Testament symbol of God as spouse of Israel,[4] and with the help of many New Testament passages it speaks of "Christ . . . the Bridegroom; the church . . . the Bride." The Roman statement draws this conclusion:

That is why we can never ignore the fact that Christ is a man. And therefore, unless one is to disregard the importance of this symbolism [Christ as Bridegroom, Church as Bride] for the economy of Revelation, it must be admitted that, in actions which demand the character of ordination and in which Christ himself, the author of the Covenant, the Bridegroom and head of the Church, is represented, exercising his ministry of salvation — which is in the highest degree the case of the Eucharist — his role (this is the original sense of the word *persona*) must be taken by a man.[5]

This theme of God, Spouse of Israel, originated in Canaanite liturgy and is often applied to Christ, Spouse of the Church, within a distinctive liturgical setting. The New Testament introduces this nuptial theme in the midst of a heavenly or earthly banquet, celebrating the marriage of the King's son (Mark 2:19; Matt 22:1-4; Rev 19:7). The motif of God or Christ as bridegroom is thus linked with a long biblical tradition about the heavenly or eschatological banquet and leads into the liturgical commemoration of the Eucharist (Is 25:6; Ps 22:27; Matt 26:29).

The argument here is fundamentally liturgical and sacramental: the contention of the *Declaration* is that the sacramental signing of Christ's role, especially and supremely in the eucharist, would be obscured if the presiding minister were to be a woman. Citing a variety of texts from the Second Vatican Council and subsequent official Roman documents, the *Declaration* argues that the presiding minister only represents the church because he first represents Christ as head of the church. What is at stake, above all, is that the role of Christ in liturgical action, especially that of the eucharist, be clearly and unmistakeably signed: ". . . the priest is a sign, the supernatural effectiveness of which comes from the ordination received, but a sign that must be perceptible and which the faithful must be able to recognize with ease.''[6] The *Declaration* is suggesting that the role of Christ as head and shepherd of the Church is signed in clear distinction from the priest's representing the Church as body and bride of Christ.

While the argument is fundamentally liturgical and sacramental, the *Declaration* does not support its position with more appeals to liturgical text and rite. The eucharistic liturgy is directly mentioned only once, when the document asserts that the priest takes the role of Christ when he pronounces the words of consecration. And the footnote reference is not to the texts and gestures of the Roman liturgy (nor to any other), but to the *Summa Theologiae* of St. Thomas Aquinas.[7] If the distinctive role of Christ as head and shepherd of the church is so clearly signed in distinction from the church's role as body and bride of Christ, it could be expected that liturgical gesture and text would reflect that distinctive role. In fact, it could be expected that it would be clearly mirrored in liturgical texts, for it is in its verbal and oral articulation that a sacramental sign is given its most specific perceptible meaning. The classic concern with the "matter" (action, things) and "form" (words) of sacramental activity was grounded in this understanding of a sacramental sign.

Yet the *Declaration* gives no indication of liturgical texts which would support its suggestion that in the act of consecration at the eucharist the priest represents Christ the head and shepherd of the church in distinction from his role as representing the church as the body and bride of Christ. It is the view of this writer that no such textual support is to be sought because there is none to be found. There is no point in the eucharistic liturgy at which the priest represents Christ the head in contradistinction to his representing the church. These roles are signed together, inseparably, and without sharp distinction between them. A major weakness of the *Declaration*'s liturgical and sacramental argument is that it has no basis whatsoever in the prayer texts of the Roman rite or the texts of the eucharistic liturgies of any other churches whose apostolic succession Rome acknowledges.

Conventions of piety often hold such power, even over the perceptions of the literate and the articulate, that the assertion of the preceding paragraph is probably not wholly acceptable as a bald statement. We are, perhaps, schooled less by what the liturgy says and does than by a long history of liturgical passivity on the part of the laity which obscured the role of the people in the liturgy. Centuries of a Latin liturgy have especially schooled Roman Catholic piety to be more attentive to what appears visually at the liturgy than to what is said. Within the context of such a piety, the *Declaration*'s suggestion that the priest represents Christ as head and shepherd of the church when he pronounces the words of consecration seems to be a reasonable, even obvious suggestion. If one attends to the eucharistic action primarily with the eye, it *looks* as if the priest takes on a distinctive role when he "pronounces the words of consecration." The point of what follows in this chapter is to indicate that what may seem obvious is not, and that the liturgical texts say something quite other than what the *Declaration* says about the representation of Christ at the eucharist.

III

The *Declaration* describes the priest as taking the role of Christ above all in pronouncing the words of consecration.[8] Whether "words of consecration" refers to the eucharistic prayer as a whole or to the institution narrative alone is not entirely clear. Christian antiquity, at least until the fourth century, universally viewed the entire prayer as consecratory. Western theological reflection, for a variety of reasons that need not be pursued here, had by the high middle ages singled out the institution narrative as "words of consecration." More recent theological reflection, attentive to the nature and structure of the eucharistic prayer, has returned to the older view.

The effect of that reflection can be seen in the Anglican-Roman Catholic dialogue on eucharistic theology, which views the whole prayer as consecratory.[9] The Roman Missal of 1970 seems to incorporate both views, describing the eucharistic prayer as one of "thanksgiving and sanctification,"[10] while also describing the institution narrative as "institution narrative and consecration."[11]

If the *Declaration*'s expression "words of consecration" means the whole eucharistic prayer, the priest's representation of Christ is clearly conjoined integrally to his standing as representative of the church. The eucharistic prayer is also offered in the first person plural ("we"), and is intelligible only as a prayer offered on behalf of the whole church. As the Roman Missal says so well, "The meaning of the prayer is that the whole congregation joins Christ in acknowledging the works of God and in offering the sacrifice."[12] On a view of the whole eucharistic prayer as consecratory, there is no basis for the suggestion that there is a clear and distinctive signing of the priest's role as representing Christ as head and shepherd of the church apart from the priest's representing the church as body and bride of Christ. Both roles are enacted together.

But it is doubtful that the *Declaration* is referring to the eucharistic prayer as a whole when it refers to the "words of consecration." Since the *Declaration* cites no liturgical text and no work of theological reflection (as distinguished from official documents) since that of Durandus of Saint-Pourcain (d. 1332), and appeals to the *Summa Theologiae* of St. Thomas Aquinas, it can be assumed that the *Declaration* maintains the medieval view of the institution narrative itself as "words of consecration." If this is the case, it is not enough merely to cite the integrity of the eucharistic prayer as spoken in the name of the whole church. The authors of the *Declaration* seem to view the institution narrative in some sort of disjuncture from the rest of the prayer — rather, perhaps, as the General Instruction of the Roman Missal singles out the institution narrative as *consecratio*. Neither the consensus of Christian antiquity nor current reflection is taken into account by the *Declaration*'s apparent view of consecration.

In view of this, it may be asked whether the *Declaration* can be met on its own grounds by citation of other sources. And indeed it can. In the Roman liturgy the institution narrative does not stand in any sort of disjuncture from the rest of the eucharistic prayer. And at no point in the prayer does the priest speak directly in the name of Christ. He continually speaks in the name of the church. Even the institution narrative, which quotes the *verba Christi*, is spoken in the third person: it is a quotation within a narrative recital addressed as part of a prayer to God the Father, and it is encompassed within a prayer spoken in the name of the whole church. The *Declaration* contends that the priest represents the church because he first represents Christ himself as head and shepherd of the church.[13] It is not the purpose of this paper to discuss the theological truth of this assertion. But on the level of *sign*, in what is said and done at the act of eucharist, the exact opposite is the case. It is only by praying in the name of the church that the priest enacts his role as consecratory representative of Christ.

This is all the more evident in the distinctively Roman pattern of eucharistic prayer — notably in the ancient Roman Canon (now Eucharistic Prayer I of the Roman Missal), but also in the newer prayers of the Roman eucharistic liturgy. The institution narrative is preceded by an invocation (*Quam oblationem*) that the gifts will become the body and blood of Christ, an invocation that is offered in the name of all:

Quam oblationem tu, Deus, in omnibus, *quaesumus*, benedictam, adscriptam, ratam, rationabilem, acceptabilemque facere digneris: ut *nobis* Corpus et Sanguis fiat dilectissimi Filii tui, Domini *nostri* Iesu Christi.	*We pray*, O God, that above all you would be pleased to make this oblation blessed, approved, right, spiritual, and acceptable, so that it might be *for us* the Body and Blood of your Son, *our* Lord Jesus Christ.[14]

In the classic Canon, the corporate character of the invocation is reinforced by the petitionary *quaesumus* (*we pray*), as it is in the newer

Prayers II and IV of the Missal. Similarly, the invocation before the narrative in Prayer III uses *Supplices . . . deprecamur* ("beseeching . . . we pray"). Moreover, the institution narrative is linked to the invocation which precedes it. In the classic Canon, the narrative begins *Qui pridie* ("Who, on the day . . ."), and the antecedent of the pronominal reference to Christ is the invocation which prays that the offering of the Church will become the body and blood of Christ. A virtually identical pattern is present in the other eucharistic prayers of the Roman rite.

Textually, then, the institution narrative is wholly dependent upon the invocation which precedes it, and the narrative is unintelligible except as a continuation of the invocation. The narrative does not stand alone or in disjuncture from the rest of the eucharistic prayer. Thus in the articulation of the eucharistic prayer in the Roman rite no clearcut distinction is made between the priest's representing the praying church and his representing Christ the head and shepherd of the church. The two roles are enacted simultaneously. Even on a view which insists on pinpointing a temporal moment of consecration with the recitation of the *verba Christi*, there is still no disjunctive representation of Christ as the head and shepherd of the church apart from the priest's representation of the church as the body and bride of Christ. In reciting the institution narrative, the priest continues to speak on behalf of the praying church.

It can well be asked whether the *Declaration* does not reduce sacramental sign to dramatic pictorial tableau or to enacted allegory when it singles out the priest's role in pronouncing the "words of consecration" as signing his representation of Christ the head and shepherd of the church. The priest's offering of the rest of the prayer is surely as much a representative sign of the presence of Christ the head and shepherd of the church who stands before the Father as is the priest's role in reciting the institution narrative. Singling out the consecratory moment devalues the sign that the rest of the prayer is. To offer prayer "through Christ our Lord" surely cannot *exclude* Christ under his aspect of being head and shepherd of the church. It is precisely because he is head of the church that prayer can be offered in this fashion.

Conclusion

A major defect of the *Declaration*'s argument is that it speaks of an aspect of sacramental signification as if it could be singled out in a particular moment of eucharistic celebration, in distinction from other moments of eucharistic celebration which express other aspects. That is to say, the *Declaration* speaks as if it assumes that at one particular moment one aspect of the representation of Christ is signed, while at other moments, other aspects are signed. The *Declaration* fails to recognize

that in all liturgical action, at all times, the priest represents simultaneously both the church and Christ its head and shepherd. Further, the
Declaration overlooks the tradition of liturgical prayer by which the
priest represents Christ only by speaking in the name of the church. In
so doing, the *Declaration* verges dangerously close to saying that a
priest can act as priest without speaking and acting in the name of the
church. Yet the pattern of the church's prayer is such that the priest acts
as priest only because he speaks in the name of the church.

What appears, then, on the level of sign in the church's prayer pattern
is that the priest represents Christ because he represents the church.
There is no moment in the eucharistic action when the priest represents
Christ in any way apart from the church. There is no liturgical prayer,
and in particular there is no eucharist, which is not the action of the
church. Attention to the sacramental signs actually used in the Roman
liturgy indicates the weakness of the argument against the ordination of
women on the grounds that they do not have a "natural resemblance" to
Christ the head and shepherd of the church. There is no separate and
clearly distinct sign of Christ the head being represented at the eucharist
apart from the representation of the church. And since, on the level of
sign, the representation of Christ is grounded in representation of the
church, it would seem that a woman could perform the priestly role of
representing Christ as well as a man.

8

RABBINICAL TRADITION
ON THE ROLE OF WOMEN

by

Hayim G. Perelmuter

It will be useful in looking at the problem of ordination and a religious leadership role for women in the Church, to examine the experience of Judaism in this direction. There is much both faiths have in common on this subject and many areas in which they differ.

For the Church, priesthood was seen as a continuation of the model developed in the Old Testament. It saw itself as the successor to Israel into history in its role as elect of God, with priesthood as a central role of linkage. In scripture, the model for the priest was male, and there was no room for a woman to function in this role.

For the Synagogue, the destruction of the Temple was a traumatic experience, an interruption to be restored only by the Messianic era in the end of time. New models for leadership emerged through Rabbinic Judaism. What now became central were the knowledge of the Torah, the capacity to interpret it, and the authority to deal with it that came from ordination.

The emphasis on maleness, nevertheless, was common to both Synagogue and Church, and the role for women was one that needed to be worked out in a painstaking way, with much soul-searching and inner struggle.

For the Church, priesthood was a continuing reality. For the Synagogue, on the other hand, it became a memory, preserved in a sense of awareness of descent from the priesthood. The descendants of the priestly family possessed the right of precedence in being called up to the Torah and blessing the congregation on the three pilgrim festivals:

Passover, Tabernacles and Shavuot. They were subject, if they wished to retain their status of ancestral purities, to the same laws as were their priestly forebears.

Yet for Judaism, the emphasis is plainly on the Rabbinate and its role, and it is here that the struggle for the participation of women develops.

I

Leadership models for women are clearly to be found in the Old Testament and Rabbinic Judaism, but not in sufficient emphasis to qualify for the kind of role which is being sought after in our day.

Certainly Eve plays no minor role as she moves from the role of man's helpmate to the shaper of his destiny. In a way, the story of the Fall is intended as a corrective to that view. The matriarchs, each in their way, show a sense of creative independence, and Rebecca's role in achieving primacy for Jacob is a case in point (Gen 27).

There is the mother of Moses, Jochebed (Ex 2:1-10), and his sister Miriam[1] who play significant leadership roles in the shaping of his career. There is Deborah, of course, who acts as leader and judge, clearly a figure of strength and of influence (Jdg 4-5). There is the Queen Mother Athaliah,[2] to say nothing of Jezebel,[3] both of whom play such a crucial part in the affairs of state. There are Bathsheba[4] and Abigail[5] in David's time, and the former's role in achieving King Solomon's succession to the throne would do credit to the best political manipulators of our time. We have the wise woman in the days of Samuel; the prophetess Hulda in Jeremiah's day (2 Kgs 22:14-20).

In a time of Israel's history when prophets and judges were central to its national and religious formation, it is of no little significance that women could be recognized as judges and prophets. Not many to be sure, but that there were any at all is worthy of note.

There are, however, clear indications of a polarized view of woman in the infrastructure of the Biblical narrative. In the creation stories the view of woman before the Fall sees her as the equal of man, as his fulfillment. Then after the Fall there is a change in her status because of her sin.

In the Book of Proverbs we tend to find a negative view of woman; in the Song of Songs there is a return to the "prelapsarian view" of woman, autonomous and strong.[6]

The daughters of Zelophehad,[7] who made such a strong plea for woman's rights in inheritance, emerged in later Rabbinic tradition as experts in the interpretation of Torah. "It was taught:" the Talmud records, "The daughters of Zelophehad were wise women, they were experts, they were virtuous."[8] Not many women emerge in Rabbinic literature as experts in scholarship. Beruriah, wife of Rabbi Meir, is perhaps the best known.

She is described as an avid scholar, a perceptive student of Torah, who apparently went through the intensive three year course of study customary for disciples of Rabbis at the time. The Talmud relates how a scholar who came before Rabbi Johanan, asking him to teach him the Book of Genealogies in three months, is rebuked for his presumption with the words: "If Beruriah, who studied three hundred laws from three hundred teachers in one day could nevertheless not do her duty in three years, how can you propose to do it in three months!"[9]

Nevertheless, into the intertestamentary period and the formative years of the development of Rabbinic Judaism, clearly the role of woman becomes circumscribed and limited. When Josephus, writing about Judaism to the Roman world in the first century, boldly expresses his defense of Judaism in response to the attacks of Apion, he could write:

> . . . for, says the Scripture: a woman is inferior to her husband in all things. Let her therefore be obedient to him: not that he should abuse her, but that she may acknowledge her duty to her husband.[10]

Certainly, if we were to apply the criteria of individual human rights, the role of woman in the post-Biblical, formative Rabbinic era would have to been seen as limited, and perhaps secondary.[11] When it came to references to rights and status in courts of law, women were coupled with children and slaves in their ineligibility to testify in a court of law. They could be divorced by, but could not divorce their husbands. They could never marry again if their husband were to disappear or abandoned her. They were not required to study Torah or to perform most of the 613 commandments.

Yet the woman was honored and cherished in the society as Mother and Wife. She was protected by contract. Judaism was basically a monogamous society.

A deeper reason is seen for this special status. Rabbinic Judaism emerged as a force for Jewish survival after the destruction of the Jewish State by Rome. Survival was its goal, through Torah and family. The role of studying Torah was given to the man; of being the central force in developing and influencing the family — to the woman.

In the conflict with Hellenism, in the first pre-Christian century, the stress was on the unity and survivability of the Jewish people. Hence it became very important to ward off outside influences which could blur and dilute that identity and unity.[12] Thus a special status develops for woman to protect her, and to protect the structure of Jewish society.

The central fact is, whether viewed from a negative or a positive viewpoint, the place for woman in a ministerial role was minimal. There

were virtually no women scholars, no women rabbis, no women religious functionaires.

What we do find are women playing an economic or business role as
the husband concentrates on the study of Torah. We find, for example,
the case of an 11th Century woman in Babylonia, Wuhsha by name,[13]
who appears in court, makes a will, takes part in commercial transac-
tions, heads a committee for the repair of a synagogue building, and
dedicates a Torah scroll.

We learn, that in Renaissance Italy, permission was given occasionally
to women to act as *Shoḥet* (a ritual functionary, usually male who
slaughtered fowl and domestic animals to provide the community with
Kosher meat).

In the Response of Isaac di Lattes, a Rabbi in Mantua, we find the
formula of permission for a woman to function as a religious functionary
in this role. He writes:

> Just as man fulfills his role to the highest degree by devoting himself to
> study [of Torah], searching after wisdom and probing into the causes of
> all phenomena, so it is the glory and the grandeur of woman to remain
> in the home to give guidance to her children and to prepare food for the
> household. Therefore the management of the household devolves upon
> her. Now since it is the woman's responsibility to prepare meals for her
> husband and to care for her flock, her little children, and to raise them
> as flower beds that they may become strong to serve their Creator,
> should they desire to eat dressed meat properly slaughtered, she cooks it
> and prepares the table. Now, in order that a stranger may not come into
> her house [to be with her] in performing the act of ritual slaughter as
> required by our holy Torah, *it has been a practice for the daughters of
> Israel to study the laws of ritual slaughter.* And this worthy and virtuous
> maiden in Israel, who is not lacking in worth and grandeur has studied
> the laws of Ritual Slaughter [of permitted animals and birds for food],
> has mastered the material in the appropriate manuals, and has become
> proficient in them through instruction from the venerable Rabbi ———,
> who attests to her proficiency and validates her work as acceptable. *I
> therefore give her my support, and open the door to her, permitting her
> to perform this holy task* to feed others, provided only that she perform
> in the presence of an expert to determine whether she faints or not [i.e.
> whether she can really stand the gaff!], she must do this twice a day,
> morning and evening for the first three months, then once a week for
> the following year, and thereafter once a month for the rest of her life,
> that she not forget what she has learned. Her deeds will praise her in
> the gates, she will eat of the fruit of her hands, and she will merit a good
> marriage, sons who will study Torah and perform good deeds in Israel
> in the lifetime of her father and her mother, her brothers and sisters,
> uncles and aunts, who will behold the good things that come to her, and
> will rejoice. Amen.[14]

I have translated and cited this episode because it reflects the subtle
change in attitude to ministry by woman in a male oriented religious

culture, and within the legal framework of the accepted tradition. One must remember that the proper preparation of meat for the table was an injunction rooted in the Bible and related to the Temple cult. The animals brought to the Temple for sacrifice, were as we read in the Book of Samuel, slaughtered by the priests, who kept a small portion, returning the rest to the one who brought the offering so that he and his family could partake of it.[15]

This priestly activity became the task of a specially trained religious functionary who had to master a tractate of the Talmud which dealt with this both from a religious and technical point of view. This functionary was usually a male. To permit a woman to do this was in reality a departure from norm, and we must note how this departure is justified by attempting to portray and defend the traditional role of woman!

II

To take a leap from the sixteenth century to the nineteenth century is not as long a leap as the years suggest. For, from the point of view of Jewish history, the middle ages extend from the eighth century when the Talmud was completed, up to the eve of the French Revolution, during which time most of the world Jewry lived under Talmudic law.

It is with the French (and American) Revolutions, that the ghetto walls began to fall, and the opportunities for the entry of the Jew into the world of western culture appeared. The price of the "ticket of admission to European civilization," as Heine put it, was the acceptance of individual freedom at the price of national identity.

Thus many Jews tended to see themselves a French (or German, or British, or American) Jew of the Mosaic persuasion, and Reform Judaism appeared on the scene, in an attempt to refashion Judaism in consonance with the new spirit of the new times.

Here were new views for emancipation of men and women; new ideals of equal status; new dreams touched off by the Romantic movement. Mary Wollstoncraft Shelley dreamed of the liberated woman in England; George Sand, in France, made her claim for emancipation in men's garb! Rahel Herz and her Jewish compatriots presided over salons which were centers of literary, artistic and political creativity.

Since Reform Judaism saw itself as a new incarnation of prophetic Judaism, reborn for a new Messianic day, it declared itself emancipated from the "bonds" of Rabbinic law, and could legislate freely for the future.

Early in the nineteenth century it proclaimed equal status for men and women within Judaism. By mid-nineteenth century it had declared that women could be ordained as Rabbis. The first woman Rabbi was so ordained in American Reform Judaism in — 1973! That it took more than a century to implement this declaration speaks volumes for the tension between legislation and custom in any religious movement, even the most liberal.

At the present time there are four or five ordained women Rabbis in the American Reform movement. One of them, Sally Priesand, the first to be ordained[16] (1973), was elected in June of 1977 as the first woman to serve on the Executive Committee of the Central Conference of American Rabbis. Almost one third of the enrollment in the four branches of the Hebrew Union College — Jewish Institute of Religion, the American Seminary that trains Reform Rabbis, are women. So in this wing of Judaism, it would appear that the breakthrough for women in the ministry has been achieved.

A closer look at the process will be helpful. For one thing, the first woman known to have filled any rabbinical function in modern times was Hannah Rachel Werbermacher[17] (1805–1892) who was known as the Maid of Ludomir. She became famous as a Talmudic scholar, and was consulted by a great number of *hasidim*, who regarded her as a saint. She wore a prayer shawl, put on phylacteries, said Kaddish and attended services regularly. But she never received ordination. In the 1930's Regina Jonas was the first woman to be ordained a Rabbi in Germany. However, she never led a congregation. She died in a concentration camp under the Nazis.

We must note it took almost a century for the first woman to be ordained as Rabbi in the Reform movement. For as early as 1846, the Breslau Synod passed a resolution:

> that woman be entitled to the same religious rights and subject to the same religious duties as man. . . . that women are obliged to perform religious acts as depend on a fixed time, insofar as such acts have significance for our religious consciousness.[18]

It stopped short, however, of including ordination.

It took American Reform Judaism, in the spirit of American liberalism and freedom, to take that step. In 1892, three years after its founding, the Central Conference of American Rabbis (C.C.A.R.), the central body of Reform Rabbis, passed a resolution which repeated the spirit of the Breslau resolution, equal rights for women, but still no mention of ordination.

It was not until 1922 that the question of ordination was confronted head on at a session of the C.C.A.R. Here the question was dealt with directly. Prof. Jacob Lanterbach presented a lengthy responsum on the question, and came to a cautiously negative conclusion on the grounds that it might jeopardize the authority and historic character of ordination. He was opposed in the debate by Prof. David Neumark, who argued:

> You cannot treat the Reform rabbinate from the Orthodox point of view. Orthodoxy is Orthodoxy and Reform is Reform. Our good relations with our Orthodox brethren may still be improved upon a clear and decided stand upon the question.

Therefore, a resolution, approving the ordination of women, was overwhelmingly passed, with two negative votes cast by Prof. Lanterbach and Rabbi Barnet Brickner.

So there was the resolution, but still no ordained Rabbis. A few women here and there took full Rabbinic courses hoping to be ordained. Between 1922 and 1932 three or four women were graduated without ordination from the New York and Cincinnati schools of the College-Institute.

In 1935, the daughter of a Rabbi enrolled at the New York School (Jewish Institute of Religion) took the full course, asked for ordination, and after a faculty battle it was denied by a narrow majority. The student received a Master of Hebrew Letters degree but no ordination.

In England, in the early twenties, the Hon. Lily Montagu, one of the founders of the World Union for Progressive Judaism, was elected as "lay preacher" of her congregation and served for many years as its spiritual leader and preacher. She had no ordination from a theological seminary, although in later years she was given an honorary D.H.L. degree from Hebrew Union College.[19]

But still no ordination of women. Finally the man who voted against ordination of women in 1922, came out for it in 1955. In that year, Rabbi Brickner, who had by this time become President of the Central Conference of American Rabbis, called for a reconsideration in his presidential address. Acknowledging his opposition in 1922, he added: "But since then our needs have changed and I have changed my mind. Many Christian Protestant denominations have also changed their minds and now ordain women."

Earlier in 1955, Harvard Divinity School had voted to admit women to qualify for ordination, and the General Assembly of the Presbyterian Church had made a similar decision. He, therefore, recommended the appointment of a special committee to study the matter and to report at the next conference. The following year a report was brought in, giving its approval to the 1922 resolution and suggesting that the time of ordination had come. This report was received, and tabled for further discussion.

No additional resolution seemed needed, for the 1922 resolution was clear enough. All that remained was implementation, and in 1967, a woman was admitted to the Rabbinic program, fulfilled the requirements and was ordained by Dr. Nelson Glueck, who had served as a member of the 1956 committee.

The hand of custom hung heavy even over a movement that had hitched its wagon to the star of change.

III

In the traditional wings of Judaism (Orthodox and Conservative) the movement toward the religious equalization of woman's role has moved much more slowly.

The restraints in Jewish law, the paramount role for the male despite a protective role for woman remained. The part assigned to women in synagogue worship remained secondary. They were kept separate in worship service, and in some situations even veiled from view.

Yet as one moved into Western societies, with their tendency to a more liberated view of woman, one saw evidences of changing attitudes.

The Conservative movement, although it saw itself as living under the authority of the *Halacha* (religious law), nevertheless, conceded some change in religious practice. The elimination of separation of seating in public worship was the major change it made when it first appeared on the American Jewish scene at the turn of the century. Some Conservative congregations (but not many) went so far as to introduce the organ as an instrument of musical accompaniment in worship.

In the Conservative movement there were gradations of subtle change. The faculty of its theological seminary tended to adhere most closely to the Orthodox position; the rabbinate tended to be sensitive to constructive change within the tradition; and the laity was flexible in its own practice while insisting on the maintenance of traditional patterns by its functionaries.

But here, as in the Orthodox world, the pressures for change were constant. Many Jewish women were involved in the woman's liberation movements. Many women of Conservative and Orthodox backgrounds moved ahead in the academic and professional world, and began to press for more significant roles in their religious lives.

Responding to this pressure in the Conservative movement, the Rabbinical Assembly's Committee on Law and Standards ruled that women could be counted as members of the quorum (*minyan*) for group prayer.[20] This has not yet won widespread acceptance in the movement, yet it is indicative of a process of change that is not likely to be stemmed. Just over the horizon, demands that women serve as cantor and as rabbi are surfacing. Women have long been students in the Teacher's College of the Jewish Theological Seminary, but some are now knocking insistently upon the doors of the Rabbinic division for admission.

Philip Sigal of the Law Committee put it succinctly, after giving the full measure of legal arguments for the inclusion of women in the religious quorum when he wrote:

> To disqualify women from sharing in the right to constitute an assembly or a worship community is to offend them without reason. Even if we categorize the disqualification of women to constitute a quorum as *minhag* (custom) it is a *minhag* which has lost its reason and its appeal.[21]

The issue has surfaced and keeps reappearing. It is a constant theme in scholarly and popular journals; it emerges at assemblies and conferences of religious and law bodies across the spectrum of Jewish life.

Not even Orthodoxy is immune from these stirrings. Here, however, the emphasis is more on removing certain disabilities in legal status and in participatory roles in the synagogue. Orthodox women who have made their way in the professional and academic world are leaders in this advocacy for their advancement in religious status.

Particularly symptomatic of this is the very sober and penetrating analysis by the Dean of Stern College, an Orthodox sponsored woman's college in New York.[22] That the article was written at all is evidence of the stirrings on this question within the Orthodox camp.

Writing in *Tradition, A Journal of Orthodox Thought*, Dean Saul Berman deals with the problem in all its complexity. He examines the discontent with the role of women in traditional Judaism, analyzes the legal components which Jewish law assigns to women, evaluates the justice of complaints, and makes some "modest proposals."

The issues as Dean Berman sees them involve: a sense of being deprived of opportunities for positive religious identification; disadvantages in civil law, especially in the role of the abandoned wife; and the rabbinic perception of the nature of women and the role to which they are assigned.

There ought to be a moratorium on apologetics and a determination to do something about the most serious problems, Berman believes. He very clearly suggests a direction for Orthodoxy:

> It is vital for us to examine these laws and social practices which seem to be unjust to women. When all is said and done, those laws were the total preoccupation of centuries of Jewish sages and scholars through whose interpretative skills capital punishment was virtually abolished; through whose legal authority the task of transformation and eventual elimination of slavery was accomplished; and through whose social awareness a Jewish welfare system came into existence, which is unmatched to this day for its sensitivity to the feelings of the poor.[23]

Reform could proceed *de novo*, though it was not immune from the pressures of custom. For Orthodoxy, he sees the response to the problems in the slow and steady working out of the situation, by bending, without breaking the law to meet new situations.

What this portends for the ministry role for women, especially ordination, in the development of Orthodoxy is not promising in the long run. But what can be expected is a facing up to and gradual change of some aspects of the legal role of women, and a gradual freeing up of women for more of a role in public worship. At the very least, it may be said that the problem is beginning to be faced and discussed.

Conclusion

One thing is clear, and it would seem to be operative not only in the experience of Judaism, but in the experience of many other religious and cultural movements.

It has to do with the delicate balance between custom and law and their development. Accepted customs sometimes harden into and find their expression in law. Law, in its turn, comes under the constant pressure of newly emerging customs.[24]

You do not make a law, a Rabbinic maxim once observed, unless a consensus of the people is willing to accept it![25] And when the law is in existence, if consensus rejects it, it becomes ultimately necessary to change the law.

When Rabbi Joseph Karo wrote his code of Jewish law in the sixteenth century, he did not take into account the folk practices of Polish and German Jewry. It became acceptable to them only when Rabbi Moses Isserles (1526–1571), a great Rabbinic leader of East European Jewry, included them.[26]

There are now women rabbis in Reform and Reconstructionist Judaism, women ministers in many Protestant denominations. As one observer wryly put it: "While women ministers are getting the pulpits with less status, less money, and less hope for advancement, they have nevertheless made it to the bottom rung."[27]

How many palm trees await how many Deborahs to sit under them and judge, we do not know. But what we do know is that the process moves forward, the pressures are irresistible, and law and custom in their interaction will create situations where woman's drive for ministry will ultimately find its fulfillment.

PART FOUR

PASTORAL

AND

PSYCHOLOGICAL DYNAMICS

9

HUMAN CONFLICTS
WITHIN CHURCH MINISTRY
AND THE ORDINATION OF WOMEN

by

Sebastian MacDonald, C.P.

The ordination of women to the priesthood is a current problem for the Roman Catholic Church. I propose to look at it from a pastoral perspective. In doing so, I am working on the supposition that the Holy Spirit is present in the ministerial setting, embellishing it as the liturgy for Pentecost recalls, shedding light, bestowing comfort, providing refreshment. Because this is a presupposition, I will not be adverting to it in the remarks that follow.

With this supposition in mind, however, we can accept with equanimity one commonly held position today, namely, that the Scriptures do not answer the question about the legitimacy of ordaining women to the priesthood. Though we ordinarily look to the Word of God for guidance in coping with life's major problems, in the issue under consideration, there is insufficient evidence to conclude that the Scriptures prohibit, for instance, the ordination of women to the priesthood.[1]

I

The rich resource of the Bible, then, will be probed no further here; this has already been done earlier in the volume. Let us turn our attention to another familiar place where faith assures us that the Spirit of God is operative: tradition. Tradition has emerged as the major factor in this issue.[2] Again, however, decisive arguments pro and con cannot be found within it. In using it we will have to model ourselves on the gospel figure, the head of the household "who can bring forth from his storeroom both the new and the old" (Matt 13:52).

It is not inappropriate to speak of these treasures of tradition as data, that is, facts and figures, or information, that can be appealed to for support. Data is the substance out of which reasons are fashioned. In a question begging clarification, such as the ordination of women, reasons are a determinative factor in the clarification process. But the task of sifting the data and shaping it into forceful reasons is a difficult one.

But it can be done. This is the opinion of the authors of the recent Vatican document on the ordination of women. While acknowledging that Scripture is not conclusive, they propose tradition as probative. Its mainline message, in their opinion, is the appropriateness of the male sex for priesthood, because in this way "natural resemblance" to Christ is best preserved.[3] I do not intend to explore this particular focus of the tradition; it too is being investigated elsewhere in this volume. My interest rather is the procedure followed in gathering the data that has gone into fashioning the reason (the male sex of Christ) against the ordination of women.

The data used to substantiate this prohibition is significant. It includes not only the reason of "natural resemblance" but a series of interpretations of scriptural data, developed in tradition, entailing Christ's deputation of only men as the Twelve,[4] Paul's careful usage of "God's fellow workers"[5] to specify his male disciples, and the subsequent array of statements from the Fathers and medieval theologians against the ordination of women.

A major difficulty lies with the method employed by the Congregation for the Doctrine of the Faith in using this data and so presenting its arguments. This data is to be located in the "theological places,"[6] a revered source for theology, where the Holy Spirit addresses believers in significant ways.[7] The Congregation associates these "places" with tradition. In doing so, in my opinion, it unduly narrows the field of human experience that is involved. It is not that important authorities have been overlooked. Rather, the notion of tradition is overly restricted to the Fathers and the theologians.[8] Data derived from contemporary science has not been utilized sufficiently in assessing the reasons against the ordination of women.

In developing this criticism, I will not concentrate on the omitted data, but will proceed indirectly by describing the way the Church is gradually coming to grips with pertinent, more contemporary data in its recent official documentation. The 1968 encyclical *On the Regulation of Birth* (*Humanae Vitae*) and the 1975 *Declaration on Sexual Ethics* both represent a healthy move toward a fuller recognition of the data that pertains to human behavior. *Humanae Vitae*, for instance, is sensitive to the problems associated with responsible parenthood (*cf.* paragraph n. 2) and the qustions to which these give rise (n. 3). In a similar way, the more recent *Declaration on Sexual Ethics* pays considerable attention to "observations in the psychological order" (n. 8) concerning homosexuality and masturbation (n. 9), and to studies on the fundamental option (n. 10) regarding the question of serious sin.

Yet despite this growing awareness, there is still some diffidence in dealing with the data positively and constructively, as, for instance, by more vigorously integrating it into the doctrinal corpus as explanatory reasons for the conclusions that are reached.[9] What is happening, instead, is that this data is usually not preferred over against the traditional interpretation of Scripture and the usual understanding of tradition (the Councils, Popes, Fathers, liturgy, Sacred Congregations and theologians).[10] The present *Declaration on the Question of the Admission of Women to the Ministerial Priesthood*, and its *Commentary*, continues to follow this more restricted pattern in its understanding of "theological places."

II

The teaching Church does not yet seem comfortable, by and large, with certain kinds of data bearing upon human conditions and conduct. I see several reasons for this hesitancy.

There is a propensity to preserve harmony and consistency between the data, the reasons fashioned out of it, and the principles and norms, or conclusions and applications that help constitute official doctrine or positions.[11] Underlying this is a fundamental viewpoint on reality itself, entailing a firm conviction that Divine Providence "reacheth from end to end *mightily*, and ordereth all things *sweetly*."[12]

Nicholas Crotty adverted to this attitude several years ago in addressing the issue of evil in human action. Citing Noldin's manual of moral theology,[13] he remarked on the commonly held position that, in the objective order, there can never be conflict between moral values.[14] This is because the moral order is immediately subject to God's government. It cannot be allowed that God be the cause of conflict in the objective order; such a principle would imply that He is responsible for the inevitable loss of goodness or for any injury that occurs in resolving the conflict.

Such a viewpoint pervades the present document on women ordination. It influences the choice of data that enters into the formulation of reasons against ordaining women. I will not exhaustively pursue this point, but will offer several illustrations of it. At the very outset the

Declaration speaks of the equality that is to result between men and women, which "will secure the building up of a world that is not levelled out and uniform but harmonious and unified" (par. 1). Further on, speaking of the fact of the Incarnation of the Word in the male sex, it remarks that "it is, indeed, in harmony with the entirety of God's plan as God Himself has revealed it" (par. 28). The accompanying *Commentary* points out that "the equality of Christians is in harmony with the complementary nature of their tasks" (p. 26).

Though I too may be selective in the data I glean from the documents in question, I submit that there is a strong influence at work here that bears close attention in evaluating the argumentation against the ordination of women. It is strong enough to eliminate contrary data.

In conjunction with this propensity for seeking harmony are the appeals to the fittingness found between the sacrament of Order and the calling of men only (*Commentary*, p. 11), and the analogy of faith (p. 11), explained in terms of " 'this natural resemblance' which must exist between Christ and his minister" (p. 12).

Closely linked to this principle of "harmony" is another reason why the Church seems to experience difficulty in dealing with certain kinds of data. Church documents generally disregard "conflict" as a principle or way of understanding God's design for us, and our attempts to respond to Him. Crotty indicts Catholic moral theology for such a failure, as it struggles with the issue of evil surrounding us and our complicity in it. He complains that the moral principles in use seek to extricate us from responsibility for much of the evil that is objectively involved in our behavior and conduct.[15] There is an overriding concern not to give objective recognition to the role that conflict plays in moral theology. As it is, such conflict is confined to subjective factors at the level of individual action. There principles such as that of the twofold effect and probabilism (to cite merely one of the moral systems involved here) are employed to interpret the responsibility of the individual moral agent for the evil that is bound to occur in the conflict. In ways such as this the moral tradition of the Church has sought to curtail and confine moral responsibility for the evil that so often accompanies human action at the individual level.

This orientation toward conflict helps to explain the caution evident in the *Commentary* about discontinuity with past tradition concerning the ordination of women, and the fear of introducing something new. This appears in the rhetorical question: "But what the Church has never done — is this any proof that she cannot do it in the future?" (p. 22) The evident determination here to avoid a break with the past appears to me as an example of the Church's attempt to deny the possibility of conflict at the objective or doctrinal level, and thereby curtail and restrict the unfortunate impact (a kind of evil) that would ensue. By the same token, however, this denial of conflict with tradition affects the procedure the Church follows in dealing with the data pertaining to such issues as the ordination of women.

Besides the two principles, one of "harmony" and its reverse side, "avoidance of conflict," there is a third aspect to note: the tendency to an exclusively *a priori* reasoning in handling practical pastoral concerns. It is seldom evident that the pastoral situation enjoys a priority in helping to fashion the principles that guide Church policy. The recognition of "the help which the Church receives from the modern world"[16] is certainly not indicated in the *Declaration* being considered here. The frequently cited role of custom in the genesis of Church law is a slow and disorganized procedure, but it does show how lived experience provides data for the formulation of policy. An instance of this was the extension of the Sunday precept to assist at liturgy into Saturday evening; this was an accommodation of a pastoral nature to the weekend leisure habits that prevail in the modern world.[17] When "practice" is referred to in the *Declaration*, it is that of the Apostles (pp. 7–8): "This practice of the Church therefore has a normative character: in the fact of conferring priestly ordination only on men . . . This norm . . . has been and is still observed because it is considered to conform to God's plan for His Church."

Charles Curran, speaking from the perspective of moral theology, has been a consistent critic of the tendency within official Church teaching to be non-historical and too exclusively deductive.[18] This and the other two reasons already cited in this chapter lead me to question how adequate is the data-base out of which the *Declaration* fashions reasons to deal with the issue of women's ordination. Though the negative conclusion it has reached may be justified, there is a problem with the procedure. The basis for gathering data is overly restricted. It comes as some surprise that the Congregation itself, in the Commentary, admits "such a quest [for reasons to substantiate the conclusion] is not without risk" (p. 30). But, then, the remark is made: "It is well known that in solemn teaching infallibility affects the doctrinal affirmations, not the arguments intended to explain it" (p. 30).[19] In addition to the dubious propriety of this reference to infallibility in relation to the non-infallible *Declaration*, there is a frank admission that the reasons advanced in the *Declaration* may lack the force of cogency. But this deficiency is offset, so the argument runs, by an appeal to "profound fittingness" (p. 30) and "analogies of faith" (p. 31), which I have previously described as instances of an inadequate harmony-principle at work.

This exclusive reliance on fittingness and analogy is appropriate where "the properly supernatural content of [the] realities" (par. 34) reach far

beyond the competency of "the human sciences." For an issue, however, such as the leadership-role of women, where the secular world
with its politics, economics and social practice has made considerable
progress, the Church can learn very much and obtain abundant data to
clarify the issue of ordination. Admittedly, clarity is not always the out-
come of such investigation. Nonetheless, such an effort is the more
promising and credible procedure to reach conclusions on the question
of women's ordination. Unfortunately, the harmony-principle tends to
shunt aside the data of human experience where tradition not only lives
but also faces conflicts and develops new consensus. A fuller appreciation of human experience will throw light on this contention.

III

The constant tradition (p. 21) that proves so influential in this prohibition of ordination for women is itself the product of something prior to it.
There is certainly an experience that feeds this tradition. Here I intend
to explore at length the meaning and function of experience.

I rely in great measure on studies in the field of "experience." [20]
These investigations have coped with the vagueness that afflicts this
term due to its wide usage in popular language. In this view experience
is an interaction occurring between a person and his/her environment,
that begets new relationships. These, in turn, possess the creative potential for further interactions of the same kind. [21]

The primary emphasis in this description is on the *active* element in
experience. It attempts to offset the common understanding that experience results from a more or less *haphazard passive* accumulation of
events in the life of an individual or institution. If there is a thread of
unity, it is none other than the identity of the individual or institution
serving as the repository of these widely divergent experiences. Over
against this common viewpoint, a highly active role is assigned to experience by someone such as Dewey. It consists in a vigorous interaction
between an agent and the environment, organized in a way to make
something happen, such as a new relationship. Behind this description of
experience lies an approximation to the laboratory model in which experiments are conducted to test hypotheses. But there is also a strong
mandate to assume responsibility for the kind of experience we undergo.

In terms of this understanding, the issue of ordaining women assumes
a different significance from what it has in the interpretation of tradition
presented in the *Declaration*. The experience of being a woman reflected
in this tradition is a truncated one because it is a passive construct, consisting of data that has arisen haphazardly. Or, to speak more precisely,
the historical experience appealed to was under the control of unknown

forces redolent of ignorance, passion and taboo. These effectively stunted the experience of what it means to be woman, and it is this imperfect and incomplete tradition that is presented in the document under consideration.[22]

In this setting, it is being a man that approximates the experience of being fully human. Being a woman is a lesser condition. The experience that substantiates these views is obviously incomplete, and needs to be supplemented by an active interpretation of what it means to be a woman. This is a task which the *Declaration* has not addressed. As a result, it is deprived of the kind of data needed to fashion cogent reasons for any conclusions about the ordination of women.[23]

In seeking a more complete experience on behalf of women, there is a pastoral implication for the mission of the Church. This must include a serious dialogue with the world, as part of that environment in which women interact. Pope Paul VI spoke of this mission in his first encyclical letter.[24] Such a dialogue is essential for gathering a data-base on the role of women in the family, industry, the business world, politics, and any other phase of society where women live and work. If the Church regards this data as irrelevant to the issue of women's ordination,[25] it is foreclosing consideration of a considerable amount of experience capable of raising serious questions for investigation.[26]

In the last analysis, this appeal to such an interpretation of experience looks to those new questions and the new data that are emerging. It is my contention that the Church in the name of harmony and the analogy of faith has permitted only a limited access to experience and so has seriously narrowed the base for constructing any arguments pro or con in regard to women ordination. Should the total experience of being a woman undergo investigation, the conclusions may change. A total experience comprises a continuity between the secular and ecclesiastical spheres of woman's experience, and thereby broadens the base of data to be examined.[27]

Such a broadened experience will resist the harmonizing tendencies observable in many church documents. This is because new dimensions of experience beget new interactions and new problems in the issue of ordaining women. The potential conflict latent in these problems, if honestly confronted, will generate the kinds of reasons needed to handle the issue effectively.[28]

The underlying conflict, when the total experience is examined, is the man-woman problem.[29] There is a continuum between the secular aspect of this problem, and the ecclesiastical. Woman's experience of being dominated and exploited by men cannot be compartmentalized in such a way that what occurs in secular society has no reference in religious society. And it is just as inappropriate for the Church to seek to harmonize the secular aspects of this experience as it is to do so with the ecclesiastical aspects. The mission of the Church urges otherwise.

If the Church seriously attends to the total experience of women, largely one of inequity, the hidden problems will emerge and lead to the kind of investigation that would never be possible in a procedure seeking to harmonize a narrowly based experience. The reasons operative on behalf of fittingness and analogy lose some of their significance when placed in the context of the experience of being woman, that spans the religious and secular spheres. For, in this context, the issues of domination, exploitation, discrimination and injustice are clear. They are as endemic to the Church as to secular society at large, and the Church renders all of us, especially women, a service in acknowledging the problem and committing her resources to respond to it.

A positive regard for experience and its problems entails a greater role for conflict in the development of Church policy. The role of harmonizing divergences under such overarching considerations as the Will of God will be significantly reduced. No longer, then, will one seek to minimize the presence and influence of evil, both premoral and moral, in human experience. An orientation towards harmony may well explain why the Church countenanced such things as slavery, colonization, the crusades and the inquisition in the course of history — all associated with varying degrees of premoral and even moral evil that were not confronted adequately or soon enough.

If the Church were more attuned to the conflict nature of these and similar occurrences, it would more quickly be caught up in the helpful procedure of isolating the evil that is involved, and realistically weighing it in the balance against the good that is being achieved. Moral responsibility lies in this careful weighing of good and evil. So far as the ordination of women is concerned, the Church best situates itself to make a response when it considers the total experience of being a woman, including the conflicts and problems. For these enable the evils of her situation to clearly emerge, and thereby pave the way for the Church to pastorally minister to those who are afflicted, persecuted and suffering.

IV

The issue of the ordination of women touches the nature of the Church's identity and mission. This is so, not simply because half of its membership is women. There are more basic reasons than that.

For instance, Church mission is involved because the status of women in the modern world challenges it to evaluate its effectiveness on their behalf, in the face of its refusal to ordain them priests. Can the Church be faithful to what it is all about, in terms of representing the care, concern and compassion of Jesus Christ today? Mission means ministry and service on behalf of the needs of the world. The element of power, even when properly interpreted in terms of magisterium and jurisdiction, is not an adequate understanding of Church ministry, despite the tendency to make it such.[30] It is this focus on power that stands at the heart of the objection to ordaining women to the ministry, namely, that they are not suitable subjects of such power, since they lack the natural resemblance to Jesus Christ residing in male sexuality.[31]

If ministry were understood as service, this objection would fall, since women have proven to be effective ministers in the category of service.[32] Within the ecumenical context, arguments have already been forthcoming to interpret the validity of ordination in terms of the effectiveness achieved by the ministry in question, rather than in terms of the passing on of power through the imposition of hands.[33] If the mission of the Church were described in terms of effective ministry, then the definition given at the *Call to Action* meeting in Detroit, 1976, would be pertinent: "priesthood is a special relationship of love, that is, a unique community of life, with the people of God; its essence is not a role, functions, series of actions or stereotyped expectations."[34] Women are certainly qualified for this type of ministry. Will they be called to it? If and when this occurs, the mission of the Church will be improved.

Church identity lies in its leadership function, and the issue of women's ordination raises this identity for investigation also. The primary leadership task of the Church is to forward the cause of Jesus Christ in the present day world.[35] Here too, leadership appears in the promotion of love, peace and justice on behalf of the oppressed and burdened.

It is difficult to understand how this can be accomplished without assuming responsibility for the plight of the women of the world. Their condition is not simply one among many, but, to the discerning eye, it is a root problem, where the conflict of good and evil occurs in a radical form.[36] The inequity here, both in the Church and in secular society, is too paradigmatic for any institution to take it lightly and still maintain its credibility as a moral force in today's world.[37]

It should be noted that the insistence on the totality of this experience of being women in both church and secular society necessarily entails problems and conflicts touching on the variegated condition of women. In some instances ordination is not an appropriate response to the problem at hand. This would be especially true where the secular quality of woman's experience leaves her totally unqualified for the ministerial service of priesthood. In this case ordination is not appropriate, though some other religious ministry, corresponding to her demonstrated effectiveness, is in order. In any case, the leadership the Church assumes on behalf of women will add significantly to the identity it enjoys in the world.

Conclusion

Despite some of the remarks made in this chapter, harmony does enjoy a notable place as a fruit of the mission of the Church.[38] But, in this instance, it is a harmony *consequent* upon the resolution of the conflict between good and evil, threatening all its members, both men and women. In this role harmony has not been blind to the real hurts and injuries, suffered especially by women.

A sizeable number of these women seek ordination to the priesthood. This is undoubtedly a problem. In this *Declaration* the Church has begun to take it seriously; hopefully it will continue in this vein. It renders a service to a divided world by seeking to reconcile the divisions within itself.[39] Such reconciliation may not necessarily entail ordination of women. But, until the problem is confronted in all its complexity, an adequate solution will not be forthcoming, and the Church will be failing in its mission to the world. The question must be properly posed in order to orient the process of response in the proper way. Otherwise women and men will continue to live with an unanswered question, and sustain an experience of suffering that spans the continuum of church and secular society. Such pain and suffering is incompatible with the Catholic tradition, graced by the presence of the Holy Spirit, Who is the promise of solace, comfort and refreshment to us all.

10

SYMBOLISM OF SEXUALITY:
PERSON, MINISTRY AND WOMEN PRIESTS

by

Thomas More Newbold, C.P.

It would seem to be obvious that there are some things that a man —
as a *male* — and a woman — as a *female* — either simply cannot do, or,
in terms of what is fitting and appropriate, *should* not do, or wisely
would not try to do. But I think that common consensus would exhaust
the list of such things very quickly. And present debate makes it clear
that ordination of women to the priesthood would not make that consensus list. The question here is: why not?

Are there any particular or special roles and functions which are
closed or should be forbidden to any human person by reason of his or
her sexual anatomy? Or, more precisely: Does the sexual-anatomical
fact intrinsically imply a destiny of inclusion or exclusion from any of
the roles and functions that are by their very nature the possible roles
and functions of a human person?

Perhaps the proverbial "battle of the sexes" has raged over answers
to these questions because some (and sometimes *all*) helpful distinctions
were blotted out or blurred into the background by emotion or prejudice
or both. However, calmly reflective approaches to such questions have
been attempted from time to time; and not only attempted, but rather
thoroughly explored and vigorously, if not always persuasively, expressed.

I

Wherever and whenever human sexuality has become the subject of
serious study or discussion, three dominant approaches have emerged.

For the sake of convenience they may be designated as: the biological, the cultural, and the symbolic. The biological is that approach to an understanding of human sexuality which focuses almost exclusively on the physical endowments and differences of human persons as male and female. Large areas and long stretches of the Judaeo-Christian tradition have been dominated by this approach; and in the 20th century, it was given a particularly vivid expression and summation in the famous (and hotly controversial) dictum of Sigmund Freud: "Anatomy is Destiny." [1]

This approach would view the psychology of man and woman as derivative of the physical, and thus so dependent upon the physical that all areas of personal functioning are sharply and irrevocably defined — whether it be in the traditions of legal rights and obligations, social patterns and structures, or religious tasks and functions. This approach is given practical expression by that segment of our population which insists upon the essential and irreducible differences between male and female consciousness, and upon the necessity to conform attitudes and behavior to these differences.

In the Freudian version of this approach to human sexuality, the fate of women becomes nothing less than pathetic! — to say nothing of the provocations to exasperation and frustration. By proclaiming that "anatomy is destiny," Freud derives the psychology of the feminine human being from the contours of the female body, and specifically from what the female body lacks — a phallus. The "lack," of course, is in relation to the male human body; and thus the way is open for all the humiliating prejudices and discriminations of a male-dominated society.

In all fairness, it must be emphatically noted that not everyone in the Freudian tradition agrees with the more flagrant and negative implications of the Freudian dictum: "anatomy is destiny." Erik Erikson, for instance, is much more positive. He shifts the emphasis from what is missing to what is present: a productive inner potential in "a productive inner-bodily space"; and his interpretation is one that challenges the Freudian feminine psychology on all its major declarations and contentions. Erikson summarizes his views as turning

> . . . from the loss of an external organ to a sense of vital inner potential; from a hateful contempt of the mother to a solidarity with her and other women; from a 'passive' renunciation of male activity to the purposeful and competent activity of one endowed with ovaries and a uterus, and from a masochistic pleasure in pain to an ability to stand (and to understand) pain as a meaningful aspect of human experience in general, and of the feminine role in particular.[2]

However, even in Erikson's positive and persuasive account one senses the felt need to defend women against Freudian attack, and the implication that the feminine still requires defense and justification.

II

We turn now from the biological to the *cultural* approach for understanding human sexuality. Here we discover a decisive change of emphasis. Such representative figures of this approach as Karen Horney and Margaret Mead derive their psychology of human sexuality from the shaping influences of cultural traditions rather than from the determinism of biological structures and endowments. In this view, the assertion is made that social custom and habit have molded, if not entirely created, the psychological propensities of men and women, and that the conditions of society define and determine the masculine and feminine. The primacy of biological facts is replaced by the primacy of sociological facts.[3]

Also, in the literature of this approach to human sexuality there is (understandably and often justifiably) an element of vigorous protest against the traditionally subordinate position of women. It is argued that this socially-imposed position has created in woman a psychology of dependance and passivity which are only learned responses and not intrinsic traits of the feminine. It is also argued that, therefore, such traits can be changed if our culture changes.

In recent years the more radical implications of this cultural approach have been given very explicit rhetorical and social expression. Among the more militant women's groups, the claim is often made that there is no real difference between men and women, only the differences created and imposed by unjust male cultural standards. In practical terms this view is represented by those who attempt to obliterate the cultural and sociological differences between masculine and feminine functioning in the workaday world.

III

There is still another approach — *the symbolic* — which offers (I believe) particular hope. It effectively advances our search for answers not only to our initial questions about sexuality but also to the present controversy about ordination of women to an office held exclusively by men up till now. There are two principal reasons for this progress. The first would be that this symbolic approach does not come on the scene as just another, and competing, alternative to the biological and cultural approaches. It does serve, however, as a corrective for the rigid restrictions of the biological approach and for the excessive claims of the cultural approach. The biological approach tends to reduce all differences between men and women to anatomical endowment and the derived possibility of male/female functions. The consequence is a rigid dichotomy that often leads to (and often *has* led to) sexual discrimination. In contrast, this symbolic approach, while recognizing the difference between being male and being female, does not restrict *personal* role and function to sexual-anatomical differences.

In like manner the symbolism of sexuality provides a corrective to the cultural approach. The culturists tend to look upon any admission of difference as discrimination, and would therefore tend to deny *all* differences, or at least *reduce* all differences to cultural forces and pressures. The symbolic approach, while admitting the fact of cultural influences, makes any exaggerated claims unnecessary. It does so by recognizing, as we shall see, the psychic component of masculine/feminine contrasexuality as intrinsic to every human person. The second reason for the special hope placed in the symbolic approach is that it adds an essential dimension to our understanding and appreciation not only of human sexuality specifically but also of the human person generally, whether that person be male or female.

The few reflections offered here on the symbolic approach to human sexuality will depend almost exclusively on the contributions of Carl Gustav Jung and those who work in his tradition.[4] It is true that nowhere in Jung's writings will one find a formal and full-scale development of the symbolic approach. Yet, in the several passing comments and many random remarks which Jung makes one can find the kind of profound suggestions and original insights that open the way for such a development.

The most important of these suggestive insights is that which Jung often referred to as the "contrasexuality" of each human person.[5] By this he meant that the masculine is not the exclusive concern and reserve of the male, just as the feminine is not the exclusive concern and reserve of the female; but that *both* masculine and feminine are central, shaping factors in both sexes. Sex is of the body, since being male or being female is an anatomical fact. At the same time, sex and gender are not identical. Gender refers to attitudes and modes of behavior that are designated as masculine and feminine; and it is a familiar fact that "masculine" and "feminine" qualities coexist in each sex. Most people correspond in gender to their sexual makeup — appearing female and feminine, or male and masculine. What is not so apparent, but just as factual, is the "contrasexual" aspect of every human person. This is the psychological component which does *not* correspond to the individual's anatomical sex — namely, the masculine element in woman and the feminine element in man.

Thus, an adequate understanding and appreciation of the nature of human personhood, whether male or female, involves recognition of both the anatomical fact of being male or being female, *and* the contrasexual fact of masculine-feminine components in the human psyche of each person.

IV

Jung found it necessary to describe this twofold recognition symboli-cally, because the masculine and feminine in any man or woman is a psychic as well as a sexual and a cultural determinant of human being. Neither masculinity nor femininity can be known directly as a thing in itself but only indirectly as encountered in images, actions, and emo-tional responses.[6] They are best described as two modalities of being oneself as a person, and of giving oneself to the world and others. In Jung's terms, the masculine and feminine are "archetypal" principles and patterns of the human psyche whose polarity and complementarity will find expression in this interaction of both sexes and in the interac-tion within any individual person of the conscious ego with the masculine/feminine elements of his or her personal self.

Dr. June Singer describes some contemporary manifestations of this symbolic understanding of the human person. She writes:

> Today . . . the average woman has the opportunity to unite with her inner masculine potential in a far less restricted way than ever before. More and more women are moving away from full-time housemaking and are assuming some of the functions and modes reserved to men in the past. Women are developing business and professional skills and contributing to the economic support of their families. And many men are taking up life styles formerly denied them for reasons of convention, or economic necessity. The integration of the opposites (i.e., of the masculine/feminine psychic components) can proceed in both direc-tions.[7]

Hence, it is not surprising to find a growing number of people — both men and women — intent upon achieving (in symbolic terms) as com-plete an integration of the masculine and feminine as possible. And, in-volved in this intent, is the effort to educate people away from stereotyped sex attitudes by providing equal opportunity and responsibil-ity for both sexes in all areas of personal role and function.

An old word is now beginning to be used as a new name for this un-derstanding of the human person, and for the socio-cultural phenomena which flow from it. The word is: "ANDROGYNY." A consultation of most dictionaries will not help much. Most dictionaries propagate the inadequate, distorted notion of androgyny as referring to some kind of hemaphroditic hybrid! On the contrary, as Dr. June Singer remarks, an-drogyny is "a fundamental principle that has existed for so long that it may be said to be inherent in the *nature* of the human organism. Not reactive, but intrinsic, is the principle of androgyny."[8]

In a scholarly study of some aspects of androgyny in literature, Caro-lyn G. Heilbrun defines androgyny as a condition in which the per-sonalities of the sexes are not rigidly defined. She further describes it as a movement away from sexual polarization (not polarity) and from the arbitrary restrictions of gender stereotypes. Androgyny would mean a world in which individual roles and modes of personal behavior can be freely chosen — the implication being that the determining factors in any person's life-choices and behaviors should stem more from that person's inner structure as a human person, and not exclusively or primarily from anatomical endowments and societal expectations.[9]

Thus, androgyny is neither a novelty nor an anomaly, but the modality of being a person for any human being — male or female. It need not become a cultural fad that is being used as an excuse for abrogating traditional values. It is, rather, a human fact which demands full recognition, clear understanding, and active implementation.

V

Such considerations give both helpful clarification and normative direction when we turn our attention to the specific question of the ordination of women to the ministry of priesthood. In general, it becomes clear that the question of women's ordination is *not* a question of extending some kind of male franchise to women, but rather a cultural and ecclesial problem of recognizing a matter of human fact.

There are several reasons for this; the first being that the symbolism of human sexuality cannot be reduced to the confining and crippling dimensions of the Freudian dictum: "Anatomy is destiny." The anatomical "femaleness" of women, as well as the anatomical "maleness" of men, does not of itself involve the destiny of exclusion from symbolic human actions and functions. And since the ministerial priesthood is such an action or function, the only reason for the exclusion of either men or women would be the factual one of a normative tradition.[10]

Moreover, any argumentation for an exclusively male priesthood that is based on the principle of "natural resemblance" will be inadequate in the light of the *symbolic* approach to an understanding of human sexuality. It is easy, of course, to make flippant comments about the argument from "natural resemblance" as it appears in the *Declaration on the Question of the Admission of Women to the Ministerial Priesthood.*[11] Almost anything convenient to negative preconceptions can be read into the argument as it stands. It is much more to the point, however, to probe the implications of "natural symbol" and the modes of its function.[12]

It is not the purpose of this chapter to investigate "natural symbol"; but one of the established conclusions reached by those who have done so may be stated here as relevant to the present purpose. It is this: the "natural resemblance" of a "natural symbol" does not require that the symbolic person or function or object be a *literal copy* of the person, function or object symbolized.[13] As Jung has pointed out, the symbolic manifestation or expression of an archetype loses both vigor and viability, meaning and vitality if it becomes a stereotype.[14] To understand the "natural resemblance" of "natural symbol" in this reduced sense would impoverish its meaning and threaten its viability, making it a stereotype that fails to represent the full range of both meaning and possibility. Thus, it is certainly a fact, as the *Declaration* asserts,[15] that Christ the Lord, in His male Personhood, is the archetypal symbol of priesthood; but to conclude that this fact requires an exclusively male priesthood is stereotypical reductionism (a stereotype) when considered in the context of the symbolism of human sexuality and personhood.

Before all else, a man is a male *PERSON* and a woman is a female *PERSON*. This means that *both* men and women have always in common that capacity for full humanness and for the full range of symbolic action and function that the primacy of personhood involves. The value and validity of the symbolic approach to human sexuality lies precisely in this: that it never denies the anatomical destiny of being male and female, but at the same time it never loses sight of the primacy and meaning of PERSONHOOD in both men and women. To cherish that value and respect that validity require, therefore, that the symbolism of sexuality be applied to ministerial status and functions, not within the limited sexual-anatomical perspective but within the larger and more adequate context of the *personal*.

The strength of the *Declaration*, it seems to me, lies in its forthright affirmation of the validity of the symbolic approach; its weakness lies in drawing a conclusion based on the assumptions about human sexuality that are proper to the biological and cultural approaches only. This leaves the *Declaration* open to the accusation of being a "sexist document," and one that emphasizes "sexuality over humanity."[16] While neither of these accusations seem to me to be a full and fair assessment of the *INTENTION* of the *Declaration*, both have some basis in the tone and text of the document. For while the *Declaration* recognizes the irreplaceable contribution of women to the ministry of the Church, and also encourages a more extensive involvement by them in ministry,[17] it still maintains an unchanged position in the face of the crucial question: Can women be ordained to the ministry of priesthood? It seems to me that, granted the document's assumptions relative to the extent and validity of the symbolism of sexuality, this position is understandable; but a full acceptance of the symbolic approach to human sexuality would not see the conclusion as defensible.

Such acceptance would open the way to a more comprehensive understanding and deeper appreciation of the roles and functions that are appropriate, fitting, and possible for the total human person, whether male or female. And in the context of such understanding it would seem that ministerial priesthood, while not the "right" of any individual,[18] could justly be designated an appropriate, fitting, and possible function for any mature, properly prepared, and ecclesially summoned human person — whether man or woman.

Conclusion

"A rebirth of vital religious symbolism, in my opinion, may result from recovery of the feminine element both in individual experience and in the religious symbols themselves. Because the feminine element is by and large de-emphasized in religious symbolism, the fullness of human experience is not represented."[19] These words by Ann Belford Ulanov speak directly to the heart of the problem. And it is heartening to hear more than just an echo of such a statement from some contemporary theologians. I shall quote but one instance here:

> . . . Is it a question of 'ordaining women to the priesthood' or should we be seeking new, as yet unexplored ways to symbolize the relation between God and people?
> I raise this question because there can be little doubt that our theological imaginations (as well as our vocabulary) have been dominated by male imagery. We have paid little attention to what might be called the femininity of God, the motherhood of God . . . I mention this, not in order to be relevant and *avante-garde*, but because our theological imagery really does affect the way we think and the way we perceive the world. Earlier in this century Ludwig Wittgenstein reminded us strongly to what degree our language and our imagery shape our world. Even from a purely psychological point of view the masculine symbols of God and His activity have colored our understanding of God as an aggressive, dominating partner in the human enterprise.
> Perhaps, then, the call to recognize the role of women in ministry is part of a larger, deeper call to broaden our understanding of who God is. This is not just a matter of extending the ordination franchise to women, but of letting our vision of God expand beyond the familiar masculine images. Seen in this light, the agitation for women in ministry is not simply a pastoral strategy for improving the Church's function in the modern day, but a serious call to continuing conversion.[20]

This expresses very well the deeper need and the more inclusive goal which together precipitate the "question of the admission of women to the ministerial priesthood." But I do not think that need will be satisfied or that goal achieved unless and until a prediction made years ago by Rainer Maria Rilke is realized. Speaking from his own experience and perception of the changing status and place of women in our culture, Rilke made this confident assertion: ". . . someday there will be girls and women whose names will no longer signify merely an opposite of the masculine, but something in itself, something that makes one think, not of any complement and limit, but only of life and existence: the feminine human being.''[21] In more direct language, this is a way of saying that the time will come in our culture when female anatomy will no longer be a destiny of exclusion from personal roles and function, whether they be secular or religious.

When and if Rilke's prediction is realized as cultural fact, the admission of women to the ministry of priesthood would cease to be a controversial issue and could become an accepted possibility. In which case, the ordination of women need not be so far down the road of historical possibility as we sometimes think; even though it may not be, as many would hope, just around the corner.

11

DIALOG WITH WOMEN
ON THEIR CALL
TO MINISTRY AND PRIESTHOOD

by

Dennis J. Geaney, O.S.A.

When Sleeping Women Awake
Mountains Will Move
Ancient Chinese Proverb

It has become conventional wisdom with many groups that the ordination of women in the Roman Catholic Church is as certain as death and taxes. The questions that remain are: Will it be this century or the next? Will it be a quiet and orderly evolution as in the Lutheran Church of America, an Episcopal scenario like the Philadelphia "eleven" and its aftermath, or Bishop James S. Rausch's prediction that for Roman Catholics to ordain women would cause "the biggest schism in the history of the Church"?[1] Will the women to be ordained emerge from homespun *koinonia* type churches, which would be a grassroots seminary, or from our professional schools of theology? Will they be "street" people or professionals?

I

In Victor Hugo's phrase the question of the ordination of women is "an idea whose time has come," which translated into Vatican II language is called "the signs of the time." The raising of consciousness through the interplay of the forces of history has its own rhythm and timetable. It is the *kairos*, the unpredictable Spirit-movement which

143

bursts upon the scene precisely at the fulness of time, rather than the *chronos*, the computerized prediction which can be programmed for any moment. It is God who makes history in his dialogue with the individual and collective human will. For the Roman Catholic Church, however, simply to accommodate itself to the flotsam and jetsam of movements and fads would be to be swept along with every political and social current out of a survival instinct. At best it could be equated with a pragmatic posture and at worst with a Machiavelian quest to maintain privilege and power.

The sociological and psychological arguments are not enough — any more than the child's argument against parental discipline that "all the other kids' parents let them do it," is enough. The public opinion poll pointing to a trajectory of gradual acceptance of Catholics for whom "it would be a good thing if women were allowed to be priests" is a valuable indicator for assessing God's continuing revelation in history, but it is not adequate.[2] The *Vatican Declaration* quite rightly argues that change must be in keeping with our divinely guarded church tradition.[3] Our failure to stay within the tradition is to lose it. It is for this reason that we must be clear about the theological assumptions which underpin our understanding of priesthood and the ordination of women.

The proclamation of the gospel and the celebration of the Jesus event in our lives have a priority over questions about style of ministry, the qualifications and the sex of those who hold office. The structures of the church must flow from and be consistent with the gospel imperatives or the heralding of the message and the gathering of the Jesus people. Ministry and priesthood are expressions of the life of the Christian community, not vice versa. The form of ministry and the shape of priesthood are determined by the exigencies of the gospel. Since priesthood is a leadership role and exists for the community, in a particular culture or subculture a male or a female priest would be the appropriate leader for ordering church life, depending on the symbolic system of the culture.

In a homily by Sister Francis Borgia Rothluebber she recounted how a sister returning from Peru told of being greeted in village after village without a priest with: "Will you offer Mass for us?" The homilist's telling argument was the rhetorical question, "For whom is the Eucharist?" In these circumstances of a patriarchal culture, this woman was seen as the fitting person to be the leader of the Eucharistic community. The Eucharist as well as the total ministry of the priest exists for the community. Priesthood is ideally defined by the local gospel community in union with the total church rather than the currently operative institution of priesthood which may have suited the priestly leadership needs of Christians of other cultures.

Baptism is not simply the sacrament of initiation which brings one into the vestibule of the church. It brings a person into full membership of a priestly people. *Mystici Corporis*, *Mediator Dei* and Vatican II describe in biblical and theological nuanced language how all the people are the people of God, but the monarchical model which began in the Constantinian era still has possession. Our present model of priesthood flows from the medieval notion of a royalty which has access to wealth, education and power, without a system of accountability to the people. Bishops and priests are the church who determine the conditions of membership for the laity. The ordination of women, therefore, can appear as a threat to the clerical estate which maintains and defends the present model of priesthood.

II

The *koinonia* model of the early centuries, which respects the institution of hierarchy, offers an alternative. It is groups of believers who gather in communities which are small enough for the members to know each other and share their faith experiences with one another and be to each other a priestly people. The decision making process resides with the group, as we see in Acts 13:1-3. It ratifies the gifts of members so that they may minister in the name of this particular community which embodies the life and Spirit of Jesus Christ. This writer has been associated, however briefly, with such communities in the United States: St. Mark's in Cincinnati, St. Andrew's in Oakland, St. Mary's in Fort Wayne, and Paulist Center in Boston. Bishop Ottenweller of Toledo is the Episcopal apostle of this model of church. The pastor of each of these parishes comes from the traditional mold but has discovered the role of pastor as enabler, and through his charism helps people discover their ministerial gifts and their call. In this model the ministry is done not primarily by the professional enablers but by the people.

As priests leave the active ministry, and creative young men by not entering seminaries do not choose to perpetuate present structures, members of *koinonia* communities are being prepared to assume many priestly functions. We have in the United States several of this new type of "seminary" opening and expanding while traditional ones are closing.

No longer are our churches filled with emigrants. The present level of education of parishoners in the United States does not signficantly separate them intellectually from their priests. Still it is necessary for the *koinonia* communities to help supplement general education of its members with Bible and historic studies according to the time frame of people who work, attend to their families and minister to the community. St. Mark's parish is sending six women to a three-year part-time Lay Pastoral Ministry Program at Mt. St. Mary's Seminary at Cincinnati. This is an accredited Master of Arts in Religion program. These are women who are already part of the life and ministry of the parish. While the goal of these women is not ordination, the parishoners already have women in prominent leadership roles, thus making a transition to women priests easier if the male clerical priests were withdrawn.

I am not naive about the implications of a priesthood emerging from the community rather than the professional school. Failure to know the history of our tradition and a critical understanding of the Bible can lead to a fundamentalism that is more rigid than present Catholicism. "Symbols without content," writes Dr. David O'Brien, "interpretation without knowledge, emotional highs on religion without sensitivity to the history or sociology of religion, all are going to end up destructive of faith and church."[4] Women presently ministering in the community are capable of this kind of sophistication without leaving the community on a permanent basis and thus lose their roots as community people. At this point we are arguing for the development of *koinonia* women ministers and/or priests through theological extension-school programs.

Regardless of the model of ministry or the educational style, the rigor of theological education must be maintained. Ministers or priests as caring people meditate religious meaning within a tradition. The style or educational methodology can and will be argued, but not the need for a disciplined approach to preparing people who will pass on the heritage. When we argue for the extension-school model for community-based education for women ministers who might be our future priests, we are not arguing for less education than the present educational requirements for priesthood. It would be a disaster to cut back on theological education simply because we are in a crisis situation resulting from cultural developments we have not yet integrated into our understandings of ordained ministry.

The *koinonia* model of church and ministry seems to fit an extension-school model of education, over against the full-time educational models which take people out of the ministry context and could make them ultimately less effective as ministers or priests. The argument is not for less professional training but rather addresses itself to the context of the learning and the acquiring of the ministerial or priestly identity through immersion in pastoral life.

It should not be assumed that when women have the same professional training as the ordained male, the hierarchy and the local community will make room for them. This route seems to demand a bloody entrance. If women have been ministering in *koinonia* communities and have over the years acquired a theological education, the local community and the universal church would be inclined to call them as it did Ambrose and Augustine. People would have become accustomed to women ministers and would be asking that they become their ordained priests. People need to experience ministry that is not rooted in one sex.

III

In our mainline Protestant Church and now in the Roman Catholic Church in the United States, the A.T.S. Master of Divinity program which requires a college education and at least three years of graduate or professional training has become the norm for ordination for ministers and priests. However, Catholic women who are entering the field of professional pastoral ministry in the Roman Catholic Church are seeking credentialing in a number of ways. Sisters and lay teachers in our Catholic school system from kindergarten to university may indeed see themselves as called to the teaching ministry, but they do not talk about it as a path to ordination. Many sisters have left the Catholic school for precisely this reason. They desire to be out of the highly structured classroom and relate to people in a total context of life in which they can offer meaning, comfort and challenge stemming from the gospel in a more explicit context.

The largest category of the new non-clerical pastoral professionals is the Director of Religious Education. In a small diocese like Grand Rapids, Michigan, there are twenty-two full-time D.R.E.'s, mostly lay. In the present decade what began as a vague and undefined role is now becoming an American Catholic Institution. As D.R.E.'s stay in a particular parish for a number of years, they become more and more seen by the community not simply as professional educational administrators but as parish ministers. They seem to want to keep their role restricted and not assume responsibility for the entire parish, nor are they on the whole interested in ordination for the priesthood for themselves.

While the job offers a low salary, it is attracting a core of lay people who have degrees in theology from our Catholic universities and colleges and from Catholic and non-denominational schools of theology. Within this increasing cadre of professionals are a pool of competent women who have a strong ministerial and priestly identity whom the local community or the larger church could call upon to assume the ordained priestly office. Presently they stand with their sisters who seek ordination. Most seem to prefer the anonymity of their private lives while they use their work-life to break open the Word of God to parishioners through volunteer lay teachers whom they instruct in training programs and workshops.

There is another segment of women, mostly sisters in an age bracket that is skewed to the shady side of life who are pastoral visitors in hospitals and nursing homes. Older sisters work out of their life experience

and their religious commitment. These sisters are not interested in ordination for themselves or their work. Sister Thomasine McMahon of the
Cathedral parish in Oakland is an unusual parish minister. She has
trained a core of lay volunteer parish visitors. She expressed to me with
great anguish a situation in the hospital in which she could give communion and hold the hand of the person but could not give the sacrament of
the sick to the dying person nor find a priest who could come to the
hospital. She is not asking to be ordained a priest or deacon but won-
dered why our sacramental theology and canon law limits her ministry
and frustrates her as a minister. Could not such a person be commissioned in the name of the Church to offer general absolution and the
sacrament of the sick in such cases? We ask our theologians if more
limited or more specific types of priestly ministry would be consistent
with our Catholic sacramental tradition.

Some younger sisters and a smaller number of lay women have taken
academic quarters and full years of Clinical Pastoral Training to prepare
themselves for professional chaplaincies. Whether such people should be
admitted to holy orders depends on one's understanding of ordination.
Ordination to this writer implies a leadership role in the total community
besides a public and permanent commitment to ministry in the Roman
Catholic Church. It implies that the person has a vision of who Jesus
Christ is and how his Spirit is alive in the world, a person who can
articulate this vision for others in symbols that speak to our culture, a
person who has the charismatic gift of bringing unity to a community
which is symbolized in the sacramental celebration, particularly the
Eucharist. Every hospital chaplain need not be ordained, but it would be
fitting for the head of the pastoral care department, the woman or man,
who exercises these functions and has these gifts to be the public symbolic representative of Jesus Christ for the hospital's Catholic community.

IV

Under our present model of local church and the A.T.S. Master of
Divinity (M.Div.) educational model for ordination to the priesthood,
and assuming we follow the patterns of the Lutheran and Episcopal
church, the first women to be ordained in the Roman Catholic Church
will be graduates of our Catholic and non-denominational schools of
theology. Therefore, we need to look at these schools and their women
students.

A decade ago only Protestant and non-denominational schools were
open to Catholic women who wished to prepare for ministry or priesthood in the traditional way churches affirm as educational preparation
for ordination. Catholics are the largest denomination at a number of

non-denominational schools such as Chicago and Harvard. The fifty-six students enrolled at Harvard Divinity School are in an assortment of degree programs at the doctoral and master levels with a variety of goals, only one of which might be ordination. From the doctoral programs at these schools are coming our present and future supply of women professors of theology; at the master's level some are preparing to be teachers of theology, D.R.E.'s, and others to qualify for priesthood. One of the male students has been accepted for ordination by a Catholic bishop. Women M.Div. graduates must wait for the waters to be stirred.

Our Catholic schools of theology have made remarkable strides in the past five years in opening degree programs in their schools to women. The majority of the schools run by religious orders are also open to women. In 1977 Weston College had thirty M.Div. non-clerical candidates. The number of diocesan schools that are open to women is likewise rapidly expanding. Newark, Milwaukee, Detroit, Cincinnati, and Orchard Lake offer a variety of degree programs for women. Increasingly schools promote the extension-school model for married women with families and single people who cannot afford a full-time program.

V

Who are these women who have graduated from or are attending these professional schools of theology? The author of this chapter interviewed women at the four major centers of theological education in the United States: Chicago, Berkeley, Washington, D.C., and Boston. Ten interviewers will be capsulized.[5] Some were very brief; others involved two sessions.

Susan Sherwood is a 1976 graduate of the Pacific School of Religion (P.S.R.). She had a traditional twelve-year Catholic education in a lower middle-income family in New York. Her desire to be a priest came while in high school but was put aside as a whim. While studying psychology at Berkeley she realized that ministry spoke to ultimate meaning in a way that psychology could not. She was offered a scholarship at P.S.R. While a student she preached, led prayer groups and did hospital chaplaincy. She has a strong priestly identity and feels called to priesthood. Presently she is head of a pastoral care department in a Catholic hospital. She has a strong identification with her Catholic tradition, and has no desire to change denominations to be ordained.

Karen Wells is a 1976 graduate of Harvard Divinity School. She grew up in a family in which one parent was Catholic. Her religious training was Sunday Mass and C.C.D. She attended a Protestant college where she met a chaplain who introduced her to Harvard Divinity School where she enrolled. She found that her Catholic tradition and faith were supported while a student at Harvard. Upon graduation she became employed by a diocese as a Catholic chaplain on a secular campus. She is unmarried and desires· much to be a priest to support her pastoral work. She preaches every other Sunday in the local parish church, is a counsellor and spiritual guide. She speaks about ministry and sacraments in a more spiritual context than the structured categories of the priest who is inclined to see his ministry in terms of status and power, even though it be sacramental power. She is not looking for the priesthood for personal affirmation but to complete or bring to another level the priestly ministry she is presently performing. While she is presently a celibate, she will not wait forever for the church to ordain celibate women.

Sister Marie Wilkins is in her late thirties. After a stint as a high school teacher, she went to St. Louis Divinity School to study scripture. After one year she became intrigued with the possibility of being a professional minister. She is presently employed by a diocese as the Catholic chaplain at a commuter campus which has no tradition or need for a liturgical expression of Catholic faith. She has enrolled in a Doctor of Ministry program which accepts her experience as a minister and her previous theological studies as the equivalent of a Master of Divinity. "I do not need to be ordained to be a minister. I am a minister of the word of Jesus Christ. No church can prevent me from the expression of that vocation."

Shirley Waters, age 26, grew up in a traditional ethnic family that had a strong identification with the local ethnic parish. After twelve years of Catholic education she went to a state college to become an English major and ultimately to study for a doctorate. In her senior year, she had a vocation crisis which she shared with the Catholic chaplain and ultimately with her family. She was being called from a vocation of teaching English literature to one that involved inter-personal relationships. In time she began to see it as a call to ministry. She applied and was accepted at a Catholic theology school. She insisted on an M.Div. program after they had already enrolled her in an M.A. tract. At the end of the first year, she took a year off to work and marry. I met her while in her last year at another Catholic theology school. She is presently a part-time campus minister. "The ordination of women has not been a real big issue for me. I have so many other things to deal with. I feel there are many styles of ministry, but I don't feel a need to be validated until I run into this situation where the ministry I am doing is not validating me. Right now I think I would have difficulty in a parish because of the priestly role and authority. I feel I would have more freedom in a campus situation."

Sally Cassidy, age 25, is a second year student at the Church Divinity School of the Pacific. I met her at a *koinonia*-type parish where I assisted with the daily and weekend liturgies. There was something about the way she carried the book in procession and read the scriptures that gave her a priestly identity. When I explained to the Sunday congregation at the end of a liturgy that she was studying at Episcopal school for ministry in the Roman Catholic church, the congregation roundly applauded. She was not posturing for an audience but ministering out of some mysterious depths.

She comes from an Irish Catholic family. Her parents separated when she was young. She had sixteen years of Catholic education. During the last six she was not a practicing Catholic. She left for Europe after graduation to "get it all together." While she was in Germany she was sitting on the bank of a river and began to weep profusely. This was the religious experience that turned her life around. She became a Vista volunteer and gradually began to read and reflect on God and life issues. She enrolled in Drew University School of Theology and found herself to her surprise in a Methodist seminary. She transferred to the Berkeley Episcopal school where she receives a sizable scholarship. She feels called to the priesthood, finds the study of theology exciting, volunteers one day a week at the *koinonia* parish as the "on-call priest" for the day. She feels called to the priesthood but understands the reality of church polity.

Sister Mary Theresa Feltus, age 35, comes from a large, middle-income family. She entered at age 18 and taught for twelve years. While engaged in formation work for her community she found she had ministerial skills as a spiritual director and the facility for giving group retreats. The community accepted her petition to go to a Catholic school for professional ministry. While at school she assisted a *koinonia* community and further developed a ministerial and priestly identity. After graduation she accepted a position as campus chaplain at a Catholic university. She takes her turn preaching, conducts penitential services, gives spiritual direction, and directs prayer retreats. As we spoke about priesthood her voice began to quiver. "I am hearing confessions now. I am offering forgiveness. People say, 'I feel the Lord has forgiven me in your listening to me.' I cannot sacramentalize or celebrate it." She was close to tears. She sees herself as a priest in her heart, but she says she will not join the Episcopal church to externalize it.

Caroline Sullivan, age 45, is married and the mother of a family that is well on its way to adulthood. She has taught homiletics in a Catholic seminary, has done extraordinary creative liturgical work in a *koinonia* community. At last she has an opportunity to study theology as a full-time student at a Catholic school which is in driving distance from her home. Theology intrigues her in a way that does not capture the imagination of the average male seminarian. She is highly supportive of the system which makes intellectual demands on students for ordination.

She made it clear that she is not interested in ordination. I took it as the statement of a realist who does not want to get locked into using her energies in fighting a cause, when she could be giving her undivided time to ministry and her family. She strongly affirms the M.Div. for the student who is interested in ministry but not ordination. She is taking all the courses a priest candidate takes, including celebration of the sacraments. She feels that as a full-time minister she will be at times a leader of prayer and paraliturgical celebrations. She is open to employment as a parish associate.

Mary Louise Kirby, age 28, is a part-time M.Div. candidate in a diocesan seminary. She thought of being a sister while in high school. She was turned on in college by a joy-filled theology professor. She is presently a teacher in a Catholic high school. She has no intention of seeking ordination. "It frightens me to think that all our ordained men will go away. I have been drawn to ordination, but pastorally it still frightens me. I am afraid of what it will do the the church."[6]

Susan White is from the South, a graduate of a Catholic college in 1975. She was unemployed and wanted to do something meaningful so she started teaching Sunday school. She became ever more enthused. She took a teaching position in a Catholic high school but now wants to be in pastoral ministry. I met her as an applicant for full-time M.Div. study at a Catholic theology school. She is applying for the financial support of her diocese which is supporting two other lay women who are pursuing ministry degrees. One of these is Susan Sendelback, 23, a student at the Catholic University's theological school. "She was a student at the University of Georgia four years ago when — as a result of her ministerial work within her prayer group and in campus ministry — her friends began to urge her to realize her gifts for ministerial leadership."[7] "I knew I needed my bishop's support." With his endorsement access to Catholic University became a reality. She says, "Women entering the ministerial role leads to a more compassionate, sensitive role — your mere presence softens the clerical approach."

Ella Harris, fiftyish, is a successful black business woman who is tired of making money and wants to work full-time as a parish associate. She is a born Catholic, divorced, but not remarried. She is a leader of the charismatic prayer movement of her diocese, working closely with the priest diocesan director. She is presently taking a year of pastoral studies at a Catholic theology school and works part-time as an associate pastor for her field project. She is emphatic about not wanting to be a priest but identifies herself very clearly in clergy meetings as an associate pastor. "Priests are shocked when they hear me say it. I want to be an associate pastor to help develop the spiritual life of the parish. My biggest obstacle is not being black, but being a woman."

From these interviews and others several impressions have been etched on my consciousness.

1. This movement among women toward ministry is Spirit born. In many cases the religious experience leading to the decision was described or alluded to. There are no cultural supports to enter this profession. Parents, schools, and church are not encouraging it. Society offers no rewards to such people.

2. This consciousness-raising in which religious experience took the shape of a ministerial vocation began to surface in the early seventies. Prior to this time dedicated women in the church either sought their identity as sisters or saw themselves as auxiliaries of the clerical priesthood. Today women in ministry have an autonomy that has its origins in the uniqueness of their own charisms, which they put at the service of the entire Christian community.

3. Ministry rather than ordination is the primary thrust and motivation. Ordination is an important symbol for women seeking ordination as well as those who are not. Until some women are ordained, all women will be in the category of second-class citizens and second-class ministers. Ordination, not degrees, is still the union card.

4. For some women ordination is a deeply felt need. It was mostly felt by campus ministers and hospital chaplains who are doing all the traditional priestly functions except leading the Eucharistic prayer and performing other sacramental rituals.

5. The women I interviewed seem to be more mature than their male counterparts in theology schools. Because they are breaking into a twentieth-century male preserve, they have developed strengths and insights that males have not been forced to wrestle with.

6. Below the surface there are deep layers of anger. This varies with the length of experience women have had in working under males. Sisters and older D.R.E.'s feel it more deeply than young lay women beginning in ministry. Hurts of past decades that were repressed are surfacing. This anger can be creative, as it is in any new movement that seeks to wipe out the injustices of the past and present. Men need to interpret the hurt and anger, not as personal attacks but the platform from which the cause for justice and renewal of ministry can be launched.

7. There is frustration among women because of the inability of the male clergy and bishops who have their hands on the levers of power to deal with women as equals both as humans and as copastors. They see clerical training and life style as inhibiting this development.

8. Women in ministry have a different mind set from priests. The priest has been trained in a sacramental theology and pastoral care that centers on the power of Jesus being exercised in ritual words and actions rather than in the totality of the human experience in which ritual words and deeds are only a part. The difference is pointed up in pastoral visitations and communion calls. The priest can make the call with his car running, while he enters the home, compared with the non-ordained minister who would allow a half hour for the call. Since a woman, as a broad generalization, is more apt to minister out of her feelings because she is more in touch with them, the style and content of the pastoral relationship can be significantly enriched.

9. Probably the deepest impression of my interviews is what women have to offer the faith community. The very hurts they experience and the pain of being frustrated are their tools of ministry. A woman ministry student said: ''I don't think of ministry as helping or caring. I think of it as living with people. Being present, being conscious means accepting another's pain, sharing my pain, that my pain is not just okay but good, helping each of us to turn away from our own situation to others is to forget mine.'' Pain as I hear it expressed, is not simply a passive endurance of fate but a strength and power to enable her to affirm herself and stay in there with the staying power of the women at the foot of the cross.

Conclusions

Two further points need to be made: one a clarification, the other a projection.

A clarification. In this paper the minister coming out of the *koinonia* community and preparing theologically through part-time study, which indeed may cover five or six years is contrasted with the three to four full year traditional M.Div. route. It need not be either/or, but rather both educational models and a variety of combinations. The local church model which stresses the ministering community as the seminary or seed bed for ministerial identity and development, if pushed to its ultimate, would give us a congregational model which can be tyrannical in its leadership and narrow in its total perspective. The Roman Catholic church has never fallen into this trap. It has always affirmed the ordained person as a person who may always be serving a local congregation but is ordained likewise for the entire church and indeed may be called to serve a church other than the one which has given her/him nuture in responding to God's call.

The ordained person should possess the ability to move to another community and offer leadership to help a new church be formed or an old church renewed. The church is always in mission and every priest is potentially a missionary. The linking of the local church to the universal church, perjoratively called the "institutional church," is particularly important to a generation which is still reacting to the heavy hand of authoritanism rather than responding to the creative power of the authority forms of the Roman Catholic church which makes local pastoral power possible and not simply dependent on the charismatic power of the local priest.

A Projection. What will be the future of these women who are presently studying in our schools? Will they be able to survive the long haul, the winters of not using their ministerial training in an ecclesial setting?

All professionals need a place to practice their art and a community of professionals with whom they can share their insights, encourage each other to learn from one another. If these are lacking, our M.Div. graduates will slip into caring positions which are not overtly ministerial in an ecclesial context. Their burgeoning ministerial identity will fade into one of the many secular helping professions, which is only tragic in view of what they might be to renewing the church of tomorrow.

When the first wave of M.Div. hit the beachheads and find that they are not wanted in Roman Catholic ministry structures, some may survive and become purified and strengthened through gorilla warfare, but it is not likely to encourage the second and third wave of women who experience a call in seminal form. It is urgent that these women form their own networks to survive as emigrants on an alien soil. Without this peer support, it is easy for people whose ideals and expectations are so high not only to give up ministry as a vocation and priesthood as a goal but to actually leave the Church. A large number of lay people who were deeply involved in the lay apostolate movements of the fifties have left the church in frustration and disillusionment or retain a marginal stance in bitterness. This can happen to our recent graduates and our present students.

It is crucial that other ordinaries like Archbishop Borders of Baltimore affirm women in ministry with positions at every level of church structure from the diocesan office to parish associate. Financial grants must be given to women who are enrolled in ministry courses. A placement service needs to be inaugurated or become a part of the present clergy personnel office. Since the ordination of women is not presently a top priority in the Church, women need more than a promise, a prayer, and a pat on the cheek. They need to be commissioned now as lay ministers in public services that tell the people in the pews that we are seriously working toward the ultimate commissioning in the church — ordination.

PART FIVE

MINISTRIES FOR TOMORROW

12

DIALOG WITH CHURCH LEADERS AND THEOLOGICAL SCHOOLS ON CHARISMS AND PRIESTLY MINISTRY

by

Alcuin Coyle, O.F.M.

Our age has been characterized by a sensitivity to the power of the Spirit. In this Spirit the Church was born at Pentecost, and this same Holy Spirit has exercised a significant role in Church development at every point in history.

From the very beginning Church structure developed in response to the Spirit. According to Robert J. Karris in the third chapter of this book, a single uniform model of ministry was something unknown in the early days of Christianity. Particular ministries developed according to specific needs of space, time and culture. Today more than every before church leaders must be attentive to new promptings of the Spirit in facing the consequent tensions between local diversity and universal unity, between past and present needs with a view toward charting the future directions of ministry and priesthood.

The question of women in the future directions of priesthood cannot be presented in its true light, except against the background of the many gifts of the Spirit distributed among all Christians, and in organic relationship with other ecclesial functions. The Church of the future, therefore, must be envisioned as a community, drawing heavily upon charismatic ministries. In order that the Church be transformed into a more adequately human social order, there must be a continuing development away from ministerial roles, identified with fixed states of life, toward functional roles assumed on the basis of personal qualifications and talents. Such a development in the direction of democratization and specialization, will offer hope for a higher level of cooperation between men and women. It removes sexual discrimination in recognizing God's call to ministry and priesthood. We are presently witnessing the beginnings of this development.

It must be acknowledged, however, that there are some in the Church who do not share this hope and others who react fearfully. Hope is not simply a flying leap into the utter openness of the future. It is based upon a long tradition back into Old and New Testament times. This book has already explored the diversity and evolution of ministries during these early ages. Hope, for this very reason, is vibrant with real possibilities. Thus, in developing a consciousness regarding women in future direction for ministry, the Church today will be required to take risks. These can be borne without fear provided there is *a real sense of history* — our ancestors too were men and women of faith (Heb ch 11–12) — and *a real sense of hope* — "the Spirit helps us in our weakness . . . [and] intercedes for the saints" (Rom. 8:26-27).

Church leaders must be confident that God, who is the author of human history — past, present and future — and who guides it to fulfillment, will enable them to achieve the openness that is necessary in responding to our future needs in ministry. This hope should stimulate Church leaders to read with courage "the signs of the times" and to project with a sense of vision the agenda prepared by the contemporary world.

The ecclesiology of Vatican II has challenged the Church to recognize "the signs of the times" and to understand the world in which we live, its expectations, its longings and its often dramatic characteristics. Prominent among the signs of the times which signal the expectations and longings of human persons today is the women's movement. The fact that the Church has taken little cognizance of the women's movement itself, and has made only perfunctory, sporadic and uncoordinated efforts to examine its own practices and attitudes, is creating a serious pastoral problem.

At the same time, progress is gradually taking place in certain sectors of the Church. For example, in many areas women are being called to collaborate with all segments of the Church in the essential work of evangelization. This is a very positive sign, but it is hardly enough. The ministry of the Church will suffer if women are given only a secondary place in its life and mission. While the state of the question rests as a task for the entire Church, bishops in particular have a very special pastoral responsibility in this regard. Likewise, seminaries and theological schools exercise a very important role in opening and facilitating new directions in ministry by women, reaching into priesthood.

The final chapter of this book, completing our investigation of women in priesthood, has a more comprehensive purpose than the preceding ones. Its special focus is on the broader issues regarding the future directions of ministry. By allowing the Spirit to speak to us within the movements of our contemporary world, its achievements and hopes, its failures and needs, we will dream about the future of religious leadership. It will be evident, as we look ahead, that women as well as men can answer the call of the Spirit within this *Sitz im Leben*. In fact, sexual differences will fade away as people are judged qualified or not for the apostolate.

The observations here will be developed within two perspectives:

1. the development of ministries within the Church;
2. the contemporary challenges placed on the role of theological schools in preparing men and women for future ministry.

The first area will trace the process from spontaneous charismatic gifts to official recognition of the lay minister, deacon(ess), and priest, of the minister celibate and married, male and female. The second and final section will point out the essential challenge of *mission* in all theological education and the concomitant need of Christian identity in the complexities of mission to the world.

I

From very early times, the Church exercised her common mission in the world by entrusting her members with various functions according to their charisms. In chapter three we learned that women featured prominently in almost all religious offices of the Church during the years after Pentecost. Consequently, besides the sacramental ministries there were always other ministries, both liturgical and non-liturgical. In the course of centuries, the sacramental ministries ceased for women, as Carolyn Osiek noted in chapter four. Even non-liturgical roles of women came to be severely restricted.

The Church today is not seeking to resurrect these defunct ministries. Rather according to her ancient pattern she inquires into the charisms of her members now and relates these to her ministerial needs today. To inquire about the modes of ministry for the future, is to ask *under what forms* the Headship of Christ will need to be represented in the communities that are taking shape today, and what distribution and diversification of ministerial tasks among men and women will be needed for the Church of tomorrow.

The Church should not be content to think that it has been handed down a universal pattern of the structure of ministry effective for all times and places. Rather, we must clearly realize that the ministries, transmitted by the living apostolic tradition, have through the centuries taken diverse forms; the particular value of any one of them remains relative in many details. The same creativity should be expected of the Church today, as characterized the Apostolic Church. The early Church gave to itself those forms of ministry which rose from the charisms of its members, men and women, and best answered the needs of the times.

The creativity and openness to new forms of ministry today is not merely an abstract possibility. It is a responsibility and task which the contemporary world places on the agenda of the Church. In this way the Church will be able to equip itself with a variety of ministries which best correspond to the contemporary needs of the people of God. In this effort, full use must be made of all ministerial possibilities now officially recognized, while keeping these open to necessary adaptation and flexibility. At the same time going beyond the necessary adaptations of traditional forms, the Church must also look to the secular world for effective models of leadership. Carroll Stuhlmueller in chapter two explored this interaction of the sacred and the secular in Old Testament forms of authority. Women provide an extraordinary example not only of secular leadership but specifically of prophetic challenge. Thus the Church can devise new forms of future ministries consonant with her nature. We need to look more closely at the relation of charisms with offices or official recognition.

All Christians are charismatic by vocation, and the Spirit distributes individual gifts to all differently. The exercise of their proper charism can be called "ministry" in the broad sense. Nevertheless, not all are engaged in the ministry of the Church in the same manner and with the same intensity. The two notions of office and charism must be distinguished according to whether services are spontaneously rendered or are entered into on a more permanent basis. This distinction hones in on the question of women's ministerial role: should its more charismatic form become more regulated and "ordained" within the Church's Magisterium?

The common and fundamental ministry of both office and charism is unity. The importance of Church unity, particularly for Roman Catholicism, was discussed at length in chapter one. Office and charism seek unity, each in its own way. Office ensures order and continuity; charism, transcending time and space, contributes to the ministry of unity through renewal, reform and development. In the Church, office has its origin primarily from the historical Christ and bears the characteristics of the Incarnation; charism has its origin primarily from the Holy Spirit and bears the characteristics of the working of the Spirit. Office represents the Headship of Christ; charism heals, renews and carries the Church forward.

In the Church, office and charism stand dialectically over against each other, differing in structure and mode of operation. The dialectic between office and charism is one of complementarity. Together they form the total ministry of the Church. Moreover, the Church flourishes best when office and charism respect each other and draw upon the resources of the other. However, there has always been, and always will be, a tension between office on the one hand, and charism on the other. This tension becomes ever more severe when charism seeks a permanent place in the Church institution and proceeds from a strong, prophetic stance. Such is the case with the charismatic role of women.

In chapter nine of this book, Sebastian MacDonald recognized the importance of *conflict* in the development of doctrine. Other chapters noted the presence of a healthy tension in the history of Israel, in the early Church, and even today.

Similar tensions are found in other spheres of human life outside the Church, and no order of law can do away with such a phenomenon. To a certain extent, tension is necessary and is often very creative and fruitful. Every time, however, that tension causes a problem within the Church, office and charism will have to find an adequate solution in a spirit of service and reconciliation, so that the tension does not result in crisis and eventual polarization. This warning is especially appropriate when we the Church respond to the women's movement.

All charismatic gifts and offices then are intended for mutual service of the community. Charisms arise from the Spirit, are discerned by the community, and are authenticated by office for the common good. When certain charisms are acknowledged officially so that they can fulfill their function in the name of the community, we have lay ministries. All members receive the Spirit and express the ministerial nature of the Church in their own sphere. Some may do so in a more stable manner, and have become visible signs of the community's own concern and commitment. The field is unlimited. Men and women fulfill these functions, as they are manifestations of the special gifts of the Spirit and are rooted in baptism. Hence, they are not derivatives from the apostolic ministry, and they do not demand any change in basic structures. All that is needed is that community leaders recognize the many services already being rendered by many of its members.

In the course of history lay ministries tended to be absorbed within the clerical office and their duties exercised primarily within the context of the liturgy. On the one hand, liturgical celebration, instead of being an action of the whole community, had become the preserve of a few ministers specifically ordained for that purpose. Liturgy was viewed in a restricted manner as consisting of the ritual performed by the ministers so that many integral elements of liturgical celebration became marginalized. Correspondingly, on the other hand, the ordained ministers came to be defined more and more in terms of their "sacred" functions in the liturgy. Therefore, the reality of lay ministries and, more important, the participation of all christians in the basic ministerial function of the Church in the world was gradually lost sight of, as all ministries became clericalized. Carolyn Osiek discussed some aspects of this clericalization in chapter four; Dennis J. Geaney investigated the gradual liberation of lay ministries in chapter eleven.

The renewal of lay ministries was introduced at Vatican II and became more specifically actualized in the post-conciliar document *Ministeria Quaedam* of 1972. This apostolic letter restored to lay people the exercise of all ministries that belong to them in virtue of the common priesthood and of charisms allotted to them by the Spirit. The document suggests the possibility of lay ministries related to the Church's charitable action. This distinction clearly indicates that lay ministries are not to be restricted to services pertaining to the liturgy. In principle, they extend to all aspects of the mission of the Church.

This is an important distinction to keep in mind, as we investigate the lay ministry of women and its possible ordination within the priesthood. The post-conciliar Church has been so preoccupied with internal structures and processes that a great deal of attention has been diverted from the important task of developing lay leadership. Moreover, during this period, many priests assumed the lay responsibility for social action, particularly in the areas of peace and justice. Overlooking the primary task of the laity, many priests became involved primarily in pursuing social causes rather than in preparing the laity to assume their proper responsibility for such issues. As a result, there is a real necessity at the present time to re-examine the question of the loss of a generation of lay leadership, and that out of such a re-examination a new sense of direction will emerge.

The ministerial opportunities, on the other hand, afforded the laity through the restoration of the Permanent Diaconate have been a welcomed development. However, this ministry could eventually prove to be a serious regression, if it creates the impression that it is through the Permanent Diaconate the laity primarily participate in the ministry of the Church. Such an impression could easily foster a rather prevalent attitude that to exercise a ministry within the Church you must be ordained. This soul-searching question must be pondered by any lay movement as it seeks ordination; women must attend to it, as the restoration of their own order of deaconess is under study and they look towards the priestly order.

The pressing task of Church leadership is to develop lay responsibility in ministry, and to devise ministries that best respond to the needs of the local Church. For it is at this level that recognition must be given to the role exercised by the laity in all aspects of the mission of the Church. *Ministeria Quaedam* is an invitation to translate into actual practice the conviction that the responsibility of the Church in her mission to the world cannot be borne by the clergy alone. The comprehensive responsibility must be shared by all Christians through a distribution of tasks and functions.

Against the background of this theology of lay ministries we consider the nature and function of the diaconate. The nature and history of this office will direct us in understanding the ministry of women and its ordination by the Church. Although the diaconate has emerged as a sacramental ministry, and consequently signifies in its own way the Headship of Christ, in its present form it does so only in a derivative and limited way, subordinate not only to the bishop, but also to the priest. It has not escaped the historical forces of sacralization, and has become predominantly a liturgical ministry.

In accordance with ancient tradition, though the deacon had a special place in the liturgical celebration, his proper place was in the world, witnessing to the service dimension of Christ and of the Church's mission, and with special concern for the poor. While the priest was primarily concerned with the ministry of Word and Sacrament, the deacon was primarily concerned with service, especially to those in need. After the first couple centuries, the deacon ceased to be a servant (minister). He became an administrator and emerged as a rival to the priest for power within the community. When the functions of leadership and administration were taken away from him, he became only a subordinate minister in the liturgy and his office became progressively superfluous.

The present notion of the diaconate is simply a rediscovery of the traditional vision that became obscured in the course of history. This new vision offers a better sense of identity to the priest as minister of the Word and Sacrament. It is also clear that the notion of diaconate understood in this way is expressive of an essential dimension of the Church. The ministry is seen neither as a means of meeting the shortage of priests, nor as a stepping stone to the presbyterate or to a married clergy, nor a mere recognition of distinguished service. The diaconate should be conferred on these persons, men or women, who are already devoted to the Church's ministry of service, one of the requirements being a certain stability in it. The establishment of such a diaconate would also lead naturally to the reality of a better developed concept of team-ministry. For this reason we look more closely at the office and ministry of priest.

Vatican II, as mentioned already in this chapter, placed great emphasis on the office and charism of the bishop on the one hand, and the charisms of the lay apostolate on the other. This latter is derived from the "common priesthood" of all. Since Vatican II, experience has shown that these directions resulted in a crisis of identity for many priests. However, as the implications of the conciliar teachings became clearer, the true role of the priest emerged as one of unifying spiritual leadership. This role expresses itself in the various priestly functions: prophetic, sacramental and pastoral. We need to look at these in more detail, in order to perceive the proper role of women within the priesthood.

The most significant change in the concept of the priest today is the fact that the priest is seen in terms of "mission to the world." This on-going task requires a challenging dialog and respectful cooperation with all other members of the community. This two-fold process expects a rather realistic problem assessment on the part of priests. The temptation to accept prestige and privilege, as well as the inclination of people to bestow benefits on them are diminished when professional competence is seen to be more important than symbolic roles. This is very important for the problem of the man-woman relationship in the Church.

The new emphasis upon service and cooperation has helped precipitate the wide-spread identity crisis of priests who have discovered that they are less qualified to serve the community than many competent laity. In this age of specialization, many priests find themselves in the position of non-professionals engaged in a variety of fields that can be better handled by non-clerical specialists, whether men or women. The recognition of this fact is leading to an atmosphere conducive to a re-thinking of the meaning of ministry. There is a growing realization that there exists in fact a diversity of ministries. Competent men and women are functioning already in a variety of these ministries, in positions of leadership and responsibility.

At this point of time there is a great need for diversification of the traditional form of priestly ministry, which in turn would imply on the part of some priests a certain specialization designed to meet precise pastoral needs of a local church. There are also certain difficult situations which call forth new forms of priestly life and ministry. This idea, particularly in the case of women who aspire to priesthood, was introduced in the first chapter of this book.

In these situations, the procedure will have to be experimental and by way of carefully proposed pilot projects. These challenges become apparent when we consider the total mission of the Church both to the rural and urban situation. Here is where the exceptional expertise of many women must be considered.

In the rural areas where the christian community is scattered over a wide territory, the Eucharist is celebrated only occasionally. The ministry of the few available priests then becomes seriously inadequate. In such a situation, new forms of priestly ministry and new styles of Eucharistic piety are required in order that spiritual leadership can reach outward to the farms and ranches, to the owners and share-croppers.

A new model for the ministry of men and women could be introduced gradually in the following way. First, lay ministries could be installed, chosen from among the leaders of the local community. At a second stage, suitable persons from among them could be ordained to the diaconate. As a final stage, deacons who have proved themselves as spiritual leaders in their respective communities, and are found suitable for this ministry, could be presented as candidates for ordination to priesthood, even though married or of the female sex. They would continue to exercise their secular profession on a part-time basis. Here we would see celibacy no longer as a requisite for priesthood, although the tradition and noble witness to celibate life, as we will point out later in this chapter, would continue for priests serving other ministries.

By way of contrast to rural areas, another type of situation is seen in the pluralistic society of our cities. In the urban areas there is a growing tendency for homogeneous groups, based on various professional and other factors, to seek community at the level of the group. Diversification in the exercise of the priestly ministry seems necessary to reach out to the pastoral needs of these groups. Priests will have to specialize in their ministries, for example, to workers, to students, and to professional people. Since the homogeneous groups cut across parish boundaries, the ministry of those specialized priests will extend across larger areas. The expertise for these works will also cut across sexual barriers. The present organizing of parishes marked by geographical boundaries will remain, but the exercise of the ministry in the city will become much more flexible. This will require that the entire pastoral clergy of the city share a common vision of their task and learn to operate as a team with an appropriate division of responsibilities.

Any discussion on new directions of priestly ministry calls for some reflection on the future role of celibacy. This has special relevance both for those who have accepted celibacy and for those who continue to envision it as only one of their options for the future. In terms of the future, I would plead for a disjunction of ministry and celibacy both with regard to the marriage of ministers and the admission of married people to ministry. In the light of recent experience, it would appear that this would be a more realistic policy for the future.

There is very little point in placing celibacy in opposition to marriage by posing the question "which of the two represents the greater or more noble aspect of Christian life?" By doing this, one would only postulate propositions that cannot be demonstrated. One cannot adopt this kind of generalization in the matter of celibacy. Nevertheless, experience testifies that celibacy can be lived in an adult and balanced manner by certain people because through the Spirit they have given it a precise meaning in their lives.

Some see celibacy as a means of being available for serving the world. Without any attachments, they are free to go wherever they are called. Others regard celibacy as a privation motivated by eschatology, *i.e.*, by the fact that we are living in the "no yet" — in the expectation of the return of the Lord. Again, others desire to remain celibate on account of a special relationship and consecration to the person of Christ. Some make the option because they desire to balance the tendency of giving an absolute character to marriage and sexuality. Others live out their celibacy as a means of directing themselves to the kingdom of God, to the values of another order. For these, celibacy is a way of making the contingent character of the world come into their lives. It is quite evident that these expressions of the meaning of celibacy, as well as the values that are being lived, can turn celibacy into a way of life that is rich and full of meaning for the apostolate.

There are also several possibilities regarding the specific form of celibacy itself. The first is the desire to observe this way of life in solitude. While some look for a strong, cohesive community in order to serve the world and kingdom of God, others seek more flexible communities where each one is open to the other in common prayer and reflection yet can develop individual, apostolic ministries. It is clearly important that celibate priests reflect profoundly on the variety of these forms with a view to finding new avenues. It is quite obvious that celibacy calls for a spiritual maturity, a free choice and the example of others who have lived it in an authentic manner. It is a charism that must be approached as a whole way of life, rather than a mere absence of marriage.

An objective observation on the past and present shows that the state of celibacy can be a most fruitful sign and a source of reflection for many who are called to ministry. Inasmuch as it also represents a special charism in the Church, celibacy can direct the faith of all toward God, the ultimate mystery that constitutes the profound sense of our being. It is our hope that present and future directions on priestly life and ministry will not be directed solely to the solution of problems, but to the needs that must accompany those who are trying to make their lives an authentic witness in view of the kingdom, and for those who are preparing themselves for such a choice.

The preceding paragraphs apply equally to men and women. They reflect on the common ministerial gifts spread among the Church. Some men and women exercise their charism principally through a close and

continuous involvement in secular affairs. They are called to lay ministries. Other men and women are more attached to the Church, yet not so
much in a sacramental way but as a way of manifesting the Church's
concern and service towards the poor and the deprived. These represent
the traditional office of deacon(ess). A more sacramental role is undertaken by the priest. We have seen the priest exercise these liturgical
functions, married or celibate. Each imparts its own quality to the
priesthood.

All of the gifts, which are consecrated by the Church in lay ministry,
diaconate or priesthood, as celibate or married person, can be possessed
by women. Women, therefore, ought to be tested like men for church
office, so that the apostolate will adequately meet all needs and reflect all
gifts. Because this book investigates the specific role of women in future
directions of priesthood, we turn now to examine their charism and call
to office.

During the early days of Christianity, women exercised various forms
of ministry and service. There were deaconesses, generally widows, who
carried out various liturgical, pastoral and diaconal tasks. During the
course of the centuries, many circumstances contributed toward bringing
a different state of affairs to prevail where ministry became a masculine
privilege. During the last few decades, however, there has been a
marked change in the conception of human sexuality and the role of
women on the basis of the behavorial sciences and experiences. Thomas
More Newbold explored a number of these issues in chapter ten. The
traditional pillars of culture — class and immutable social roles — are
beginning to crumble. Different professions and social functions are now
perceived differently as a result of the fact that they are being exercised
in an enriched manner by both men and women. It would be most ad-
vantageous for the Church to accept these social advances and thus appeal to the responsibility of women.

The present situation of women in the Church is an ambiguous one.
On the one hand, women exercise many important functions in the
Church, while on the other, they are denied all official ministries, ordained and non-ordained. The time has come to seriously face this situation and to recognize the validity of ministry for women in the Church.
The exigencies of the present time, both in the world at large and in
many local churches, demand such a recognition.

There is a growing awareness of the equality of women in all spheres.
The call experienced by many women to dedicate themselves to the
service of others in various ministries has had serious repercussions on
discussions regarding ministries in the Church. Women are full members
of the Church. Discrimination against them, exclusively on the basis of

sex, will deny to the Church the particular gifts and charisms of women. Aptitudes should be recognized by the Church, no matter who manifests them.

If a woman has the required qualities for ministry, she should be welcomed and accepted by the local community. Each local church should initiate a process of dialog and collaboration between men and women in ministry that will dissipate the fear of otherness, as well as inhibitions and resistance. Such a line of action will bring about an eventual awareness of constructive confidence. The presence of women in a variety of ministries will also lead to new dimensions of team-ministry and to a progressive change in the self-image of the priest. The Church, particularly in its theological institutions, should gradually prepare for the change when women will take their rightful share in the ministry of the Church.

The incorporation of women in the ministerial service of the Church suggests at times sacred ordination as opportune. Many in the Church are aware of the weaknesses of the traditional theological objections to the ordination of women, particularly from the doctrinal and biblical levels. Moreover, there are indeed many psychological and sociological factors that have clouded the theological issue, and these dimensions must be given consideration, particularly in virtue of sociological conditions of time and place. Consequently, because of the convergence of so many factors involved, this book has endeavored to clarify the fundamental nature of the problem of ordaining women to priesthood. In the meanwhile, the admission of women to all of the other ministries has the backing both of theology and tradition.

There is no serious reasons to exclude women from any creative ministries, and in particular from the diaconate. There are women who have a specific charism for service to the Church, but not within the celibate community. At the present time, there is no alternate form of a recognized ministry available for them. If the diaconate were open to these women, whether married or single, it would enable them to express this particular charism fully and authentically in a new witness and service to the local and universal Church.

Finally, from an ecumenical point of view, we are brought face to face with the fact that ministry is a service that has been obscured by the rigidity that governs the man-woman relation in ecclesial ministry. Many Christian Churches have already recognized this fact. The Roman Catholic Church can hardly continue to reject as absolutely impossible something that is already becoming possible within Christianity. In the future, the Church must continue the dialog with the experience and experiments of women in ministries in other ecclesial communities. This is a matter that can brook no further delay.

II

Theological schools are at the heart of any endeavor to foster and facilitate new directions for future ministries. We turn our attention to their role and purpose. These institutions must be willing to recognize the fact that formation to ministry is no longer to be designed along the lines of a strictly uniform pattern. Theological schools should evaluate their present goals in the light of contemporary ministerial needs, and consequently provide an openness to specialization that will allow a diversity of programs both on the academic and pastoral levels, as well as in the formation of pastoral life-style. In this way, women would have access to training and formation programs for personal and spiritual development, as men generally have at the present time.

There is a real necessity to integrate formation efforts in any future preparation for men and women to ministry. This vision animating such a formation is one fostered by a unified spiritual leadership — a ministry richly diversified and embodied in a variety of concrete tasks and service. What, we ask, are some of the contemporary challenges facing theological schools during the post-conciliar period as a result of new directions of ministry? I would like to propose some challenges for your consideration. It will be evident that women as well as men would qualify. Therefore, our discourse from this point onward will generally not allude specifically to men or women.

The ecclesiology of Vatican II provided a model of "the Church as mission" which is most integral to the question of theological formation to ministry. Vatican II viewed "Church" and "World" not as static categories. The Church exists in the world as the presence of God's meaning for humankind, and is grounded in the ministry of Christ's service for the life of the world. Jesus Christ came into the world as one who serves, to bring God's love and salvation to men and women and to reconcile one another into a new humanity, freed from every type of alienation. This ministry of Christ to all that is human is continued by the Church. The Church, therefore, is turned to the world, and all members share and express their ministry to the world in a variety of ways.

Within this ecclesiology, the Church has a new vision of its relationship to the world. *It is essentially mission in character*. The mission is to bring the healing power of God to bear on all aspects of human life and the problems facing contemporary humanity. In order to foster this vision, theological schools must recognize that their service, like the Church's, is essentially mission. *Theology*, even the most rigorous academic theology, is not simply preparation for ministry; *it is mission itself*. Therefore, to study theology is to engage in mission. This is why theological education hermetically sealed from the climate of modern technology and science, and the empirical outlook this has generated, could not possibly equip a man or woman for future ministry within the Church. Theological education does not simply provide a body of esoteric knowledge whereby the student is constituted a professional or an expert in order to hand out information at a lower level. The minister is not in relation to the people as doctors are in relation to their patients. For the most part, the laity are already on the mission in another form when the minister comes to them.

Men and women, preparing for ministry, must be made familiar with the climate of contemporary thinking and how committed Christians pursue the missionary task of the Church in their daily lives. Thus, while it is desirable that theological education take place in the context of the larger academic community, this must not be considered the sole context.

Pastoral field work, preferably in an urban situation, and under competent direction, should be incorporated into the very structure of theological education. This should take place before and during any intense theological training. It should be concerned specifically with the problems of modern life and how the Gospel can shed light on these issues. Above all, it should search out the theological and moral dimensions of social issues and problems. Thus, emphasizing that theological formation must not be isolated from modern thought and life, we are indicating also that the theological school is not the unique locus of theological education. Reflection on the relation of faith to experience is itself of the very structure of theological education.

In the preparation for ministry, a fundamental aim of the theological enterprise should be the inculcation of a true and profound sense of Christian identity. There is no such thing as purely academic truth in theology. Theology is a service of the Word of God, and as such, it is only a different modality from the proclamation of "The Word." There must always be a sustained attempt to penetrate into the meaning of the mystery revealed in Jesus Christ, which leads the student to grasp the workings of grace in his or her own life as well as within the world at large. Arising from this, the task of theology is to bring the great tradition of the Christian faith — biblical, historical and theological — to bear on the issues of the contemporary world. The study of theology is, therefore, a dialog between past and present, with a view to planning for the future.

In order to integrate this role of theology for men and women candidates to ministry, there is also a great desire and need for a new spirituality for the future. The old spiritualities are insufficient. The East has produced a spirituality that has tended to the extreme of spiritualism, which does not give serious consideration to the reality of the world, of work, of everyday life. Western culture has produced a materialistic ethos, which does not consider realistically the profound multileveled dimension of human existence. It cannot countenance transcendence. In practical terms this means the discovery of a way to find where God is in the loneliness of the modern city and in the expanse of rural existence. This task calls for sensitive and creative leaders, who look to the theological schools for information and formation.

In preparing for religious leadership, our theology of redemption and our theology of creation should sharpen our focus on personal qualities within men and women. Theology should hopefully touch and provoke a call to real spiritual leadership — a leadership to minister to people, to help them become aware of their gifts, and how they can serve the Kingdom.

Leadership is based on the fact that God has called us to do His work, and has given us whatever we need to respond effectively. He has invited us to join in His style of personhood, which is life-affirming and life-creating, active in this world and yet always reaching beyond it. The apostles became aware of their potential in being called by Christ. He made the Samaritan woman aware of who she was, aware of her poverty, but also of her potential. Jesus made her respond to Himself. To call one another to life in Christ Jesus — this is one of the most basic tasks of ministry. It means to help one another discover the real meaning of life so that each one may become the unique creature God created in a relation of love with all other creatures. It is a leadership that demonstrates the ministry of healing and compassion, and makes the forgiveness of the Father something visible and credible. At a point of time when so many people feel unaccepted and alienated from family, community and country, it becomes a ministry that gives special witness to the charism of unity, so conspicuous in the nature of the Roman Catholic Church and of its priesthood.

Leadership within this age of the Church has taught us a great deal about ecumenism — that all who call upon the name of the Lord constitute His presence in the world. It is of far greater significance than anything that divides us at the practical or theoretical levels. An ecumenical theology does not merely mean a deep knowledge of doctrinal differences. It develops a theology with emphasis on the principle that what unites the followers of Christ is greater than what divides them. The unity we have discovered to be present is not of our making — it has always been there. How this develops depends on all of us, but particularly on our religious leaders.

Ecumenical theology, moreover, must not be restricted to the Christian presence. It must include the wider religious dimensions represented by the great religions of the East. At a time when the presence of Christianity is more manifest on every continent, and is giving continued expression to our faith in relation to many non-Western traditions, theologians should emphasize the necessity of understanding the implications of world-pluralism in theology. Furthermore, since the fundamental issues which confront the world are global in scope and character, it is of the greatest importance that Christian Churches of diverse national, class and theological backgrounds find ways to listen and to learn from one another. In this way the future minister of the Church will be prepared theologically from a world perspective.

Conclusions

This book has scanned the entire Biblical-Christian history in order to discern how religous leadership emerges from the charisms of the spirit, scattered throughout the world in each distinct gift of life.

> God looked at everything he had made, and he found it very good. (Gen. 1:31)

> Yes, we know that all creation groans and is in agony even until now. Not only that, but we ourselves, although we have the Spirit as first fruits, groan inwardly while we await the redemption of our bodies. . . . And hoping for what we cannot see means awaiting it with patient endurance. (Rom 8:22-25)

In this final chapter our eyes look to the future. We peered across the horizon for signals of things to come; these appeared in the many, unrecognized and "unordained" manifestations of human talents. Many of these have already advanced to professional careers in the secular arena, and yet Church authorities seem to stand back — hesitant, fearful, at times friendly but awkward, at other times suspicious and hostile.

We hear again the pagan Jethro saying to the great Moses:

> You are not acting wisely. . . . You will surely wear yourself out, and not only yourself but also these people with you.

> The task is too heavy for you; you cannot do it alone. Now listen to me, and I will give you some advise, that God may be with you. (Ex. 18:17-19)

Church leaders are guided by Pope St. Peter I in their response. Many in the Church, who had known the Lord Jesus during his earthly life, objected to Pope Peter: "You entered the house of uncircumcised men and ate with them" (Acts 11:3). In fact, Peter did more than that. He had given "orders that . . . [without any further ado, the household of the gentile Cornelius] be baptized in the name of Jesus Christ" (Acts 10:48). Peter's ultimate justification for breaking rank and doing what even the Lord Jesus had never done lay in the surprising charisms of the Spirit:

> If God was giving them the same gift he gave us when we first believed
> in the Lord Jesus Christ, who was I to interfere with him. (Acts 11:17)

It took the early Church several, painful decades before the new mission
to the gentiles was fully endorsed. St. Paul addressed this question in his
major epistles to the Galatians and Romans. The Church explored tradition. It obeyed Jesus' injunction:

> Search the Scriptures
> in which you think you have eternal life —
> they also testify on my behalf.

In this book distinguished scholars have investigated Old and New Testament, the early Church Fathers, the ongoing tradition and its stabiliza-
tion in theology, Church law and liturgy. Conflict and symbolism
emerged as strong factors, especially in transitional moments like our
own; these aspects of Church life received special attention. Yet, all of
these elements were pitched in continual dialog with today, whether that
be through Jewish history, psychological studies or pastoral interviews.

This study, "like a dragnet thrown into the lake" of Biblical and
Church life, has "collected all sorts of things." We are consoled by
Jesus' words that such is "the reign of God." Such an abundant harvest
raises all sorts of problems. We have too much, even of good things; so
it seems anyway, as we vacillate what to do before the teeming charisms
of the Spirit which the dragnet collected. The speculative line turns into
personal tragedy, when it is made to read: we have too much, even of
good people, especially of the female sex, as we look to future directions
of priesthood.

Our problem was the early Church's trauma as well. What were they
to do about the gentiles, all those good people waiting to be summoned
to Christianity and to Church leadership.

> Then one night Paul had a vision. A man of Macedonia stood before
> him and invited him, "Come over to Macedonia and help us. (Acts
> 16:9)

Our response ought to be the same as Paul's:

> We *immediately* made efforts to get across to Macedonia, concluding
> that God had summoned. . . . (Acts 16:10)

Yet, the struggle continued in the early Church, and so Matthew made a
significant adaptation to Jesus' parable about the dragnet. While Jesus
concluded to the eschatological judgment, Matthew drew our attention
back to the age of the Church:

> Every scribe who is learned in the reign of God is like the head of a
> household who can bring forth from his storeroom *both the new and the
> old*. (Matt 13:52)

This book has dealt mostly with the old; the Church is always fearful, as it was even in apostolic times, to proceed in paths beyond those where the footprints — the norms — of Jesus were visibly present. While investigating the old, we spotted continual signals of the new. The Old was not seen as specific details restricting the movement of the Church but as models for the Church's recognition of the Spirit now. Because of the old, the Church was continually bringing forth the new.

The Jew is always seen in visionary form. We, too, like Paul of Tarsus, "had a vision." In the final chapter we attempted to journey into the future directions of the priesthood. This path led us through the way of God's creation where the Spirit is groaning for recognition. We proceeded from charismatic gifts to official Church recognition, from lay leadership to the ordained form of deacon and priest, from the charisms of celibacy and marriage, to their presence in men and women. We delayed over women and their future role in ministry and priesthood.

From the mind and hopes of women we can view the purpose and work of theological schools. Such a vision places expectations upon them. Theology becomes mission, not only to bring the Church's healing to all aspects of life but to recognize the Spirit's presence in the Macedonian as well as in the "household of Cornelius." A Christian identity is imparted to the transcended gifts of the Spirit and a new, rich, vibrant unity is achieved not only across the Church but throughout the world.

It must be unity in Christ Jesus. "Baptized into Christ," wrote St. Paul, "all of you . . . have clothed yourselves with him. There does not exist among you Jew or Greek, slave or free person, male or female. All are one in Christ Jesus . . . [and] descendants of Abraham" (Gal 3:27-29)

As charisms unite in Jesus, they emerge in all the areas of leadership where Jesus speaks, forgives, rules, consecrates and calls home. The groanings of the Spirit of Jesus call us to dialog about the future directions of priesthood. Among the old and the new are the gifts of life, male and female, created together by God in the divine image. *"God found it very good"* (Gen 1:31).

Part Six

BIBLIOGRAPHY

13

PUBLICATIONS: 1975–1977

by

Hyang Sook Chung Yoon

The following bibliography furnishes the reader with the sources of important, currently available material, pertinent to the topic of ordination of women predominantly from Roman Catholic perspective in the United States.

Since several comprehensive bibliographies, listed below and extending through 1975, are readily obtainable, we focus on publications from January 1976 till November 1977 and on significant titles omitted in the 1975 bibliographies. This bibliography can be used most effectively in conjunction with Anne Marie Gardiner's selected bibliography (1965–1975) in her work, *Women and Catholic Priesthood: An Expanded Vision.*

I. BIBLIOGRAPHIES

BARNHOUSE, RUTH TIFFANY. MICHAEL FAHEY, S.J., BRIDGET ORAM, AND BAILEY WALKER, O.P. "The Ordination of Women to the Priesthood: An Annotated Bibliography," *Anglican Theological Review* (Supplementary Series), No. 6 (June, 1976) 81–106.

GANGHOFER, ODILE. *The Woman in the Church/ La Femme dans L'Eglise.* Strasbourg, France: Cerdic-Publications, 1975.

GARDINER, ANNE MARIE, S.S.N.D., ed. "A Selected Bibliography (1965–1975)" *Women and Catholic Priesthood, An Expanded Vision: Proceedings of the Detroit Ordination Conference.* (New York: Paulist Press, 1976) 199–208.

KENDALL, PATRICIA A. *Women and the Priesthood: A Selected and Annotated Bibliography.* Episcopal Diocese of Pennsylvania, 1976.

MORGAN, JOHN H. AND TERI WALL, ed. *The Ordination of Women: A Comprehensive Bibliography (1960–1976).* Wichita: Institute on Ministry and the Elderly, 1977.

II. BOOKS

AUBERT, JEAN-MARIE. *La Femme: Antiféminisme et Christianisme.* Paris: Cerf/ Desclee, 1975.

BROWN, RAYMOND E., S.S. *Biblical Reflections on Crises Facing the Church*. (New York: Paulist Press, 1975) 45–62.

BURGHARDT, WALTER, S.J., ed. *Women: New Dimensions*. New York: Paulist Press, 1976; reprint from *Theol. Studies* 36 (# 4; 1975).

CORIDEN, JAMES, ed., *Sexism and Church Law*. New York: Paulist Press, 1977.

GRYSON, ROGER. *The Ministry of Women in the Early Church*. Collegeville, Minn.: Liturgical Press, 1976; *Le ministère des femmes dans l'église ancienne*. Gembloux: Editions J. Duculot, 1972.

HEYWARD, CARTER. *A Priest Forever*. New York: Harper and Row, 1976.

JEWETT, PAUL K. *Man as Male and Female*. Grand Rapids: William B. Eerdmans' Publishing Co., 1975.

KRESS, ROBERT. *Whither Womankind? The Humanity of Women*. St. Meinrad, Inc.: Abbey Press, 1975.

LAKELAND, PAUL. *Can Women Be Priests?* Theology Today Series, No. 34. Hales Corners, Wi.: Clergy Book Service, 1975.

MICKS, MARIANNE, AND CHARLES P. PRICE, eds. *Toward a New Theology of Ordination: Essays on the Ordination of Women*. Somerville, Mass.: Greeno, Hadden & Co., 1976.

PROCTOR, PRISCILLA. *Women in the Pulpit: Is God an Equal Opportunity Employer?* New York: Doubleday, 1976.

RAMING, IDA. *The Exclusion of Women from the Priesthood: Divine Law or Sex Discrimination?* translated by Norman H. Adams from German (*Der Ausschluss der Frau vom priesterlichen Amt: Gottgewollte Tradition oder Diskriminierung?* Cologne: Bohlau Verlag, 1973.) Metuchen, N.J.: Scarecrow Press, 1976.

SCHAUPP, JOAN. *Woman, Image of the Holy Spirit*. Denville, N.J.: Dimension Books, 1975.

SWIDLER, LEONARD. *Women in Judaism: the Status of Women in Informative Judaism*. Metuchen, N.J.: Scarecrow, 1976.

SWIDLER, LEONARD AND ARLENE SWIDLER, eds. *Women Priests: A Catholic Commentary on the Vatican Declaration*. New York: Paulist Press, 1977.

TERWILLIGER, ROBERT E., AND URBAN T. HOLMES, III, eds. *To Be a Priest: Perspectives on Vocation and Ordination*. New York: Seabury Press, 1975.

WILSON, CANON HAROLD, ed. *Women Priests? Yes, Now!* Nutfield: Denholm House Press, 1975.

III. ARTICLES

BARRIOS, GEORGE A. "Women and the Priestly Office According to the Scriptures," *St. Vladimir's Theological Quarterly* 19 (1975) 174–192.

BEESON, TREVOR. "Should Canterbury Wait for Rome?" *Christian Century* 93 (September 1976) 735–737.

BOURGOIN, M. "Women Priests Celebrate Anniversary," *National Catholic Reporter* 11 (August 15, 1975) 3.

BOYS, M., SR., MUSCHAL-REINHARDT, R., PHILBIN, M., DALY, K., SR. "I Want to Be a Priest," Interviews by Saint Anthony Messenger. *Saint Anthony Messenger* 83 (March 1976) 12–17.

BRENNAN, L. "Ordination of Women: the Cultural Context," *Review for Religious* 35 (July 1976) 580–588.

BRENNAN, M., SR. "Why We Need Women priests; Interview by Sr. P. Knopp," *U.S. Catholic* 41 (February 1976) 18–23.

BRESLIN, JOHN B. "Theology and Womankind," *America* 134 (January 17, 1976) 34–35.

BROWN, RAYMOND E. "Roles of Women in the Fourth Gospel," *Theological Studies* 36 (Winter 1975) 688–699.

BURRELL, D. "The Vatican Declaration: Another View on the Admission of Women to the Ministerial Priesthood," *America* 136 (April 2, 1977) 289–292.

CERLING, CHARLES E. "Women Ministers in the New Testament Church," *Journal of the Evangelical Theological Society* 19 (Summer 1976) 209–215.

CLARK, STEPHEN B. "Social Order and Women's Ordination," *America* 134 (January 17, 1976) 32–33.

CUNNINGHAM, A., SR. "Woman's Call to Ministry," *Sign* 54 (July-August 1975) 19–22.

DEZUTTER, A. "One Thousand-One Hundred Women Signpost Road to Ordination; Conference to Promote Ordination of Women as Priests in the Roman Catholic Church," *National Catholic Reporter* 12 (December 12, 1975) 1–2.

DONAHUE, J. "Women, Priesthood and the Vatican," *America* 136 (April 2, 1977) 285–289.

DONNELLY, D. "The Advancement of Women . . . a Call of the Spirit; comment on the Vatican Study Commission Report on Women in Society and in the Church," *Catholic Charismatic* 1 (March-April 1976), 12–15.

———. "Women Priests — Does Philadelphia Have a Message for Rome?" *Commonweal* 102 (June 20, 1975) 206–210. Discussion 102 (August 1975) 323.

EDWARDS, O. C., JR. "The Failure of the Anti-Nicene Church to Ordain Women and Its Significance Today," *The Nashotah Review* 15 (Fall 1975) 325–351. Reprinted in *The Saint Luke's Journal of Theology* 18 (September 1975) 187–213.

FISHER, L. "The Angry Ladies," *Priest* 22 (January 1966) 44–48.

GOETZ, J. W. "Women Priests for a Pilgrim Church; views of Archbishop J. L. Bernardin," *America* 133 (November 1975) 380–381.

HAUGHEY, JOHN C., ET AL. "Impressions from Detroit," *America* 134 (January 17, 1976) 26–31.

HEBBLETHWAITE, P. "Women Priests?" *Tablet* 229 (July 12, 1975) 6456.

HOPKO, THOMAS. "On the Male Character of Christian Priesthood," *St. Vladimir's Theological Quarterly* 19 (1975) 147–173.

HUGHES, P. "Minneapolis and Ministry: a Personal Response," *America* 135 (December 4, 1976) 394–396.

HÜNERMANN, PETER. "Conclusions Regarding the Female Diaconate," *Theological Studies* 36 (June 1975) 325–333.

HUNT, B. "Have Women a Right to Ordination?" *Review for Religious* 35 (May 1976) 409–412.

———. "The Bible and the Status of Women: Equality-Subordination-Leadership," *The Nashotah Review* 15 (Fall 1975) 302–324. Reprinted in *The Saint Luke's Journal of Theology* 18 (Sept 1975) 164–186.

HURLEY, K. "Women Priests: The State of the Question," *Saint Anthony Messenger* 33 (March 1976) 18–22.

JESUIT SCHOOL OF THEOLOGY IN BERKELEY, CALIFORNIA, FACULTY OF. "Letter to the Apostolic Delegate," *Origins* 6 (April 7, 1977) 661–665. Reply by Abp. J. Jadot in the same issue on page 665.

KARRIS, ROBERT J. "St. Paul and Women," *Catholic Charismatic* 1 (Feb-March, 1977) 31–32.

———. "Women in the Pauline Assembly, To Prophesy, but not to Speak?" *Women Priests: A Catholic Commentary on the Vatican Declaration*, ed. by Leonard Swidler and Arlene Swidler (New York: Paulist Press, 1977) 205–208.

KILMARTIN, EDWARD J., S.J. "Apostolic Office: Sacrament of Christ," *Theological Studies* 36 (June 1975) 1243–1264.

KING, JOHN A. "Ordination of Women to the Priesthood: Some Current Roman Catholic Attitudes," *Theology* 78 (March 1975) 142–147.

KÜNG, HANS AND LOHFINK, GERHARD, "Keine Ordination der Frau?" *Theologische Quartalschrift* 157 (Spring 1977) 144–146.

LAKELAND, P. "The Ministerial Priesthood," *Way* 16 (Jan. 1976) 39–47.

LANGLEY, RALPH H. "Role of Women in the Church," *Southwestern Journal of Theology* 19 (Spring 1977) 60–72.

LEGRAND, HARVÉ-MARIE, "Views on the Ordination of Women," *Origins* 6 (January 6, 1977) 459–468.

LONGSTAFF, THOMAS R. W. "Ordination of Woman: A Biblical Perspective," *Anglican Theological Review* 57 (July 1975) 316–327.

LUNEN-CHENU, MARIE-THÉRÈSE VAN, "La Commission pontificale de la Femme," *Etudes* 344 (June 1976) 879–891.

LYLES, J. C. "Episcopalians: Wounded Healers," *Christian Century* 93 (September 1976) 803–804.

LYNCH, J. "The Ordination of Women: Protestant Experience in Ecumenical Perspective," *Journal of Ecumenical Studies* 12 (Spring 1975) 173–197.

MCLAUGHLIN, ELEANOR L. "Christ My Mother: Feminine Naming and Metaphor in Medieval Spirituality," *The Nashotah Review* 15 (Fall 1975) 366–386.

———. "The Christian Past: Does It Hold a Future for Women?" *Anglican Theological Review* 57 (January 1975) 36–56.

MEYER, ERIC C. "Are There Theological Reasons Why the Church Should Not Ordain Women Priests?" *Review for Religious* 34 (November 1975) 957–967.

MURPHY-O'CONNOR, JEROME. "The Non-Pauline Character of 1 Corinthians 11: 2–16?" *Journal of Biblical Literature* 95 (December 1976) 615–621.

MUTHIG, J. "Biblical Commission Says Scripture Doesn't Settle Ordination of Women," *Our Sunday Visitor* 65 (June 27, 1976) 3.

———. "Vatican Official Says Papal Study Will Not Change the Fact Women Can't Be Priests," *Our Sunday Visitor* 64 (December 7, 1975) 1.

NORRIS, R. "On the Maleness of Christ," condensed from *The Anglican Theological Review* 6 (June 1976), in *Theology Digest* 25 (Spring 1977) 11–14.

NOVAK, M. "Dual-Sex Eucharist," *Commonweal* 103 (July 8, 1977) 813–816.

———. "On the Ordination of Women," *Commonweal* 104 (July 8, 1977) 425–427.

OSIEK, CAROLYN. "The Church Fathers and the Ministry of Women," *Women Priests: A Catholic Commentary on the Vatican Declaration*, edited by Leonard Swidler and Arlene Swidler (New York: Paulist Press, 1977) 75–80.

PAGE, ROBERT J. "Chicago and Philadelphia: Moral and Theological Reflections," *The Nashotah Review* 15, no. 3 (Fall 1975), 437–447. Reprinted in *The Saint Luke's Journal of Theology* 18 (September 1975) 299–309.

PAWLIKOWSKI, JOHN. "Let's Ordain Women," *U.S. Catholic* 40 (May 1975) 12–13.

PLOWMAN, E. E. "Episcopal Church: Women Are Winners," *Christianity Today* 21 (October 1976) 48–52.

RAHNER, KARL. "Rahner: Women Priests," *National Catholic Reporter* 13 (October 7, 1977) 7, 14; trans. and abbrev. from "Priestertum der Frau?" *Stimmen der Zeit* 195 (May 1977) 291–301.

RAJA, R. J. "Pauline Women: A Probe into Women's Ministry," *Ministries in the Church in India*, ed. by D. S. Amalorpavadass (New Delhi 110001, India: C.B.C.I. Centre, Ashok Place, 1977) 213–220.

SHEETS, J. "The Ordination of Women," *Communio* 3 (Spring 1976) 3–15.

————. "Ordination of Women: the Issues," *American Ecclesiastical Review* 169 (January 1975) 17–36.

SLUSSER, M. "Fathers and Priestesses: Footnotes to the Roman Declaration," *Worship* 51 (September 1977) 434–445.

STEVENSON, W. TAYLOR. "A Case for the Ordination of Women," *The Nashotah Review* 15, No. 3 (Fall 1975), 448–457. Reprinted in *The Saint Luke's Journal of Theology* 18 (September 1975) 310–319.

STUHLMUELLER, CARROLL. "Women Priests: A Biblical Response Within Roman Catholicism," *Catholic Charismatic* 1 (February-March 1977) 12–15.

————. "Internal Indecisiveness," "Bridegroom: A Biblical Symbol of Union, not Separation," and "Leadership: Secular Gift Transformed by Revelation," *Women Priests: A Catholic Commentary on the Vatican Declaration*, edited by Leonard Swidler and Arlene Swidler (New York: Paulist Press, 1977) 23–24, 278–283, 307–309.

SWIDLER, ARLENE. "Catholics and the E.R.A.," *Commonweal* 103 (September 1976) 585–589.

SWIDLER, LEONARD. "Catholics Can't Ordain Women?" *National Catholic Reporter* 12 (September 1976) 16–17.

TERRIEN, SAMUEL. "Toward a Biblical Theology of Womanhood," *Religion in Life* 42 (Autumn 1973) 322–333. Reprinted in Barnhouse, Ruth Tiffany, and Holmes, Urban T., III, eds., *Male and Female: Christian Approaches to Sexuality*. New York: Seabury Press, 1976.

URBAN, LINWOOD. "A Dialogue Concerning the Ordination of Women," *The Nashotah Review* 15 (Fall 1975) 391–404. Reprinted in *The Saint Luke's Journal of Theology* 18 (September 1975) 253–266.

WALKER, WILLIAM O., JR. "1 Corinthians 11:2-16 and Paul's Views Regarding Women," *Journal of Biblical Literature* 94 (1975) 94–110.

WIJNGAARDS, J. N. M., "The Ministry of Women and Social Myth," *Ministries in the Church in India*, ed. by D. S. Amalorpavadass (New Delhi 110001, India: C.B.C.I. Centre, Ashok Place, 1977) 213–220.

WILLIS, E. "Women Priests: A Risk Too Dangerous to Take?" *Theology* 78 (July 1975) 370–376.

WINIARSKI, M. "Sister Says Ordination of Women Necessary," *National Catholic Reporter* 11 (October 3, 1975) 16.

WINSLOW, DONALD F. "Priesthood and Sexuality in the Post-Nicene Fathers," *The Nashotah Review* 15 (Fall 1975) 352–365. Reprinted in *The Saint Luke's Journal of Theology* 18 (September 1975) 214–217.

"Women in the Church: Symposium," including "Women, Ordination and Tradition," by F. Cardman. "Some Practical Observations," by L. Spear. "Dual-Sex Eucharist," by M. Novak. *Commonweal* 103 (December 17, 1976) 807–816.

"Women's Rights in the Church: Symposium," including "Men Best Symbolize Christ," by D. Burrell. "Vatican Makes Relative Symbols Absolute," by Sr. M. Farley. "Women, Just Be Saints," by C. McCarthy. "Why Are Women Sons of God," by A. Swidler. "Clericalism Hurts Men too," by Bro. H. McCabe. "Jesus had Feminine Qualities, too," by L. Swidler. *National Catholic Reporter* 13 (April 1, 1977) 9–16.

IV. STUDY REPORTS

HELMSING, CHARLES H., AND ARTHUR A. VOGEL. *Pro and Con on Ordination of Women: Report and Papers from the Anglican-Roman Catholic Consultation*. New York: Seabury Professional Services, 1976.

Society for Promoting Christian Knowledge. *A Critique of Eucharistic Agreement*. London, 1975.

———. *Modern Ecumenical Documents on the Ministry*. London, 1975.

"The Ministry," in *One Baptism, One Eucharist and a Mutually Recognized Ministry: Three Agreed Statements*. Department of Faith and Order (Paper No. 73) Geneva, 1975.

Sexisim in the 1970's. Discrimination Against Women: a Report of a World Council of Churches Consultation, West Berlin, 1974. Geneva, 1975.

POTTER, PHILIP A., ed. *The Ecumenical Review* 27, No. 4 (October 1975).

V. DOCUMENTATION

Anglican-Roman Catholic Consultation, "Statement on the Ordination of Women," *Origins* 5 (November 20, 1975) 349–352.

BERNARDIN, J., ABP. "The Ordination of Women: A Statement by the President of the National Conference of Catholic Bishops." *Commonweal* 103 (January 16, 1976) 42–44. Replies by B. Cooke, D. Donnelly, J. Ford, G. Tavard in the same issue on pages 44–47.

Pastoral Commission of the Sacred Congregation for the Evangelization of Peoples, "The Role of Women in Evangelization," *Origins* 5 (April 22, 1976) 702–707.

PAUL VI, POPE. Letters between Pope Paul VI (Nov. 30, 1975, March 23, 1976) and Frederick Donald Coggan, Archbishop of Canterbury (July 9, 1975, February 10, 1976) concerning the ordination of women. *L'Osservatore Romano* (English) No. 36 (440) (September 2, 1976) 3.

Pontifical Biblical Commission Report. "Can Women Be Priests?" *Origins* 6 (July 1, 1976) 92–96.

Sacred Congregation for the Doctrine of the Faith, *Declaration on the Question of the Admission of Women to the Ministerial Priesthood*, with a Commentary. Washington, D.C.: United States Catholic Conference, 1977. Also available in *L'Osservatore Romano* (English) No. 5 (462) (February 3, 1977) 6–12 and *The Pope Speaks* 22, No. 2 (1977) 108–122. The official Latin document was published under the title, "Declaratio circa quaestionem admissionis mulierum ad sacerdotium ministeriale," *Acta Apostolicae Sedis* LXIX (28 Februarii 1977) 98–116. This document was actually "approved confirmed and ordered to be published" by Pope Paul VI on October 15, 1976 and was issued (in Latin, "datum") that same day from the Sacred Congregation of Doctrine. It was not released to the public until late January 1977.

ABBREVIATIONS

A.A.S.	*Acta Apostolicae Sedis*
Amer. Eccl. Rev.	*American Ecclesiastical Review*
ANF	*Ante-Nicene Fathers*
C.B.Q.	*Catholic Biblical Quarterly*
Commentary	Commenatry on the Declaration of the Sacred Congregation for the Doctrine of the Faith on the Question of Admission of Women to the Ministerial Priesthood. Published with the *Declaration* by the United States Catholic Conference, Washington, D.C., 1977.
Declaration	Declaration on the Question of the Admission of Women to the Ministerial Priesthood, from the Sacred Congregation for the Doctrine of the Faith, 1977. Printed in the appendix to this book and cited according to numbered paragraphs.
DTC	*Dictionnaire de Theologie Catholique* 16 vols. Paris: 1903–65.
Flannery	*Vatican Council II The Conciliar and Post Conciliar Documents*. Austin Flannery, O.P., General Editor. Collegeville: Liturgical Press, 1975.
JBL	*Journal of Biblical Literature*
NT	New Testament
OT	Old Testament
Theol. Studies	*Theological Studies*

NOTES

Notes to
Chapter One, pages 5–21

[1] *Commentary*, p. 21, "It was difficult to leave unanswered any longer a precise question that is being posed nearly everywhere and which is polarizing attention to the detriment of more urgent endeavors that should be fostered."

[2] *Commentary*, p. 20.

[3] It is interesting to note that the English translation of the *Declaration*, plus *Commentary*, was released before the Latin text was circulated in the *Acta Apostolicae Sedis* LXIX (28 Feb 1977) 98–116. The latter, official publication did not include the *Commentary*. This fact seems to admit that English-speaking countries, particularly the United States, constitute the eye of the hurricane.

[4] *Cf., O'Osservatore Romano*, English edition, January 20, 1977; February 3, 10, 17, 24, 1977; March 3, & 17, 1977; May 12, 1977.

[5] The Latin phrase makes this part of the case all the more crucial; it states: "Quae Christus et Apostoli fecerunt, norma sunt perpetua."

[6] It is strange that the *Declaration* treated "Tradition" before the "Bible." Because the reasoning from tradition is plagued by serious difficulties ("the undeniable influence of prejudice unfavourable to women" in the writings of the Fathers), the Sacred Congregation may have decided to introduce it first and then to proceed with its stronger reasons.

[7] In Latin: "non agnoscere admittendi"

[8] In Latin: "aestimat oportere, pro praesentibus adiunctis"

[9] In Latin: "Numquam sensit"

[10] In Latin: "magisterium numquam necesse habuerit"

[11] In Latin: "Haec vero omnia — id fatendum est — non quidem talem evidentiam affereunt, ut cuique proxime perspicua sint"

[12] In Latin: "ut norma *habitus est*"

[13] In Latin: "quia *putatur* conformis esse"

[14] In Latin: "Tunc vero non intenditur, ut argumentum demonstrativum afferatur . . ."

[15] This indecisive style of the *Declaration* becomes all the more evident if it is compared with that normally employed by papal documents. See fn. 18 below for a quotation from Pope St. Pius X.

[16] "cum nequaquam appareat quomodo huiusmodi sententia componi queat cum iis quae fontes revelatae veritatis et acta Magisterii Ecclesiae proponunt . . ." *Enchiridion Biblicum*, ed 3 (Romae: 1956) n. 617.

[17] John J. O'Rourke, "Some Considerations About Polygenism," *Theological Studies* 26 (1965) 411–2, ". . . these words of Pius XII are not to be understood as declaring absolutely that polygenism is irreconcilable with the Catholic doctrine of original sin. . . . The Holy Father apparently wanted theologians to examine the teaching of revelation and the magisterium." A similar interpretation of the Encyclical is given by Karl Rahner, *Theological Investigations* Vol I (Baltimore: 1961) 236–7; Peter de Rosa, *Christ and Original Sin* (Milwaukee: 1967) 112–3.

[18] Although the Biblical Commission was established by Pope Leo XIII, October 30, 1902, according to his apostolic letter, *Vigilantiae* (*Rome and the Study of Scripture*. p. 30–35; Latin text, *Enchiridion Biblicum*, n. 137–148), its authority was strengthened by Pius X, Nov 18, 1907, in his *Motu Proprio*, entitled *Praestantia Sacrae Scripturae* (*Rome and the Study of Scripture*, p. 40–42; *Enchiridion Biblicum*, n. 283–288), in which he wrote: ". . . all are bound in conscience to submit to the decisions of the Biblical Commission, which have been given in the past and which shall be given in the future, in the same way as to the Decrees which appertain to doctrine, issued by the Sacred Congregations and approved by the Sovereign Pontiff; nor can they escape the stigma both of disobedience and temerity nor be free from grave guilt as often as they impugn these decisions either in word or in writing; and this, over and above the scandal which they give and the

sins of which they may be the cause before God by making other statements on these matters which are very frequently both rash and false."

[19] The English translation of these decrees is found in *Rome and the Study of Scripture*, 6 ed (St. Meinrad, Ind.: Grail, 1958) 116–7. For the Latin text, see *Enchiridion Biblicum*, ed 3 (Romae: 1956) n. 181–184.

[20] Not only did Pius XII release the encyclical *Divino Afflante Spiritu* (Sept 30, 1943), but during his reign both the secretary and the sub-secretary of the Biblical Commission commented upon the earlier decrees and their continued force in Catholic exegesis. They state that the decrees will tend to remain valid, in so far as they propose matters connected directly or indirectly with the truths of faith; in so far as they take up, for instance, literary or historical details, then the interpreter has full liberty to follow scientific investigation. *Cf.*, E. F. Siegman, "The Decrees of the Pontifical Biblical commission: A Recent Clarification," *Catholic Biblical Quarterly* 18 (Jan 1956) 23–29; see also J. Dupont, "A propos du nouvel Enchiridion Biblicum," *Revue Biblique* 62 (1955) 414–419.

[21] One of the most advanced documents on biblical studies, issued officially by any Christian denomination, is that by Pope Paul VI, "Instruction Concerning the Historical Truth of the Gospels," *Acta Apostolicae Sedis* 56 (1964) 712–718; English translation in *The Bible Today* n 13 (Oct 1964) 821–828; text and commentary by Joseph A. Fitzmyer, "The Biblical Commission's Instruction on the Historical Truth of the Gospels," *Theological Studies* 25 (Sept 1964) 386–408.

[22] Bishop Joseph L. Hogan of Rochester, N.Y., writing in the diocesan newspaper, *Courier-Journal* (Feb 9, 1977), "noted that ordinary, non-infallible teachings of the Church have been revised by Rome in the past in light of later discussions and study. One has only to recall how the Vatican II document on Divine Revelation reversed the earlier positions opposing a critical approach to the New Testament, the way the decree on Ecumenism changed the hostility towards Protestant churches enshrined in Pius XI's *Mortalium Animos*, and the radical shift from previous denunciations of modern civilization to a modified optimism

evident in the pastoral Constitution on the Church in the Modern World. The ensuing dialogue on Roman documents has been very important."

[23] The wider question, involving the reconciliation and mutual contribution of Bible/Church and world/secular culture, is explored more fully by Carroll Stuhlmueller, *Thirsting for the Lord* (Staten, N.Y.: Alba House, 1977) Part V, "The Challenge."

[24] The report of the Pontifical Biblical commission, published in an appendix to this volume, carefully traces the development of religious leadership and eucharistic ministry in the New Testament and thereby shows that our contemporary forms of priesthood are rooted in the Bible but cannot be read back into the New Testament meaning and function of the "twelve," disciple, apostle, prophet, presbyter, etc.

[25] In my judgment it is not coincidental that the removal of the Blessed Sacrament from the main altar in the post-Vatican II period corresponds with a deterioration of unity within the Catholic church. It is beyond the scope of this book to investigate the relationship of these two phenomena.

[26] The intricacies of the Greek middle voice, in the case of the verb *poieō*, as explained by Max Zerwick, S.J., *Biblical Greek*, English edition adapted from the fourth Latin edition by Joseph Smith, S.J. (Rome: Biblical Institute Press, 1963) n. 172. Zerwick maintains, in many New Testament passages, the classical usage whereby "the middle voice . . . has for object a noun denoting action, with which it forms a periphrasis equivalent to a simple verb."

[27] The *Declaration*, section 6, par. 38, states: ". . . the priesthood does not form part of the rights of the individual, but stems from the economy of the mystery of Christ and the Church. The priestly office cannot become the goal of social advancement; no merely human progress of society or of the individual can of itself give access to it; it is of another order." Advocates of women ordination respond that no one has an absolute right to priesthood but that women as well as men have a right to be tested for priesthood. In chapter two, section I, of this book Carroll Stuhlmueller discusses in detail the relation of sacred offices with secular offices and their de-

pendence upon the latter in their origin and development.

[28] Robert J. Karris refers to these three stages of gospel composition in chapter three, section II and fn 12. See also fn 20 in this chapter.

[29] The relation of women ordination to the Old Testament prophetic championing of the poor is developed in this book, chapter two, section I.

Notes to
Chapter Two, pages 25–45

[1] D. L. Baker, *Two Testaments: One Bible* (Downers Grove, Il: InterVarsity Press, 1976, is valuable for its full bibliography on the Christian interpretation of the Old Testament; its explanations, however, are inadequate. For a critical investigation, see Robert B. Laurin, *Contemporary Old Testament Theologians* (Valley Forge: Judson Press, 1970). For a good practical example, see Elizabeth Achtemeier, *The Old Testament and the Proclamation of the Gospel* (Philadelphia: Westminster, 1973) and Lucien Deiss, *God's Word and God's People* (Collegeville, MN: Liturgical Press, 1976).

[2] The *Declaration* of the Sacred Congregation for the Doctrine of the Faith totally ignores the Old Testament except for occasional references. These do not occur in sections 2 and 3, where the Bible is investigated explicitly.

[3] *Cf.*, 2 Tim 3:15-16, "Likewise, from your infancy you have known the sacred Scripture [the Old Testament, for Paul is referring to Timothy's years as a Jew], the source of the wisdom which through faith in Jesus Christ leads to salvation. All Scripture is inspired of God and is useful for teaching — for reproof, correction, and training in holiness so that the man of God may be fully competent and equipped for every good work." Also Jesus' words in Matt 5:17-18, "Do not think that I have come to abolish the law and the prophets. I have come, not to abolish them, but to fulfill them. . . . Until heaven and earth pass away, not the smallest part of a letter,

shall be done away with until it all comes true."

[4] Elements of Old Testament priesthood transferred to Christian priesthood were: celibacy (in that the Jewish priest had to be continent while functioning at the altar); perpetual (the Jewish priest was born into the priestly tribe or family and so retained the priestly office perpetually like his birthright); separate caste (again by reason of birth in Old Testament times, and in postexilic times by reason of the theocratic state at Jerusalem); little or no property (for Old Testament references see fn 52).

[5] *Cf.*, ch. 8, section 1; also Clarence J. Vox, *Woman in Old Testament Worship* (Delft: Judels and Brinkman, 1968); J. Edgar Bruns, *God as Woman, Woman as God* (New York: Paulist, 1973); J. de Fraine, *Women of the Old Testament* (De-Pere, Wisc: St. Norbert Abbey Press, 1968); A. Feuillet, "La dignité et le role de la femme d'aprés quelques textes pauliniens: comparison avec l'Ancien Testament," *New Testament Studies* 21 (1974/75) 157–91.

[6] The difficulties of transposing biblical sentences and ideas to our twentieth century world are eloquently described by D. Nineham, *The Use and Abuse of the Bible* (New York: Barnes & Noble, 1977) ch 1 "Introduction: Cultural Change and Cultural Relativism." Unfortunately, Nineham fails to answer his serious problem, principally because he overlooks the ongoing presence of Israel and Church where biblical traditions are continuously reinterpreted and where liturgical worship grants an important role of symbolism. The Report of the Biblical Commission on the ordination of women admits in its introductory section: "The question asked (Can Women be Priests?) touches on the priesthood, the celebrant of the eucharist and the leader of the local community. This is a way of looking at things which is somewhat foreign to the Bible."

[7] The Report of the Biblical Commission plainly states its own difficulty: "Yet one question must still always be asked: What is the normative value which should be accorded to the practice of the Christian communities of the first centuries?"

[8] Writers like Hans Küng leave the impression that the ideal form of Church order is that of 1–2 Corinthians since it's closer to

Jesus' lifetime, while the church administration according to the pastoral epistles represents a later less perfect form. The earliest forms are not necessarily purer and closer to the will of Jesus but represent one model among others from which the church of any age can draw upon for its own effective pastoral ministry.

⁹ *Cf.*, Vatican II, *Dei Verbum* (Apostolic Constitution on Divine Revelation), ch 2, no 8, "This tradition (expressed in a special way in the inspired books) which comes from the apostles develops in the Church with the help of the Holy Spirit. For there is a growth in the understanding of the realities and the words which have been handed down. This happens through the contemplation and study made by believers, who treasure these things in their hearts (cf. Lk. 2:19, 51), through the intimate understanding of spiritual things they experience, and through the preaching of those who have received through episcopal succession the sure gift of truth. For as the centuries succeed one another, the Church constantly moves forward toward the fullness of divine truth until the words of God reach their complete fulfillment in her."

¹⁰ The date 1943 marks the issuance of Pius XII's encyclical magna carta on biblical studies, *Divino Afflante Spiritu*. It should be pointed out that the three most important documents on the Bible come from Pius XII and from Paul VI. Under the latter's pontificate, Vatican II's Constitution on Divine Revelation was released. Earlier, on April 21, 1964, in the first year after his election, he approved an *Instruction on the Historical Truth of the Gospels*, certainly reflecting the most up-to-date scientific study on the formation of the gospels.

¹¹ The *Declaration* confined itself almost exclusively to the theological question of women ordination. Because the Bible itself is primarily a pastoral document and because here lies the principal competency of the church and magisterium, the *Declaration* would have been more convincing had it addressed itself to the readiness of the church for this type of change in priesthood and the effect of such upon the sanctifying mission of church leaders.

¹² Because Roman Catholic priesthood is closely connected with sacramental and especially eucharistic liturgies, the proper understanding of symbols is crucial. Sacraments are invalid, if symbols are broken (i.e., to use milk instead of water for baptism); they can be valid and yet productive of little good if the symbolism is poorly expressed (i.e., to administer the Eucharist with haste and anger, or to fail in integrating the Eucharist with the liturgy of the Word).

¹³ On this point, our study differs from a statement in the *Declaration*, sec. 6, par. 35: "Thus one must note the extent to which the Church is a society different from other societies, original in her nature and in her structures." — The position of this chapter, that basic styles of leadership were not immediately revealed by God but were found pre-existing among neighboring peoples is substantiated by the classic study of Roland de Vaux, O.P., *Ancient Israel* (New York: McGraw-Hill, 1961), available in a two-volume paperback. The French title indicates the subject matter more accurately: *Les Institutions de L'Ancien Testament*.

¹⁴ G. von Rad, *Genesis* (Philadelphia: Westminster Press, 1973) 175, writes: "This chapter contains some of the most difficult and most debated material in the patriarchal history, indeed, in the entire historical part of the Old Testament." At first it seems that this chapter can be removed from the book of Genesis and the entire narrative proceeds even more smoothly. Yet, many of its details have been corroborated in the startling discoveries at Ebla in NW Syria, according to an oral report of Mitchell Dahood at the annual convention of the Catholic Biblical Association, Detroit, Michigan, August 16–19, 1977.

¹⁵ *Cf.*, Leopold Sabourin, *The Psalms*, 2 ed (New York: Alba House, 1974) 358.

¹⁶ *Cf.*, J. A. Fitzmyer, "Further Light on Melchizedek from Qumran Cave 11," JBL 86 (1967) 25–41.

¹⁷ *Cf.*, David M. Hay, *Glory at the Right Hand: Psalm 110 in Early Christianity* (Nashville: Abingdon, 1973).

¹⁸ For the difficulties of the transition from the leadership of the judges to that of royalty, difficulties which are reflected as well in the complex text of 1 Samuel with its pro- and anti-monarchic texts, see J. Blenkinsopp in the *New Catholic Commentary on Holy Scripture* (New York: Nelson, 1969) p 305–7; or W. Wifall, *The Court His-*

tory of Israel (St. Louis: Clayton Publishing House, 1975) 21; H. W. Hertzberg, I & II Samuel (Philadelphia: Westminster, 1964) 71.

[19] An exceptionally brilliant account how God's will was achieved in a human situation as convoluted as a Russian novel is presented by G. von Rad, "The Beginnings of Historical Writing in Ancient Israel," The Problem of the Hexateuch and Other Essays (New York: McGraw-Hill, 1966) 166–204.

[20] We note the traumatic problem of the late royal period, experienced particularly by the prophets: were the promises about David and Jerusalem unconditional? Could Jerusalem possibly be destroyed? While Isaiah 1–39 holds for its inviolability, Jeremiah held that it could collapse as did Shiloh (Jer 26; 7).

[21] In Is 11, the prophet finally admitted that God could cut down the Davidic dynasty, so that nothing is left but a hidden root (Jesse, David's father). Eventually God would send the Spirit so that new life would appear as a tender shoot.

[22] Cf., R. E. Murphy, "Introduction to Wisdom Literature," Jerome Biblical Commentary (Englewoods Cliff, N.J.: Prentice-Hall, 1968) ch 28, n 4; H. Duesberg and I. Fransen, Les Scribes Inspires, 2 ed (Belgium: Editions de Maredsous, 1966) 15–95. William McKane, Proverbs (Philadelphia: Westminster, 1970) 51–208 on "International Wisdom."

[23] As examples, see 2 Sam 12:11; 21:1; Ez 20:25-26; cf., W. Eichrodt, Theology of the Old Testament (Philadelphia: Westminster Press, 1967) Vol II, p 153–4; P. van ImSchoot, Theology of the Old Testament (New York: Desclee, 1965) 106–7.

[24] Cf., R. de Vaux, Ancient Israel, Vol I, p 7–8.

[25] A similar tradition, attributing the order of elders directly to God, is given in Deut 1:9-18.

[26] Cf., Acts 11:3; 14:23; ch 15–16; 1 Tim 5:17, 19; Jam 5:14.

[27] Archbishop William Borders' pastoral letter, August 19, 1977, stated very succinctly the principal thesis of our chapter: "Every faith community in each period of history must understand the mission of Christ and his message in relationship to its culture and age. Yet the church must grow and therefore change. As an instrument of the Holy Spirit, the church proclaims, protects and penetrates the truth of the Father's revelation; but never in any formulation will the church express the totality of revealed truth. The church must speak within a cultural pattern so that eternal truths are expressed within the confinement of space and time. The church penetrates and modifies an existing culture but does not substitute another for it. The church accepts what is good in all cultures. It tries to change those things which wound the lives of people, becoming, as Jesus challenged us to be, a leaven for society" Origins NC Documentary Service 7 (Sept. 1, 1977) 168. We have developed these ideas at greater length in Thirsting for the Lord (New York: Alba House, 1977), especially in ch 17 "The Process of Humanization."

[28] We attempt to compare these two styles of prophetical action in "Prophecy in Israel," Perspectives on Charismatic Renewal, ed. by Edward D. O'Connor (University of Notre Dame Press: 1975) 13–35. The emergence of charismatic leadership within the Church today is discussed in this book by Dennis J Geaney (ch 11) and by Alcuin Coyle (ch 12).

[29] This name, "classical prophet," was established by W. Eichrodt, Theology of the Old Testament (Philadelphia: Westminster Press, 1961) Vol I, p. 338.

[30] An important book, linking prophecy with Israel's traditions and law, is by Richard V. Bergren, The Prophets and the Law (Cincinnati: Hebrew Union College, 1974).

[31] James A. Sanders, "Hermeneutics in True and False Prophecy," Canon and Authority, ed. by G.W. Coats & B.O. Long (Philadelphia: Fortress Press, 1977) 31.

[32] i.e., oracles against the nations (1:3–2:16), each introduced by "For three crimes . . . and for four, I will not revoke my word"; two series of thirteen oracles each (3:1–5:9 & 5:10–10:14); the visions (7:1-3, 4-6, 7-9; 8:1-3; 9:1-4); another series of four oracles (8:4-14); concluding oracle of destruction and restoration (9:5-15). Each of these subdivisions possesses internal features of well organized structure.

[33] Cf., Paul D. Hanson, The Dawn of Apocalyptic (Philadelphia: Fortress, 1975); G.W. Ahlström, Joel and the Temple Cult of Jerusalem (Leiden: 1971).

³⁴ A good exposition, when and how earlier traditions were transmitted, redacted, and given a firm place within Israel's growing "canon" is provided by P. Grelot, "The Formation of the Old Testament," *Introduction to the Old Testament*, ed. by A. Robert and A. Feuillet (New York: Desclee, 1968) 556–605.

³⁵ *Cf.*, Elizabeth Carroll, "The Proper Place for Women in the Church," *Women and Catholic Priesthood*, ed. by Anne Marie Gardiner (New York: Paulist, 1976) 21–22. This question has already been discussed in ch. 1 of this book.

³⁶ W. Eichrodt, *op. cit.*, 206–210, places the intuition of "God as personal" as the basic revelation of God in the old Testament, more crucial for understanding Old Testament theology than any other divine attribute.

37 From this fact there developed the system of types and antitypes, as well as of promise and fulfillment.

³⁸ The element of surprise in Israel's development is expressed in the Hebrew word *pith'om*, to be translated "suddenly" or "by surprise." It occurs in Is 48:3 & Mal 3:1.

³⁹ For this insistence upon first creation (i.e., founding of city and temple) and upon the New Year's festival, see my work, *Creative Redemption in Deutero-Isaiah* (Rome: Pontifical Institute Press, 1970) 74–82. The difference with Israel's religion is presented by R.A.F. MacKenzie, *Faith and History in the Old Testament* (Minneapolis: 1963).

⁴⁰ The importance of the exodus or journey motif in the New Testament can be seen in the travel-motif of the gospels, especially of Luke; it constitutes one of the dominant themes in the Epistle to the Hebrews, this time in terms of God's people on a procession towards the Holy of Holies with Jesus at the head already behind the veil (Heb 9:11).

⁴¹ Here we depend principally upon the doctoral dissertation, defended before the Pontifical Biblical Commission by Aelred Cody, *A History of Old Testament Priesthood* (Rome: Pontifical Biblical Institute Press, 1969); R. de Vaux, *Histoire Ancienne D'Israel* (Paris: Gabalda, 1971); id., *Ancient Israel* (New York: McGraw-Hill, 1961), in paperback edition, Vol 2, "Religious Institutions"; also James C. Kelly, *The Function of Priest in the Old Testament* (Pontificium Athenaeum Antonianum, 1973). The first two works include extensive bibliography.

⁴² *Cf.*, Marshall D. Johnson, *The Purpose of the Biblical Genealogies with Special Reference to the Setting of the Genealogies of Jesus* (New York: Cambridge University Press, 1969).

⁴³ *i.e.*, 1 Chron 1–9.

⁴⁴ *Cf.*, R. de Vaux, *Ancient Israel*, Vol I, p 6, "Individuals, too, can be incorporated into a tribe either by adoption into a family . . . or through acceptance by the sheikh or the elders. Even here the principle is safeguarded, for the newcomer is attached 'in name and in blood' to the tribe; this means that he acknowledges the tribe's ancestor as his own, that he will marry within the tribe and raise up his family inside it. The Arabs say that he is 'genealogized' (root: *nasaba*). With a whole clan the fusion takes longer, but the result is the same, and the newcomers are finally considered as being of the same blood."

⁴⁵ G. von Rad, *Genesis*, 2 ed. (Philadelphia: Westminster Press, 1972) 145.

⁴⁶ A. Clamer, *La Genèse* (Paris: Letouzey et Ané, 1953) 224.

⁴⁷ Even a cursory reading of Gen 49:5-7 and Deut 33:8-11 will manifest two pronouncedly different attitudes towards Levi. Gen 49 reflects not only the earlier curse and displacement suffered by Levi but also the later jealousy towards its priestly privileges in the southern kingdom of Judah.

⁴⁸ *Cf.*, R. de Vaux, *Ancient Israel*, Vol II, p 370–1.

⁴⁹ Although royalty performed liturgical acts, they were seldom called "priests," probably because the hebrew word for priest, *kohēn*, means "to serve."

⁵⁰ The Jebusite origin of Zadok is defended by A. Cody, *op. cit.*, 88–93.

⁵¹ Sebastian MacDonald in ch 9 of this book will explain the role of "conflict" in theological development.

⁵² *Cf.*, Deut 12:12; 14:27, 29; 18:1-2; Num 18:20; Josh 13:33; Ps 16.

⁵³ *Cf.*, David M. Stanley, "Conception of Salvation in Primitive Christian Preaching," *CBQ* 18 (July, 1956) 231–254; J. Schmitt, "L'Eglise de Jérusalem ou la Restauration d'Israël d'après Act 1–5," *Re-*

cherches de Science Religieuse 27 (1953) 209–18.

54 These ideas of symbol are drawn from my introduction, written for Joan Schaupp, *Woman, Image of the Holy Spirit* (Denville, N.J.: Dimension Books, 1975). *Cf.,* Thomas Fawrett, *The Symbolic Language of Religion* (Minneapolis: Augsburg, 1971); L. L. Mitchell, *The Meaning of Ritual* (New York: Paulist, 1977); Cyprian Vagaggini, *Theological dimensions of the Liturgy* (Collegeville: Liturgical Press, 1977). Symbolism is discussed from a lirtugical viewpoint by Ralph Keifer (ch. 7) and from the psychodynamic aspect by Thomas More Newbold (ch. 10), in this book.

55 *Cf., Declaration,* sec. 5, par. 25–33.

56 An important Hebrew word for temple, *miśkan,* etymologically means "desert tent." After the settlement in the Holy Land it was reserved for the liturgical tent or temple. Only in the very late postexilic age did it revert back to signify secular homes. In any case, the original natural form was not preserved (desert tent) but its original significance (God's providing for his people) was maintained. *Cf.,* Frank M. Cross, Jr., "The Priestly Tabernacle," *Biblical Archaeology* 10 (1947) 45–68, reprinted in *The Biblical Archaeologist Reader* 1 (Garden City, N.Y.: Doubleday Anchor Books, 1961) 201–228.

57 This statement about heaven's breaking the bounds of earthly sexuality can be directed towards the importance of a celibate presence within the priesthood on earth. Earthly symbolism must point to the heavenly. This symbolism too must be maintained but not at too high a cost for preserving "natural resemblance," because "virginity" undergoes its own transcendent history in the Bible. For instance in Rev 14:4, *all* the elect must be adults, male and virgins, if natural resemblance is insisted upon. The text reads: *hoi meta gunaikon ouk emolunthēsan, parthenoi gar eisin;* a very literal translation is: "these are the men who have never been defiled with women, for they are virgins." Because "virgins" and "defilement" must be taken figuratively, so as to stir serious thought and application among *all* the faithful, the symbolic expression in the church must avoid excessive literalism or extreme forms of "natural resemblance."

58 *Cf.,* Phil 4:8, ". . . your thoughts should be wholly directed to all that is true, all that deserves respect, all that is honest, pure, admirable, decent, virtuous, or worthy of praise."

Notes to Chapter Three, pages 47–57

1 *Declaration,* sec. 2, par. 10.

2 *Declaration,* sec. 3, par. 14.

3 Elisabeth Schüssler Fiorenza, "Women Apostles: The Testament of Scripture," *Women and Catholic Priesthood: An Expanded Vision, Proceedings of the Detroit Ordination Conference* (ed. Anne Marie Gardiner; New York: Paulist Press, 1975), 94–102 (95).

4 Fiorenza, "Women Apostles," 95–96. For the detailed analyses behind her statements, see her "Presencia de la mujer en el primitivo movimiento cristiano," *Concilium* 111 (1976), 9–24. For more popular presentations of her views, see "Women in the New Testament," *New Catholic World* 219 (No 1314, Nov./Dec., 1976), 256–260 and "Understanding God's Revealed Word," *Catholic Charismatic* 1 (No 6, Feb./March, 1977), 4–10.

5 From the opening quotations (notes 3 and 4) and from subsequent references to her work, the reader will be able to discern the place which Fiorenza occupies in contemporary NT criticism and in the recent discussions about what the NT says about the ordination of women.

6 "Pro and Con: The Ordination of Women in the New Testament," *Toward a New Theology of Ordination: Essays on the Ordination of Women* (ed. Marianne H. Micks; Charles P. Price; Alexandria, VA: Virginia Theological Seminary/Somerville, MA: Greeno, Hadden & Co., 1976), 1–11.

7 "What in Scripture Speaks to the Ordination of Women?" *Concordia Theological Monthly* 44 (1973), 5–30 (6). See also *The Priest and Sacred Scripture* (ed. Eugene H. Maly; Washington, DC: United States Catholic Conference, 1972), 3. It is a shame that this magnificent study, commissioned and presented by the United States National Conference of Catholic Bishops, has

been so widely neglected in scholarly and ecclesiastical circles.

[8] In an unpublished paper given at Villanova University during the summer of 1977 and entitled "Ecclesial Recognition of the Ministry of Women: New Testament Perspectives and Contemporary Applications," Reumann refers to the work of Phyllis Trible, e.g., "Depatriarchalizing in Biblical Interpretation," *Journal of the American Academy of Religion* 41 (1973), 30–48, and intimates that a change in colored glasses from the "priesthood/priestess" model to a depatriarchalizing model may allow readers to see an old and familiar landscape in a new light (9–10).

[9] *Declaration*, sec. 4, par. 19.

[10] Quoted from Wayne A. Meeks, "The Image of the Androgyne: Some Uses of a Symbol in Earliest Christianity," *History of Religions* 13 (1973/74), 165–208 (168). This quotation, while found in a number of rabbinic sources, is perhaps most conveniently available in the Babylonian Talmud, Menahot 43b. In chapter 8 Hayim G. Perelmuter explains in greater detail how various sectors in Judaism have responded to the role of women in the post-biblical age.

[11] *Declaration*, sec. 2, par. 13.

[12] For the ecclesiastical approval of the use of these methodologies, see Vatican II's *Dogmatic Constitution on Divine Revelation*, paragraph 19 and the 1964 "Instruction Concerning the Historical Truth of the Gospels" from the Pontifical Biblical Commission which was approved by Pope Paul VI. This latter document is most conveniently available in William G. Heidt, *Inspiration, Canonicity, Texts, Versions, Hermeneutics — A General Introduction to Sacred Scripture* (Old-New Testament Reading Guide 31; Collegeville: Liturgical Press, 1970), 111–119. For a superb treatment on the question of the relationships between Jesus, the Twelve, and the apostles, see Jerome D. Quinn, "Ministry in the New Testament," *Biblical Studies in Contemporary Thought: The Tenth Anniversary Commemorative Volume of the Trinity College Biblical Institute 1966–1975* (ed. Miriam Ward; Burlington, VT: Trinity College Biblical Institute/Sommerville, MA: Greeno, Hadden, & Co., 1975), 130–160 (131–137).

[13] *Declaration*, sec. 3, par. 14. For an appreciation of the critical methodologies being discussed here and their application to Gospel texts, see Norman Perrin, *Rediscovering the Teaching of Jesus* (New York: Harper & Row, 1967).

[14] See Raymond E. Brown, *Priest and Bishop: Biblical Reflections* (New York: Paulist Press, 1970), 47–73; Beda Rigaux, "The Twelve Apostles," *Apostolic Succession: Rethinking a Barrier to Unity* (Concilium 34; New York: Paulist Press, 1968) 5–15. To understand how moderate the position of Brown and Rigaux really is, one should contrast it with Walter Schmithals, *The Office of Apostle in the Early Church* (trans. John E. Steely; Nashville: Abingdon, 1969).

[15] *Declaration*, sec. 2, par. 12–13.

[16] The weakness of the *Declaration*'s argument is patent if one reads Romans 16:7 to refer to a woman, Junia, who is an apostle. See Fiorenza, "Women Apostles," 96.

[17] Raymond E. Brown, *Biblical Reflections on Crises Facing the Church* (New York: Paulist Press, 1975), 54.

[18] Brown, *Crises*, 52–53.

[19] In passing, it should be mentioned that the *Declaration*'s principle of fidelity to the example of the Lord is not sufficiently precise or clear. By what principle has it selected one factor, maleness, as the one to which the Church must be faithful and excluded others of similar importance to which the Church does not have to be faithful, e.g., the Twelve were Jews, not Gentiles; bearded, not clean-shaven; married, not subject to mandatory celibacy?

[20] "Ecclesial Recognition," 14.

[21] *Declaration*, sec. 4, par. 20; sec. 5, par. 28; sec. 6, par. 28. See the high value placed on this passage by Fiorenza, "Women Apostles," 95; Meeks, "The Image of the Androgyne"; R. Scroggs, "Woman in the NT," *Interpreter's Dictionary of the Bible, Supplementary Volume* (Nashville: Abingdon, 1976), 966–968 (966).

[22] *Declaration*, sec. 4, par. 20.

[23] *Declaration*, sec. 6, par. 36.

[24] See Fiorenza, "Women Apostles," 95–96. For the arguments that Gal 3:28 is a pre-Pauline baptismal formula, see Robin Scroggs, "Paul and the Eschatological Woman," *Journal of the American Academy of Religion* 40 (1972) 282–303

(291–293); Scroggs, "Paul and the Eschatological Woman: Revisited," *Journal of the American Academy of Religion* 42 (1974) 532–537 (533); Meeks, "The Image of the Androgyne," 180–181, 203 n 153; Hans Dieter Betz, "Spirit, Freedom, and Law: Paul's Message to the Galatian Churches," *Svensk Exegetisk Årsbok* 39 (1974) 145–160 (147–151).

[25] "Women Apostles," 95.

[26] See the accurate, if slightly overdrawn, remarks of John McKenzie: "We have rigorously universalized I Cor 14:33-36 far beyond its context; we have not been equally rigorous with Gal 3:28, a verse which admits the ministry of women as clearly as any biblical passage admits anything." See his "Ministerial Structures in the New Testament," *The Plurality of Ministries* (*Concilium* 74; New York: Herder and Herder, 1972), 13–22 (22).

[27] For a more popular presentation of my views on this subject, see "St. Paul and Women," *Catholic Charismatic* 1 (No 6, Feb./March, 1977), 31–32.

[28] There is considerable scholarly doubt today whether Paul wrote more than the indisputedly authentic "Big Seven": Romans, Galatians, 1–2 Corinthians, Philippians, Philemon, and 1 Thessalonians. It is sound methodology to use with caution data from the disputedly genuine Pauline letters in the construction of an argument that such or such a point is Pauline, for it is not commonly accepted that this data actually stems from Paul.

[29] See, e.g., Scroggs, "Eschatological Woman," 284 and Fuller, "Pro and Con," 8.

[30] *Declaration*, sec. 3, par. 14–17.

[31] "What in Scripture," 5.

[32] *Declaration*, sec. 3, par. 17; sec. 4, par. 20.

[33] See the excellent, but as yet unpublished paper delivered by Mary Ann Getty at the Cleveland conference on the Ordination of Women, February, 1977: "New Testament Reflections on Women and Ministry." In a sustained argument of twenty-five pages Getty rightly and tellingly scores the *Declaration* for this methodological shortcoming. In the NT there are the ministries of apostle, prophet, teacher, deacon, presbyter, and bishop — to name only the ones most familiar to us today.

[34] *Declaration*, sec. 3, par. 16.

[35] "Ecclesial Recognition," 21.

[36] For an overview of the data under discussion see the article by E. Earle Ellis, "Paul and His Co-Workers," *New Testament Studies* 17 (1970/71), 437–452.

[37] *Declaration*, sec. 4, par. 20.

[38] The *Declaration* treats these passages in sec. 4, par. 20. Both the *Declaration* (apparently) and I cannot follow the lead of William O. Walker, Jr., "1 Corinthians and Paul's Views Regarding Women," *Journal of Biblical Literature* 94 (1975) 94–110, who solves the problems generated by 1 Cor 11:2-16 by arguing that the passage is a later interpolation. See the effective counter-arguments of Jerome Murphy-O'Connor, "The Non-Pauline Character of 1 Corinthians 11:2-16?" *Journal of Biblical Literature* 95 (1976) 615–621. I do not adhere to the position of Scroggs, "Eschatological Woman," 284, that 1 Cor 14:33b-36 is a post-Pauline gloss. See the persuasive argument of Meeks, "The Image of the Androgyne," 203–204, that 1 Cor 14:33b-36 is Pauline.

[39] See the arguments of Scroggs, "Eschatological Woman," 297–302 and Meeks, "The Image of the Androgyne," 199–203.

[40] *Declaration*, sec. 4, par. 20.

[41] "Women in the Pauline Assembly: To Prophesy, but not to Speak?" scheduled to appear in the forthcoming commentary on the *Declaration* edited by Arlene and Leonard Swidler.

[42] *Declaration*, sec. 4, par. 20.

[43] "The Image of the Androgyne," 204.

[44] See Elaine H. Pagels, "Paul and Women: A Response to Recent Discussion," *Journal of the American Academy of Religion* 42 (1974), 538–549, esp. 544–548: Paul is a man in conflict who champions liberty, but is also desirous of order. Pagels' insight into Paul is shared by Reumann, "What in Scripture," 30, who expresses it in terms of "realized eschatology" and "eschatological reserve": "First Corinthians 11, on this reading, turns out to be the key passage: Paul allows women to pray and prophesy in church, because it is a prompting of the Spirit that moves them; this overcomes all the inclinations from his Jewish heritage; at the same time he regulates this ministry, like all gifts of the Spirit,

so that it will really build up the body of Christ, the people of God, and not cause offense at the wrong points."

45 For a similar conclusion, see A. Feuillet, "La dignité et le rôle de la femme d'après quelques textes pauliniens: comparaison avec l'Ancien Testament," *New Testament Studies* 21 (1974/75), 157–191.

46 I follow the lead of Fuller, "Pro and con," 8 in placing Colossians and Ephesians here.

47 John H. Elliott, "A Catholic Gospel: Reflections on 'Early Catholicism' in the New Testament," *Catholic Biblical Quarterly* 31 (1969), 213–223 (214). This article also contains a basic bibliography on the subject. For a very positive approach to the significance of "early Catholicism," see Reginald H. Fuller, *A Critical Introduction to the New Testament* (London: Duckworth, 1966), 166–167, 196–197.

48 *Declaration*, sec. 4, par. 20 on 1 Tim 2:12.

49 By neglecting these passages, the authors of the *Declaration* may have noticed along with others, e.g., Reumann, "What in Scripture," 12, that these texts on subordination may not be pertinent to the discussion since they refer to wives and husbands and not to women and men in general.

50 See, e.g., Scroggs, "Eschatological Woman," 284.

51 "Pro and Con," 9; see James E. Crouch, *The Origin and Intention of the Colossian Haustafel* (Forschungen zur Religion und Literatur des Alten und Neuen Testaments 109; Göttingen: Vandenhoeck & Ruprecht, 1972).

52 "Ecclesial Recognition," 23. See also Fiorenza, "Women Apostles," 97–99.

53 "Woman in the NT," 968.

54 See Meeks, "The Image of the Androgyne," 203–208.

55 "The Image of the Androgyne," 208.

56 The translation is from *Origins*, 96.

57 The translation is from *Origins*, 96.

58 The translation is from *Origins*, 96. A similar conclusion is arrived at by Manuel Miguens, *Church Ministry in New Testament Times* (Arlington, VA: Christian Culture Press, 1976), 140.

59 It should be obvious that our American circumstances do not envisage a gnostic women in every church or even every other church. Our culture does not countenance — at least legally — the discriminatory subordination of women. For a similar point, see Fuller, "Pro and Con," 9–10.

60 *The Priest and Sacred Scripture*, 39. See also McKenzie, "Ministerial Structures," 21–22.

Notes to Chapter Four, pages 59–68

1 *De praescriptione haereticorum* 41.5. Text available in *Corpus Christianorum. Series latina* (henceforth CCL) 1, 221, 12–15. All translations given in the text of this article are by the author. English text also available in its context in *Ante-Nicene Fathers* (henceforth ANF) 3, 263.

2 *De virginibus velandis* 9.1; text in CCL 2, 1218–19 and translation in ANF 4, 33. Contrary to what one might suppose today, the treatise did not argue that virgins should wear veils to distinguish them from other women, but rather that, since all other respectable women were veiled in public, consecrated virgins should be too, so as not to depart from general custom. Though *Praes.* 41.5 is cited by the Vatican *Declaration*, fn. 7, as indicative of Church Fathers' opposition to women in the ordained ministry, strangely, the more blatant *Virg. Vel.* 9.1 is omitted.

3 Exorcism as a matter of course, baptism in case of necessity. See *Apology* 23; *De corona* 11.3; *De idolatria* 11.7; *De baptismo* 17.1-3. See the discussion in Roger Gryson, *The Ministry of Women in the Early Church*, trans. Jean Laporte and Mary Louise Hall (Collegeville: Liturgical Press, 1976) 17–22.

4 The Vatican *Declaration* (7, p. 17) also cites Irenaeus, *Adversus Haereses* 1.13.2. This text describes the eucharistic rite of the Marcosian Gnostics in which a woman holds the chalice at the altar. Irenaeus, however, describes the ritual as part of a condemnation of the whole Marcosian community, not of the action of its women at the altar. This text is thus a witness to the priestly ministry of women in the Marcosian Church, but not of the Church Fathers' condemnation of such ministry.

[5] This kind of suppression of women in the Pastoral Epistles seems already to be a reaction against some form of variant Christianity that encourages women to be more active in Church life (*cf.* 1 Tim 5:14; 2 Tim 3:6-7). See M. Dibelius and H. Conzelmann, *The Pastoral Epistles* (Hermeneia: Philadelphia: Fortress, 1972), 44–49; R. Karris, "The Background and Significance of the Polemic of the Pastoral Epistles," *Journal of Biblical Literature* 92 (1973), 554–555. It is also quite possible that 1 Cor 14:34-35 is part of an interpolation from the same period and situation as is represented by the Pastorals: see R. Scroggs, "Paul and the Eschatological Woman," *Journal of the American Academy of Religion* 40 (1972), 284; for a listing of exegetes pro and con on the question, see J. Dunn, *Jesus and the Spirit* (London: SCM, 1975), 435, n 115. These biblical passages were discussed by Robert J. Karris in ch 3 of this book.

[6] *De baptismo* 17.4; CCL 1, 291, 20–292, 31. English text available in ANF 3, 677; Gryson, 18; E. Evans, *Tertullian's Homily on Baptism* (London: S.P.C.K., 1964) 37. The legend of Thecla continued on for several centuries; whether she was ever a historical person is difficult to say. It is significant that Tertullian attacked only the authenticity of the *Acts* and implied neither that they were doctrinally heretical nor that Thecla ever existed. The *Acts* in English are to be found in E. Hennecke and W. Schneemelcher, *New Testament Apocrypha* (Philadelphia: Westminster, 1965) 2, 353–364.

[7] 1 Cor 11:5.

[8] *Contra Marcionem* 5.8.11; CCL 1, 688, 7–13. English text in E. Evans, *Tertullian Adversus Marcionem* (Oxford, 1972) 561; Gryson, 19. See the account of a female visionary in *De Anima* 9.4; CCL 2, 792, 24–793, 38. English text in ANF 3, 188; Gryson, 20.

[9] Preserved only in fragments from a collection of Patristic commentaries; text ed. by Claude Jenkins, "Origen on 1 Corinthians," *Journal of Theological Studies* 10 (1908) #74, 40–42. English text in Gryson, 28–29.

[10] *Ibid.* The same argument about women prophets staying in their place is repeated in the *Apostolic Constitutions* 8.2.9., ed. F. X. Funk (Paderborn: F. Schoeningh, 1905); 1, 470; English trans. in ANF 7, 481.

[11] *Declaration*, fn. 7.

[12] *Ep* 74 (75). 10, 11; *Corpus scriptorum ecclesiasticorum latinorum* 3, 817–818. English text in ANF 5, 393.

[13] *Panarion* 42.4: "They give to women the commission to baptize."

[14] *Panarion* 49.2-3; ed. Oehler I–II, 40–42. English translations of these texts are not readily available. In dependence on Epiphanius, Augustine, *De Haeresibus* 27, reports the same information, including the account of Christ's appearance as a woman to one of the Montanist prophetesses (Epiphanius 49.1).

[15] *Panarion* 78.23; 79.1; Oehler I–II, 440–442, 446–448. The rest of ch 79, sections 2–9, is devoted to the two questions, why Mary should not be worshiped and why women should not be priests.

[16] *Panarion* 79.2.

[17] *Panarion* 79.3; and again in 79.7; *Didascalia* ch 15 in English trans. of R. H. Connolly (Oxford, 1929) 142. The same text is preserved in Greek in the *Apostolic Constitutions* 3.9; Funk, 1, 199–201; English trans. in ANF 7, 429. The *Ap. Const.* adds to the argument quotations from 1 Cor 11:3; Gen 2:21; 3:16. The same argument regarding women as teachers occurs in the *Didascalia* ch 15 (Connolly, 133) and in *Apostolic Constitutions* 3.6.1-2 (Funk, 1, 191: English trans. in ANF 7, 427–428). Since Epiphanius was a native of Palestine, it is not unlikely that he acquired the ideas from one of the Church Orders.

[18] *E.g.* 1 Tim 5:3-16; Titus 2:3; Acts 9:39; Ignatius, *To the Smyrnaeans* 13.1; Polycarp 4.3; *Shepherd of Hermas*, *Vis.* 2.4.3; Justin, *Apology* 1.67.6; Hippolytus, *Apostolic Tradition* 20, 24, 30; Origen, *On Prayer* 28.4.

[19] *Exhortation to Chastity* 13.4; *To His Wife* 1.7.4.

[20] *On a Single Marriage* (*De monogamia*) 11.1; *On Modesty* (*De pudicitia*) 13.7.

[21] Hippolytus, *Apostolic Tradition* 10 says that widows are to be "instituted" (*kathistasthai*) but not ordained (*cheirotoneisthai*) because they, like virgins, have no *leitourgia*, or official ministry. This situation seems to differ from that in Carthage as described by Tertullian.

[22] *Didasc./Ap. Const.* 3.1.1-2 (Funk 1, 182–183). Widows are not ordained: *Ap.*

Const. 8.25.2 (Funk 1. 528). In the *Apostolic Constitutions* the tendency to present widows as surpassed in importance by consecrated virgins is noticeable: see Gryson, 58–60. This differs remarkably from the *Testamentum Domini*, in which widows have the highest honorary and liturgical functions among women and are ordained (*Test. Dom.* 1.40; see discussion in Gryson, 64–69.

[23] There are only three earlier texts which may speak of deaconesses: Rom 16:1 where Paul calls the woman Phoebe a *diakonos* of the Church at Cenchreae (one of the seaports of Corinth); 1 Tim 3:11 where "women" are mentioned between two statements about deacons; the *ministrae* of the Church in Bithynia whom the governor Pliny tortures to get information about Christians (Pliny, *Epistle* 10.96.8). It is doubtful that in any of these cases anything like the full-blown order of deaconesses of the *Didascalia* is envisioned, though the text in Pliny is the most possible.

[24] It is impossible here to discuss at length the full treatment of deaconesses in these two documents. See the exposition in Gryson, 54–63.

[25] *Panarion* 79.3.

[26] The rite for ordination of a bishop begins much earlier, in chapters 4 and 5, and merges into a more general liturgical rite described in the intervening chapters.

[27] *Ap. Const.* 8.31.2 (Funk 1, 532–5); cited by Gryson, 62. Deaconesses are also included among the clergy in regulations regarding who can bless, depose, and excommunicate whom: 8, 28.1-8 (Funk 1, 530–1).

[28] *Epitome*, chapters 9–10 (Funk 2. 81). An additional complication is created, however, by the fact that the lector, who in the *Ap. Const.* receives the laying on of hands with the same expression as that used for the deaconess, is not ordained in the *Epitome* (ch 13).

[29] English text in Gryson, 63. On age limits for widows and deaconesses, see the discussion by Gryson, 63–64.

[30] The further evidence for both East and West is collected by Gryson. More detailed discussion is beyond the scope of this study.

[31] *On the Apparel of Women* 1.1-2.

[32] Origen on 1 Cor 14:34-35. See note 9 above.

[33] *Panarion* 79.1.

[34] Tertullian, for instance, was happily married, had a tender love for his wife, and considered men and women equally capable of great virtue; see F. Forrester Church, "Sex and Salvation in Tertullian," *Harvard Theological Review* 68 (1975), 83–101.

[35] *Declaration*, sec. 1, par. 6.

[36] For an excellent assessment of the diverse understandings of Tradition, see John W. O'Malley, "Reform, Historical Consciousness, and Vatican II's Aggiornamento," *Theological Studies* 32 (1971), 573–601.

[37] For the question of Tradition, we call attention to ch 6, by Gilbert Ostdiek.

Notes to
Chapter Five, pages 78–83

[1] Can. 968. — Ⅹ 1. "Sacram ordinationem valide recipit solus vir baptizatus; . . ."

[2] Sacred Congregation for the Doctrine of the Faith, *Declaration on the Question of the Admission of Women to the Ministerial Priesthood* with *Commentary*, October 15, 1976 (Washington, D.C.: USCC Publications Office, 1977). The official Latin text is found in the *Acta Apostolicae Sedis* LXIX (28 Februarii 1977) 98–116.

[3] *Declaration*, sec. 4, par. 24.

[4] "Consuetudo autem est ius quoddam moribus institutum, quod pro lege suscipitur, cum deficit lex." — c. 5, D. I.

[5] *Cf.*, Cicognani, A. G., *Canon Law*, 2d revised edition (Philadelphia: The Dolphin Press, 1935), 641.

[6] *Cf.*, Cicognani, *op. cit.*, 645.

[7] "Quum consuetudinis ususque longaevi non sit levis auctoritas, et plerumque discordiam pariant novitates, auctoritate vobis praesentium inhibemus, ne absque venerabilis fratris nostri episcopi vestri consilio et consensu immutetis ecclesiae vestrae constitutiones et conseutudines vestras approbatas, vel novas etiam inducatis; si quas forte fecistis . . . irritas decernentes." — c. 9, X, I, 4. Translated by Cicognani, *op. cit.*, 646.

[8] Can. 28. — "Consuetudo praeter legem, quae scienter a communitate cum

animo se obligandi servata sit, legem inducit, si pariter fuerit rationabilis et legitime per annos quadraginta continuos et completos praescripta."

⁹ Cicognani points out that the custom must be reasonable at the time it is established, and indicates that, at a later time, it may well become useless and even harmful, so that its contrary custom might be the reasonable thing to do. As indices of the reasonableness of a custom, he cites the fact that it does not run counter to the law of the Church or ecclesiastical authority, that it is not a source of grievance or injury to law or authority by giving rise to serious and intolerable inconveniences, that it is not opposed to the worship due to God or to the public good, that it does not sever "the nerve of ecclesiastical discipline." — Cf., Cicognani, op. cit., 650–651.

¹⁰ Declaration, sec. 4, par. 24.

¹¹ Loc. cit.

¹² Can. 27. — Ⅹ 1. "Iuri divino sive naturali sive positivo nulla consuetudo potest aliquatenus derogare; sed neque iuri ecclesiastico praeiudicium affert, nisi fuerit rationabilis et legitime per annos quadraginta continuos et completos praescripta; . . ."

¹³ Commentary on the Declaration, 21.

¹⁴ Ibid., 22.

¹⁵ Raming, Ida, The Exclusion of Women from the Priesthood, trans. Norman R. Adams, (Metuchen, N.J.: Scarecrow Press, 1976).

¹⁶ Raming, op. cit., 46–47.

¹⁷ Cf. Cicognani, op. cit., 222.

¹⁸ Ibid., 243.

¹⁹ For a thorough discussion of the Pseudo-Isidorian Decretals, see Cicognani, op. cit., 219–221, 239–248.

²⁰ Raming, op. cit., 62–63.

²¹ The same type of bias occurs, for example, in Footnote 37 to Chapter One of Dr. Raming's book. She is interpreting faculty n 28 of Pastorale munus of Pope Paul VI, scil. "Permittendi clericis minoribus, religiosis laicis, necnon piis mulieribus ut pallas, corporalia et purificatoria prima quoque ablutione extergere possint." This, Dr. Raming states, gives " 'local bishops the right to permit clergy of lower rank, (male) lay persons and also devout women, to perform the first washing of palls, corporals and purifiactors.' . . . It is instructive

to notice in this regulation the special mention of women — in itself superfluous — along with the laity: this reflects the former legal situation, which did not allow women such practice." This interpretation on the part of Dr. Raming is simply to mistranslate and misunderstand the expression religiosis laicis. Standard translations correctly render this as "lay religious." (Cf., for example, Canon Law Digest, vol VI [New York: Bruce, 1969] 375.) The term simply refers to members of religious communities, male or female, that are not clerical in nature. It includes both religious brothers and sisters. Indeed, the special mention of devout women is made to the apparent exclusion of devout men!

²² Much of this material relative to collections that are not genuine and the particular influence of the Pseudo-Isidorian Decretals relies on the notes taken from the classroom lectures of Dr. Stephan Kuttner on the history of the sources of Canon Law, Catholic University of America, 1962.

²³Cf. Cicognani, op. cit., 182–191; Raming, op. cit., 15–20.

²⁴ Cf. Cicognani, ibid., 247.

²⁵ Ibid., 247–248.

²⁶ Raming, op. cit., 9.

²⁷ Loc. cit.

²⁸ Ibid., 7.

²⁹ Ibid., 21–22.

³⁰ "Mulieres autem non solum ad sacerdotium, sed nec etiam ad diaconatum, provehi possunt, . . ." — princ., C. 15, q 3.

³¹ Cf. Raming, op. cit., 26.

³² Commentary on the Declaration, 22.

³³ Loc. cit.

³⁴ Ibid., 22–23.

³⁵ Ibid., 23.

³⁶ Loc. cit.

³⁷ Raming, op. cit., 71.

³⁸ Loc. cit.

³⁹ Ibid., 72.

⁴⁰ Loc. cit.

⁴¹ Cf. ibid., 72–73.

⁴² Ibid., 73.

⁴³ Commentary on the Declaration, 24.

⁴⁴ "Nomine incapacitatis hic venit radicalis inhabilitas ad actum, ita ut ordinationem nedum illicitam, verum etiam nullam et irritam faciat. . . . Incapacitas in

subiecta materia . . . ex iure divino positivo provenit, . . . Cum sacerdotium sit iuris divini positivi, etiam incapacitas, de qua nunc sermo est, nonnisi ex iure divino positivo profluit." Cappello, *De Sacramentis*, vol II, pars III, *De Sacra Ordinatione*, (Romae: Marietti, 1935), n 350, 307–308.

[45] Cappello cites both 1 Cor 14:34 and 1 Tim 2:11. Then he adds the remark: "SS. Patres ita interpretantur verba D. Pauli, ut excludant omnino mulieres a hierarchia ecclesiastica ac propterea ab ordinibus suscipiendis, et tamquam haereticam habeant sententiam, quae affirmat dignitatem et officium sacerdotale mulieribus tribui posse." Cappello, *op. cit.*, n 354, 311.

[46] *Cf.* notes to the Commentary on the *Declaration*, n 36.

[47] "When Paul insists on the subordinate place of the wife in domestic society, he is echoing the contemporary social structure that he knew, in which the woman was far more subject to the man than she is today. Such a view is found in . . . 1 Cor 14:34-35 . . ." Fitzmyer, Joseph A., "Pauline Theology," *The Jerome Biblical Commentary* (Englewood Cliffs, N.J.: Prentice-Hall, 1968), 79: 165.

[48] "The Church desires that Christian women should become fully aware of the greatness of their mission: today their role is of capital importance, both for the renewal and humanization of society and for the rediscovery by believers of the true face of the Church," *Declaration*, sec. 6, par. 40.

"We have a long way to go before people become fully aware of the greatness of women's mission in the Church and society, ¿both for the renewal and humanization of society and for the rediscovery by believers of the true countenance of the Church.' Unfortunately we also still have a long way to go before all the inequalities of which women are still the victims are eliminated, not only in the field of public, professional and intellectual life, but even within the family." Commentary on the *Declaration*, 36.

[49] Morrisey, Francis G., *The Canonical Significance of Papal and Curial Pronouncements*, (Toledo: Canon Law Society of America, 1974), 10.

Notes to
Chapter Six, pages 85–102

[1] P. Lakeland, "The Ministerial Priesthood," *The Way* 16 (1976) 40–41.

[2] *Declaration*, sec. 1, par. 8. For a useful summary of previous statements which might qualify as teaching of the ordinary magisterium see Haye van der Meer, *Women Priests in the Catholic Church? A Theological-Historical Investigation* (Philadelphia: Temple Univ. Press, 1973) 90–105. The only other current statements that can be taken to bear any degree of "official" magisterial weight concerning the official church exclusion of women from priestly ordination include Canon 986, par 1, commented on in ch 5 in this volume, and two references made in passing by Paul VI, in his "Address to the Members of the Study Commission on the Role of Women in Society and in the Church and to the Members of the Committee for International Women's Year" (April 18, 1975), and in his letter of Nov. 30, 1975 to Donald Coggan, Archbishop of Canterbury. These papal statements can be found in *Acta Apostolicae Sedis* [*AAS*] 67 (1975) 266 and *AAS* 68 (1976) 599 respectively. The anonymous commentary published with the USCC translation of the *Declaration* specifies that there has been no solemn decision of the magisterium in this regard.

[3] The "theological note" or degree of authority with which the Roman document is invested has been clarified by Dismas Bonner in ch 5, sec VI.

[4] K. Rahner, "Priestertum der Frau?", *Stimmen der Zeit* 195 (1977) 292–293.

[5] *Ibid.*, 293–294. This would seem to hold true even in the more restrictive reading of the theologian's role as one of seeking "to define exactly the intention of teaching proper to the various formulas" and by such "expository and explanatory additions . . . (to) maintain and clarify their original meaning," as presented by the Sacred Congregation for the Doctrine of the Faith in its *Mysterium Ecclesiae*, ch 5 (English translation: *Declaration in Defense of the Catholic Doctrine on the Church against Certain Errors of the Present Day*, Washington: United States Catholic Conference, 1973) 8. The International Theological Commission's *Theses on the Relationship between the Ecclesiastical Magisterium and Theology* (Washington:

United States Catholic Conference, 1977) provides an even more congenial role for theologians as mediating between the magisterium's authoritative presentation of the Word of God written and handed down and the faith of the People of God which is formed in concrete historical and cultural situations.

[6] *Declaration*, Introduction, par. 5.

[7] R. Gryson, *The Ministry of Women in the Early Church* (Collegeville: Liturgical Press, 1976) 112.

[8] The practice of ordaining women found in patristic times among the "heretical sects" and later among the protestant churches is noted in the *Declaration*, Introduction, 5 and 4 respectively. The document labels the practice an "innovation" in reference to the patristic period. In 4, p. 11, it calls the practice an "abuse." This question was researched by Carolyn Osiek in ch 4 of this book.

[9] *Declaration*, sec. 1, par. 6.

[10] The *Declaration*, sec. 1, par. 8, notes that the magisterium has never intervened to formulate this as a principle, though it does refer to the magisterium's occasional "witnessing" to its desire to remain faithful to the example left it by the Lord.

[11] For an excellent discussion of tradition and hermeneutics in relation to the question of the ordination of women confer F. Cardman, "Tradition, Hermeneutics, and Ordination," in J. Coriden (ed.), *Sexism and Church Law. Equal Rights and Affirmative Action* (New York: Paulist Press, 1977) 58–81.

[12] R. Gryson, *The Ministry of Women in the Early Church*, xv, 114.

[13] Thus the *Declaration*, Introduction, par. 5, "the Church does not *consider* (agnoscere) herself authorized . . ."; Sec. 1, par. 6: "The Catholic Church has never *felt* (sensit) that . . ."; Sec. 1, par. 8: "the Church *intends* (intendit) to remain faithful to the type of ordained ministry willed by the Lord Jesus"; Sec. 4, par. 24: "this norm . . . is still *considered* (putatur) to conform to God's plan for his Church." Emphasis added.

[14] *Declaration*, Sec. 2–3, 5–6, par. 10–17, 25–40. In his letter to Archbishop Coggan, Paul VI summed up the reasons thus: "She (the Church) holds that it is not admissible to ordain women to the priesthood, for very fundamental reasons. These reasons include: the example recorded in the Sacred Scriptures of Christ choosing his Apostles only from among men; the constant practice of the Church, which has imitated Christ in choosing only men; and her living teaching authority which has consistently held that the exclusion of women from the priesthood is in accordance with God's plan for his Church," *AAS* 68 (1976) 599. Confer J. Begley-C. Armbruster, "Women and Office in the Church," *Amer. Eccl. Rev.* 165 (1971) 145–157 for a handy summary of the data and the arguments pro and con.

[15] *Declaration*, Sec. 2, par. 10 and 13.

[16] *Declaration*, Sec. 2, par. 13.

[17] St. Thomas, *In IV Sent.*, dist. 25, q. 2, quaestiuncula 1[a] ad 4[um], as cited in the *Declaration*, Sec. 5, par. 27.

[18] *Declaration*, Sec. 5, par. 27; *cf.*, par. 25–33 for the complete elaboration of the representation argument.

[19] *Declaration*, Sec. 6, par. 34–40.

[20] It is interesting to note that this argument has been coopted in the *Declaration*, Sec. 2–3, par. 10–17; Sec. 4, par. 19–20, to support a deliberate choice of the exclusionist position by Jesus and the early church.

[21] See ch 3 by R. Karris in this volume; also E. Maly, *The Priest and Sacred Scripture* (Washington: USCC, 1972) 28–39, and J. Quinn, "Ministry in the New Testament," in *Eucharist and Ministry (Lutherans and Catholics in Dialogue* IV) (Washington: USCC, 1970) 69–100.

[22] Thus the Pontifical Biblical Commission, "Can Women be Priests?", *Origins* 6 (1976) 96: "It does not seem that the New Testament by itself alone will permit us to settle in a clear way and once and for all the problem of the possible accession of women to the presbyterate"; J. Danielou: "As to the possibility of women priests, there is no fundamental theological objection to it," from *Le Monde* as quoted in G. Tavard, *Woman in Christian Tradition* (Notre Dame: Univ. of Notre Dame Press, 1973) 217; Haye van der Meer, *Women Priests in the Catholic Church?*, xxii, notes that an interim progress report on a NCCB-commissioned study of priestly ministry "stated that there were no biblical or theological grounds for opposing the priestly ordination of women."

23 P. Lakeland, "The Ministerial Priesthood," 40–41 astutely observes that the two opposing camps have to be coaxed onto common ground if the deadlock is to be broken. He writes: "Realistically, since the institutional Church leans towards the *status quo*, this amounts to saying that the forces desiring change must fight it out on their opponents' battlefield" (41).

24 P. Lakeland, *ibid.*, 47: "Perhaps it is truer to say that the principal theological problem to be solved is whether the ordination of women is a theological issue at all. There is no theological value in the statement that Jesus chose only men to be his apostles; but an examination of *why* he may have done so could conceivably turn up some theological point."

25 *Declaration*, Introduction, par. 4.

26 See ch 4 by C. Osiek in this volume.

27 The chief of these other possible explanations would be a socio-cultural necessity for excluding women from the call to ministry in spite of a general acceptance in principle in other roles. K. Rahner has rightly called our attention to the fact that such contrary positions can be taken, "Priestertum der Frau", 296. Thus step two does not necessarily imply step three. Without wanting to seem facetious, one might also note that classical theology of ministry requires a divine call given to *individual* persons *apart from* their personal qualifications. The withholding of that call in the case of Jesus' Mother and other female acquaintances no matter how worthy does not of itself constitute a class exclusion.

28 Letter of Dec 11, 1210, to the Bishops of Palencia and Burgos, cited in the *Declaration*, Sec. 2, par. 13.

29 *Declaration*, Sec. 6, par. 36.

30 Not too long ago Rome reprobated a somewhat unusual theory which held that Mary was a priest. One wonders whether the motivation behind that theory was not precisely a questionable understanding that priesthood is a dignity and honor (even in the sense of an ontological perfection) and ought therefore have accrued to Mary. Confer H. van der Meer, *Women Priests in the Catholic Church?*, 151–153.

31 *Cf.* R. Norris, "The Ordination of Women and the 'Maleness' of Christ," *Anglican Theological Review* Suppl. Series #6 (1976) 69–80. There the author argues that the inclusion of "maleness" as an essential characteristic required in a minister's representation of Christ is not only an unprecedented form of the argument found in tradition (in that the maleness of Jesus was of no special christological interest to the Fathers), but that it would inevitably lead to a false and dangerous understanding of the mystery of redemption. One might ask further whether such a need for the Word Incarnate to be male in order to be God-with-us might not also imply unwanted conclusions regarding our doctrine of God.

32 This question is closely related to the christological one since Christ is the "final Adam," the summing up of renewed humanity. For a fuller discussion of theological anthropology in this context see G. Tavard, *Woman in Christian Tradition*, 187–210. Confer parallel considerations from psychology presented by T. Newbold, ch 10 in this volume.

33 Some of the more important instances of this phrase in ecclesiastical documents are: Pius XII, *Mediator Dei*, AAS 39 (1947) 553; Vatican II, *Sacrosanctum Concilium* #33 (Flannery, 12), *Lumen Gentium* #10, 28 (Flannery, 361, 385), *Presbyterium Ordinis* #2, 13 (Flannery, 865, 887); Synod of Bishops, 1971, *De Sacerdotio Ministeriali*, part 1, #4, AAS 63 (1971) 905–906; and the *Declaration*, ch 5, pp. 11–15 passim. For a brief essay sketching the history of this formula see B.-D. Marliangeas, " 'In Persona Christi', 'In Persona Ecclesiae', Note sur les origines et le développement de l'usage de ces expressions dans le théologie latine," in J.-P. Jossua-Y. Congar (ed.), *La Liturgie après Vatican II (Unam Sanctam 66)* (Paris: du Cerf, 1967) 283–288. For a commentary on the *Declarations*'s use of the formula see A.-G. Martimort, "The Value of a Theological Formula 'In Persona Christi'," *L'Osservatore Romano* (Eng. ed.) N. 10 (467) March 10 (1977) 6–7.

34 A more technical explanation would read as follows. Employing aristotelian categories of efficient and exemplar causality, standard scholastic theology saw Christ in his divinity as the principal agent of redemption and as instrumental agent in his humanity (*the sacramentum coniunctum*), who makes use of instrumental sacramental actions (*sacramenta seiuncta*) performed by human ministers according to his inten-

tion as instruments of his power. This understanding of the causal relationship between Christ and the sacramental actions is summed up in a related classical formula indicating that the effectiveness of the action comes from Christ, *ex opere operato*. The sacramental actions exercise their instrumental causality after the manner of a sign or exemplar cause, hence they must bear a natural resemblance to that which they signify. This exemplar relationship is then extended to the person of the ministering priest as a sacramental sign enacting the image of Christ. From the type of language used this imaging seems to go beyond a purely functional relationship to one with ontological roots or dimensions.

[35] *Declaration*, Sec. 5, par. 26. It might be worth pointing out here that the formula "in persona Christi" is often used with a generic reference to the exercise of priestly ministry. Whenever it is specified, it is almost invariably referring to the celebration of the eucharist, as in this text, and occasionally to the ministry of reconciliation or presiding over the Christian assembly.

[36] Vatican II, *Sacrosanctum Concilim #7* (Flannery, 4–5); Pius XII, *Mystici Corporis*, *AAS* 35 (1943) 218.

[37] A.-G. Martimort, "The Value of a Theological Formula 'In Persona Christi' ", 7, is aware of this issue in his commentary on the formula as used in the *Declaration*. I do not find his attempt to distinguish degrees of "ministering" in the place of Christ in the various sacraments that conclusive.

[38] Identification of the sacrament of marriage with the exchange of marriage vows by the marrying partners has led our tradition to identify them as the ministers of this sacrament, of which the priest is simply an official witness.

[39] For a brief survey of the issues involved see ch 4, section IV by C. Osiek in this volume; R. Gryson, *The Ministry of Women in the Early Church*, 109–110; C. Meyer, "Ordained Women in the Early Church," *Chicago Studies* 4 (1965) 298–307. Meyer notes that "to push the argument against the sacramentality of the ordination of deaconesses too far would be in fact to deny the sacramentality of the order of deacons" (301).

[40] J. Begley-C. Armbruster, "Women and Office in the Church," 151. R. Norris,

"The Ordination of Women and the 'Maleness' of Christ," 78, argues in parallel fashion that woman's baptismal share in the priestly office of Christ "creates a presumption that they are also capable of representing Christ in the role of an ordained person." See also the discussion by R. Keifer in ch 7 of this book.

[41] *Declaration*, Sec. 4, par. 18. In the title of this section and in this quotation the Latin wording primarily denotes a manner of acting (i.e., conduct or practice) rather than the inner, underlying attitude — "quae fecerunt," "modus se gerendi." These are translated by the word "attitude" in the USCC translation.

[42] Since the Council of Trent the "substance of the sacraments" has been a classical formula to designate that which is outside the power of the Church to change in the sacraments owing to their institution by Christ. Pius XII specified this further in *Sacramentum Ordinis*, *AAS* 40 (1948) 5, when he described it as "what Christ the Lord, as the sources of Revelation bear witness, determined should be maintained in the *sacramental sign*" (emphasis added). The *Declaration*, Sec. 4, par. 22, adds a further specification when it affirms that "Adaptation to civilizations and times therefore cannot abolish, on essential points, the sacramental reference to constitutive events of Christianity and to Christ himself." The "substance" is interpreted by many authors, following the lead of Pius XII, in terms of sacramental significance. Though this significance must be expressed in ritual elements of action and word, these elements are not necessarily part of that "substance" in their particular historical forms and may be subject to the Church's later determination. *Cf*. E. Schillebeeckx, *Christ the Sacrament of the Encounter with God* (New York: Sheed and Ward, 1963) 113–132, esp. 126–127 for an extended discussion of institution by Christ and the power of the Church to determine the outward shape of the sacraments.

[43] *Declaration*, Sec. 4, par. 24. D. Bonner in ch 5, sec I of this book, notes that by this passage the Sacred Congregation for the Doctrine of the Faith is preventing a custom, contrary to law, from emerging in the church.

[44] The classical work on tradition remains that of Y. Congar, *Tradition and*

Traditions. An Historical Essay and a Theological Essay (New York: Macmillan, 1966). The following briefer works are also of help: K. Rahner, "Scripture and Tradition," *Theological Investigations* VI (Baltimore: Helicon, 1969) 98–112; G. Tavard, "Scripture and Tradition," *Journal of Ecumenical Studies* 5 (1968) 308–325; K.-H. Weger, "Tradition," *Sacramentum Mundi* VI (New York: Herder and Herder, 1970) 269–274.

45 Vatican II, *Dei Verbum* #4 (Flannery, 752).

46 *Ibid*. #8 (Flannery, 754). *Cf*. K. Rahner, "Scripture and Tradition," 98–112, esp. 99–103.

47 *Cf*. Y. Congar, *Tradition and Traditions*, 338–346; G. Tavard, "Scripture and Tradition," 308–325, who describes Tradition as "the active presence of the Spirit in the Church" (319).

48 This implies an important, if not primary role of orthopraxis over orthodoxa. See also the helpful remarks of E. Schillebeeckx, *The Understanding of Faith* (New York: Seabury, 1974) 63–70 on orthopraxis as a criterion for theology.

49 Vatican II, *Ad Gentes* #22 (Flannery, 839) speaks in another context of the enculturation which must occur as the Church carries the message of the Gospel into the "great socio-cultural regions."

50 This is effectively illustrated in regard to the use of "person" in trinitarian theology by K. Rahner, *The Trinity* (New York: Herder and Herder, 1970) 103–115. *Cf*. also the Congregation for the Doctrine of the Faith, *Mysterium Ecclesiae*, ch 5, pp. 7–8, which admits the historical conditioning of the expressions of revelation and tradition.

51 For a fuller comparative discussion of the implications of this understanding of tradition for the way in which change and adaptation occur in the Church see J. O'Malley, "Reform, Historical Consciousness and Vatican II's Aggiornamento," *Theol. Studies* 32 (1971) 573–601, esp. 589ff. For an application to the theological task see K. Rahner, "The Historicity of Theology," *Theological Investigations* IX (New York: Herder and Herder, 1972) 64–82. Considering the question and re-translation and continuity in the handing on of the original message, L. Monden, *Faith: Can Man Still Believe?* (New York: Sheed

and Ward, 1970) 169, defines tradition as "the history of the encounter between the faith of the Christian community and the Christian message." One should note that this retranslation process ought not naively be envisioned as an unwrapping and re-wrapping of the internal core of revelation. Revelation is found only in historically conditioned forms of expression. Thus K. Rahner, "The Historicity of Theology," 71, writes: "This saving truth is the same within history, but while remaining the same, it has had and still has a history of its own. This 'sameness' communicates itself to us continually, but never in such a way that we could detach it adequately from its historical forms, in order thus to step out of the constant movement of the flow of history on to the bank of eternity, at least in the matter of our knowledge of truth. We possess this eternal quality of truth in history, and hence can only appropriate it by entrusting ourselves to its further course. If we refuse to take this risk, the formulations of dogma wrongly claimed to be 'perennial' will become unintelligible, like opaque glass which God's light can no longer penetrate." In this framework the Church's fidelity to the original message is much more clearly the work of the indwelling Spirit than of a literal repetition of the same formulations or expressions. Chapters 2 and 3 of this book investigated the tradition of religious leadership in biblical times and its continuous sensitivity to historical circumstances.

52 Vatican II, *Gaudium et Spes* #46 (Flannery, 948); *cf*. #47–52 (Flannery, 949–957) for the complete conciliar statement on marriage.

53 For a brief introductory statement of these sociological and structural changes see E. Schillebeeckx, *Marriage. Human Reality and Saving Mystery* (New York: Sheed and Ward, 1965) xv–xxx.

54 Vatican II, *Gaudium et Spes* #27 (Flannery, 928). A full history of the developments on slavery can be found in J. Dutilleul, "Esclavage," *Dictionnaire de Théologie Catholique* V (Paris: Letouzey, 1913), columns 457–520. H. van der Meer, *Women Priests in the Catholic Church?*, 81–86 has drawn the parallel between the cases of slavery and the exclusion of women.

55 Recall again that the first part of *Gaudium et Spes*, in which the reference to slavery occurs, develops the Church's

teaching on the dignity of the human person in response to the situation of humankind in today's world.

[56] For a full account and commentary see the following works: E.-W. Böckenförde, "Religionsfreiheit als Aufgabe der Christen," *Stimmen der Zeit* 176 (1965) 199–212; R. Coste, *Théologie de la liberté religieuse. Liberté de conscience — liberté de religion* (Gembloux: Duculot, 1969); J. Hammer-Y. Congar (ed.), *La Liberté religieuse (Unam Sanctam* 60) (Paris: du Cerf, 1967); E. McDonagh, *Freedom or Tolerance? The Declaration on Religious Freedom of Vatican Council II* (Albany: Magi Books, 1967); J. C. Murray, "The Declaration on Religious Freedom," in F. Böckle (ed.), *War, Poverty, Freedom. The Christian Response (Concilium* 15) (New York: Paulist Press, 1966) 3–16; J. C. Murray, "The Declaration on Religious Freedom," in J. Miller (ed.), *Vatican II: An Interfaith Appraisal* (Notre Dame: University of Notre Dame Press, 1966) 565–576; J. C. Murray, *The Problem of Religious Freedom (Woodstock Papers* No 7) (Westminster: Newman, 1965); J. C. Murray (ed.) *Religious Liberty: an End and a Beginning* (New York: Macmillan, 1966); H. Schlette, "Religious Freedom," *Sacramentum Mundi* V (New York: Herder and Herder, 1970) 295–298.

[57] Vatican II, *Dignitatis Humanae* #2 (Flannery, 800).

[58] E.-W. Böckenförde, "Religionsfreiheit als Aufgabe der Christen," 203. This position persisted as late as the allocution of Pius XII on tolerance, *Ci Riesce*, in 1953. See *AAS* 45 (1953) 794–802. Leo XIII had earlier recovered what seems to be the important issues behind these principles, that the sovereign freedom of God and his mastery over history must be respected and that freedom in relation to all human civil power is indispensible to the Church for it to carry out the will of its founder. See R. Coste, *Théologie de la liberté religieuse*, 336.

[59] J. Murray, "The Declaration on Religious Freedom," in J. Miller (ed.), *Vatican II*, 568.

[60] The errors proscribed include, for example, the freedom to embrace and profess that religion which the individual judges to be true (#15), that Church and state are to be separated (#55), that it is no longer fitting for the Catholic religion to be the sole religion of a state to the exclusion of other religions (#77), and that immigrants into a Catholic state be allowed to exercise their worship publicly (#78). See H. Denzinger-H. Schönmetzer, *Enchiridion Symbolorum* (Rome: Herder, 1963) nn 2901–2980 for the complete list.

[61] J. Murray, "The Declaration on Religious Freedom," in F. Böckle (ed.), *War, Poverty, Freedom*, 3–16. In regard to the first area, Leo XIII initiated the papal re-thinking of the idea of the state which was to culminate in John XXIII's *Pacem in Terris*, in which full attention has been given to the individual persons within the state, especially their freedom. See also J. Murray, *The Problem of Religious Freedom*, 47–84. In regard to the second area, it is the judgment of E. McDonagh, *Freedom or Tolerance?*, 12, that it was the work of theologians like Murray and their "insistence on the *historical nature* of previous Church-State relationships and of papal documents . . . (which) proved to be the solution to many difficulties." Emphasis added.

[62] R. Coste, *Théologie de la liberté religieuse*, 145–148.

[63] R. Coste, *ibid.*, 338–343; J. Murray, *The Problem of Religious Freedom*, 69.

[64] Vatican II, *Dignitatis Humanae* #1 (Flannery, 799): "Contemporary man is becoming increasingly conscious of the *dignity of the human person*." Emphasis added.

[65] H. Schlette, "Religious Freedom," 295–296.

[66] *Declaration*, Introduction, par. 4.

[67] Vatican II, *Ad Gentes* #22 (Flannery, 841).

Notes to Chapter Seven, pages 103–110

[1] *Declaration*, Sec. 5, par. 26.

[2] *Declaration*, Sec. 5, par. 27.

[3] *Declaration*, Sec. 5, par. 32.

[4] The origin and development of this symbol of Yahweh, spouse of Israel, was investigated by Carroll Stuhlmueller, in ch 2, sec. 3 of this book.

[5] *Declaration*, Sec. 5, par. 30.

[6] *Declaration*, Sec. 5, par. 27.

[7] *Declaration*, Sec. 5, par. 27; see also fn. 17 & 18.

[8] *Declaration*, Sec. 5, par. 26.

[9] *Agreed Statement on Eucharistic Doctrine*, 1971, frequently described as the Windsor Statement.

[10] ". . . prex scilicet gratiarum actionis et sanctificationis," *Institutio Generalis* #54.

[11] "Narratio institutionis et consecrationis," *Institutio Generalis* #54.

[12] ICEL translation. The Latin has: "Sensus autem jujus orationis est, ut tota congregatio fidelium se cum Christo conjungat in confessione magnalium Dei et in oblatione sacrificii." *Institutio Generalis* #54.

[13] *Declaration*, Sec. 5, par. 32.

[14] Literal translation.

Notes to
Chapter Eight, pages 111–120

*Bibliography

Berman, Saul J., "Status of Women in Judaism," *Tradition*, Vol. 14 No. 2, Fall 1973.
Central Conference of American Rabbis, Year Books, Vol. LXV, 1955 and LXVI, 1956.
Goitein, Shelomo Dov, "Middle Ages," *Hadassah Newsletter*, October 1973.
Greenberg, Blu and Irving, "Equality in Judaism," *Hadassah Newsletter*, December 1973.
Hyman, Paula, "Jewish Theology: What's In It For and Against Us?," *Ms.*, July 1974.
de Lattes, Rabbi Isaac b. Imanuel, *She'elot Uteshuvot* (Responsa), Friedrich Foerster Verlag, Vienna 1860.
Priesand, Sally, *Judaism and the New Woman*, Behrman: 1975.
Rainey, Anson, "Woman," *Encyclopedia Judaica*, Vol. 16, 62.
Sacks, Bracha, "Why I choose Orthodoxy," *Ms.*, July 1974.
Sigal, Philip, "Women in the Minyan," *Judaism*, Spring 1974.
Starkman, Elaine, "Women in the Pulpit," *Hadassah Newsletter*, December 1973.
Swidler, Leonard, *Women in Judaism*, Metuchen, N.J.: Scarecrow Press, 1976.

[1] Miriam interceded with the daughter of Pharaoh that the infant Moses could be returned to his mother as a nurse (Ex 2:4, 7-8). Upon the crossing of the Sea of Reeds she is called a "prophetess," leading the women in the victory refrain (Ex 15:20-21). Later she was connected in a revolt against Moses (Num 12). Along with Moses and Aaron, she was mentioned by the prophet Micah as one sent by the Lord (Mic 6:4).

[2] *Cf.*, 2 Kgs 8:18, 26–27; ch 11.

[3] *Cf.*, 1 Kgs 16:31-33; 18–19; 19:1-3; 2 Kgs 9:30-37.

[4] *Cf.*, 2 Sam 11; 12:15-25; 1 Kgs 1:5-40; 2:13-25.

[5] *Cf.*, 1 Sam 25; 27:3; 2 Sam 3:3.

[6] Leonard Swidler, *Women in Judaism* (Metuchen, NJ: Scarecrow Press, 1976) 25, 33.

[7] *Cf.*, Num 27:1-11, ch 36; Josh 17:3-6.

[8] *Babylonian Talmud*, Baba Batra, 119b (Soncino).

[9] *Babylonian Talmud*, Pesahim, 62b.

[10] Josephus, *Against Apion*, Whiston edition (Philadelphia: Lippincott, 1895) Vol. 2, 515.

[11] Earlier chapters in this book by Robert Karris and Carolyn Osiek have noted a similar decline in the status and rights of women from that in the ministry of Jesus and the early Church to that in "Early Catholicism" and the Patristic Age.

[12] *Women in Judaism*, 54.

[13] Shelomo Dov Gotein, "Middle Ages," *Hadassah Newsletter*, October 1973.

[14] Responsa, by Rabbi Isaac ben Imanuel de Lattes, Vienna 1860, 140. Italics added.

[15] *Cf.*, 1 Sam 2:12-17.

[16] "Woman in the Pulpit," *Hadassah Newsletter*, October 1973.

[17] *Ibid.*

[18] Year Book, *Central Conference of American Rabbis*, Vol. LXVI 1956, 91. See also the CCAR Year Book for 1955, 13, the Presidential Address of Rabbi Barnet Brickner which placed the issue on the agenda.

[19] *Universal Jewish Encyclopedia*, Vol. 7, 626.

[20] Philip Sigal, "Women in the Minyan," *Judaism*, Spring 1974.

[21] *Ibid.*, 182.

[22] Saul Berman, "The Status of Women in Halakhik Judaism," *Tradition*, 14, No. 2 (Fall 1973) 5ff.

[23] *Ibid.*, 10.

[24] The force of custom within Roman Catholic Canon Law is discussed in ch 5, sec 1 of this book by Dismas Bonner.

[25] *Babylonian Talmud*, Baba Kama, 79b: "You do not make a decision for the community unless the majority of the community can endure it."

[26] Chaim Tchernovitz, *Toledot Ha-Poskim* (New York: 1947) Vol. 3, 47.

[27] Efthalia Walsh, "Ever-more Women in the Pulpit," *New York Times*, Sept. 27, 1977.

Notes to
Chapter Nine, pages 123–132

[1] The Pontifical Biblical Commission concluded: "It does not seem that the New Testament by itself alone will permit us to settle in a clear way and once and for all the problem of the possible accession of women to the presbyterate." Seventeen members of this Commission voted unanimously for this statement. They voted twelve to five in favor of the statement that Scriptural grounds alone are not enough to exclude the possibility of ordaining women. *Cf. Origins* 6:6 (July 1, 1976) 92–96. Of even greater significance is the following remark: "It must be repeated that the texts of the New Testament, even on such important points as the sacraments, do not always give all the light that one would wish to find in them." *Commentary on the Declaration of the Sacred Congregation for the Doctrine of the Faith on the Question of the Admission of Women to the Ministerial Priesthood* (Washington, D.C.: United States Catholic Conference, 1977) 27.

[2] "Unless the value of unwritten traditions is admitted, it is sometimes difficult to discover in Scripture entirely explicit indications of Christ's will," *ibid*.

[3] " 'Sacramental signs', says Saint Thomas, 'represent what they signify by natural resemblance'. The same natural resemblance is required for persons as for things: when Christ's role in the Eucharist is to be expressed sacramentally, there would not be this 'natural resemblance' which must exist between Christ and his minister if the role of Christ were not taken by a man" *Declaration*, Sec. 5, par. 27.

[4] "Jesus Christ did not call any woman to become part of the Twelve," *Ibid.*, Sec. 2, par. 10.

[5] *Ibid.*, Sec. 3, par. 17. The phrase "my fellow workers," on the other hand, refers to both men and women companions of Paul. *Cf.* also the *Commentary*, 27. Robert J. Karris investigates this phrase in ch 3, sec IV of this book.

[6] *Commentary*, 21. For the meaning of this term, consult Eberlard Haible, "Loci Theologici," in K. Rahner, with C. Ernst and K. Smyth (eds.), *Sacramentum Mundi: an Encyclopedia of Theology* (New York: Herder and Herder, 1970) vol VI: 224–226. Melchior Cano (1509–1560) is often regarded as the one responsible for introducing this term into theological vocabulary, in order to compactly designate the places, in order of importance, where truth can be found. In moral theology the term "theological sources" is more common (*cf.* Noldin-Schmitt-Heinzel, *Summa Theologiae Moralis* [33], Vol I, n 10). When Noldin prioritizes seven of these sources for moral theology, the last is the procedure and practice of the church, preceded by Scripture, the Councils, Pontifical Decrees, the Code of Canon Law, the Fathers and the theologians.

[7] "This tradition which comes from the apostles develops in the Church with the help of the Holy Spirit." *Cf.* Walter M. Abbott (ed.), *The Documents of Vatican II* (New York: Guild Press, 1966) "Dei Verbum," n 8, 116.

[8] The parameters of tradition appear rather clearly in the *Commentary*, 21–24, where it seems to extend from Irenaeus to the theologians of the last century, as they are cited on page 38, fn. 36.

[9] Even the Papal social encyclicals, which have been widely praised for their attempt to confront current economic problems in our industrialized world, are undergoing criticism for their abstract

methodology and non-historical approach. *Cf.* Edward Duff, "Anniversary as Anachronism," *The Amer. Eccl. Rev.* 164 (May, 1971) 303ff. Such criticism is even more accurately levelled at the marriage encyclicals of Pope Leo XIII (*Arcanum Divinum Sapientia*) and Pius XI (*Casti Connubii*). However, Pius XII, in his 1951 Address to the Midwives, seemed to rely on relatively recent scientific information (the discoveries of Knaus in 1929 and Ogino in 1930) relative to the sterile period in the woman's ovulatory cycle, in his attempt to allow for some measure of responsible family planning on the part of Christian couples. This method came to be called rhythm.

10 *Humanae Vitae* especially has received considerable criticism for its inadequacy in dealing with scientific data pertaining to human sexuality. Many of these remarks are summarized by Richard McCormick in his "Notes on Moral Theology," *Theological Studies* 38 (March, 1977), at the following places: 102 (Kaufmann and David) and (Bleistein), 104 (Maguire), 105 (Delhaye), 107 (Auer, Korff, Lohfink). Charles Curran also, in "Sexual Ethics: Reaction and Critique," *Linacre Quarterly* 43 (August, 1976) cites similar complaints: p. 151 (Editorial in the *Brooklyn Tablet*), and 158, where he remarks: "the Congregation does not pay sufficient attention to the experiences of people and praxis . . ." For similar criticisms of *Humanae Vitae*, *cf.* C. Ryan, "Science and Moral Law," in J. P. Mackey (ed.), *Morals, Law and Authority* (Dayton: Pflaum, 1969) 79–91.

11 An indication of this is provided in the citation already quoted from the *Declaration on Sexual Ethics*, concerning the "complete harmony with the divine order of creation" (n 13).

12 According to Wis 8:1 in the Vulgate: "Attingit ergo a fine usque ad finem *fortiter* et disponit omnia *suaviter*."

13 *Cf.* the earlier, 1953, edition, at nn 65, 68 and 190.

14 Nicholas Crotty, "Conscience and Conflict," *Theological Studies* 32 (1971) 210.

15 *Ibid.*, 211–247.

16 *Cf. The Documents of Vatican II*, "Gaudium et Spes," n 44, 245–247.

17 This is implicit in the remark of the Sacred Congregation of Rites and The Commission for the Implementation of the Constitution of the Sacred Liturgy: "The purpose of this concession is in fact to enable the Christian of today to celebrate more easily the day of the resurrection of the Lord," "Instruction on the Worship of the Eucharistic Mystery," *Catholic Mind* 65 (September, 1967) n 28, 54. The way by which customs contrary to the law can become normative in the church and reverse the earlier law has been discussed in this volume by Dismas Bonner, in ch 5, sec 1.

18 *Cf.* especially his essay on "Natural Law and Contemporary Moral Theology," *Contemporary Problems in Moral Theology* (Notre Dame: Fides Press, 1970) 97–159.

19 The *Commentary* remarked earlier: "So constant has it [tradition] been that there has been no need for an intervention by a solemn decision of the Magisterium" (21), as if implying that there was an instance here of infallibility by way of the ordinary magisterium of the Church; *cf.* the implication in the question: "How are we to interpret the constant and universal practice of the Church?" (22).

20 These include especially the work of John Dewey.

21 This description is culled from many places in Dewey's writings. For instance, *Experience and Nature* (LaSalle, IL, Open Court, 1971) chapter 1: "Experience and Philosophic Method."

22 While acknowledging that "in the writings of the Fathers one will find the undeniable influence of prejudices unfavorable to women" (par. 6), the *Declaration* seeks to minimize the import of this bias by remarking: "but nevertheless, it should be noted that these prejudices had hardly any influence on their pastoral activity, and still less on their spiritual direction." If this be true, it is remarkable. In terms of the view I am here taking of experience, with an emphasis on its completeness and integrity, I would not regard this remarkable achievement of the Fathers commendable, even if it were true, since such a dichotomy in their experience of women would effectively curtail much of the interaction that lies at the root of what experience is all about. The "misogynist statements of the Church Fathers" are discussed by Carolyn Osiek in this book, ch 4; *cf.* her "conclusions."

23 Some indication of the kind of data

that is helpful in formulating reasons pertaining to the debate is provided by Andrew Greeley in an article entitled "Catholics Cling to Traditions," *Chicago Tribune*, February 22, 1977, section 3, p. 3. There he interprets data gathered by the National Opinion Research Center from 950 American Catholics, questioned on the statement: "It would be a good thing if women were to be ordained priests." He found that the results corresponded to the hypothesis that attitudes toward women were acquired very early in life from the culture and atmosphere of family experience.

[24] *Ecclesiam Suam*, August 6, 1964.

[25] This is a distinct possibility, in view of the remark: "the priestly office cannot become the goal of social advancement; no merely human progress of society or of the individual can of itself give access to it," *Declaration*, Sec. 6, par. 38.

[26] Earlier, the *Declaration* stated: "The Church's tradition in the matter has thus been so firm in the course of the centuries that the Magisterium has not felt the need to intervene in order to formulate a principle which was not attacked, or to defend a law which was not challenged," Sec. 1, par. 8. This is grist for the mill of Mary Daly, of whom Anne Patrick writes: "Daly describes her method as one of asking 'non-questions', that is, pursuing areas of inquiry that are 'invisible' to traditional methods because these areas do not fit into accepted categories of thought. This involves especially the analysis of 'nondata', the experience of women, which has largely been ignored by patriarchal systems of thought," "Women and Religion: a Survey of Significant Literature, 1965–1974," in Walter Burghardt (ed.), *Woman: New Dimensions* (New York: Paulist Press, 1977) 188.

[27] This stress on the continuity of woman's experience is needed to offset the dualism and discontinuity that is often inserted into her experience both in church and secular society, which, in turn, seems based on the deeper dualism between man and woman. Certainly, the ecclesial experience of women is not somehow made acceptable simply through being discontinuous (even if this were possible) with her secular experience. Rosemary Ruether sees the male-female dualism running indiscriminately throughout both the religious and secular experiences of woman. *Cf.*, a summary of her thought in Anne Patrick's essay above, 186.

[28] The burden of the argument here is that a conflict orientation illuminates the presence of evil in the human situation more distinctly than a harmony orientation does. Elizabeth Carroll comments on the long-range benefits accruing to the Church from its early surfacing of the Jew-Gentile problem. She relates these benefits to women with the remark: "if the narrower view had prevailed and circumcision of the foreskin of males had been made a prerequisite for baptism, women would have been denied Christian baptism." *Cf.* "Women and Ministry," in Burghardt, 95. In a more polemical tone, Elisabeth Schüssler Fiorenza succinctly underlines the advantage of a problem-orientation for theology: "theology has to abandon its so-called objectivity and has to become partisan. Only when theology is on the side of the outcast and oppressed, as was Jesus, can it become incarnational and Christian," "Feminist Theology as a Critical Theology of Liberation," in Burghardt, 40. This aspect was discussed by C. Stuhlmueller in this volume, ch 2, sec I, relating the Old Testament prophetic defense of the oppressed with the development of priesthood.

[29] *Cf.* M. Thomas Aquinas [Elizabeth] Carroll, who is convinced that "one of the prime ministries must be a healing of the man-woman situation in the church and in Society," *The Experience of Women Religious in the Ministry of the Church* (Chicago, 1974) 16. *Cf.* also Margaret Brennan, "Standing in Experience: a reflection on the Status of Woman in the Church," *Catholic Mind* 74 (May, 1976) 19–32.

[30] The current ecumenical approach to the sacrament of Orders is throwing new light on the complexity of the term "power" when applied to priesthood. *Cf.* especially the studies of Harry McSorley, "Trent and the Question: can Protestant Ministers consecrate the Eucharist?" *Lutherans and Catholics in Dialogue*, vol IV: *Eucharist and Ministry* (Washington, D.C.: USCC, 1970) 283–287, and also "The Roman Catholic Doctrine of the Competent Minister of the Eucharist in Ecumenical Perspective," *ibid.*, 124, 126, 128, 132–137.

[31] *Declaration*, Sec. 5, par. 27.

[32] The *Declaration*, Introduction, par. 2, acknowledges the service women have rendered the Church. The ecumenical context, already mentioned, lays great stress on service as constitutive of Christian ministry: "the orientation toward service, and specifically service to all mankind and not just the church, becomes a criterion of utmost importance in rethinking ministry in our day." This is a remark of Robert McAfee Brown, "Order and Ministry in the Reformed Church," *Reconsiderations: Roman Catholic/Presbyterian and Reformed Theological Conversations 1966–1967* (New York: World Horizons, Inc., 1967) 135. Daniel O'Hanlon makes the same point: "The new fact of official recognition by the Roman Catholic Church of the Protestant communities as Churches, and as means of Christian salvation, strongly suggests that there is real and effective ministry and church order in these churches," *ibid.*, 146. This takes on added significance in view of the growing role of women in Protestant ministry, as the *Declaration* itself is quick to note: "This [admission of women to pastoral office] therefore constitutes an ecumenical problem," Introduction, par. 4.

[33] O'Hanlon observes: "If order is really for service and not for power, then genuine service to the unity of the Church should be a supreme norm, a norm which may dictate the abandonment of rigid demands in all cases for an uninterrupted series of episcopal laying on of hands," *ibid.*, 152.

[34] *Cf. A.D. 1977* (Quixote Center, 1977), n 7, 6.

[35] Hans Küng makes much of this phrase in laying out a program for effective Church action: "Whenever the Church privately and publicly advocates the cause of Jesus Christ, whenever it champions his cause in word and deed, it is at the service of man and becomes credible." *Cf., On Being A Christian* (Garden City, New York: Doubleday, 1976) 524.

[36] Just how basic a problem sexism is (and whether Mary Daly is correct in calling it the basic cause of other forms of oppression) is under discussion. Anne Patrick calls for "further analysis of what is at the root of sexism, and of how sexism is related to other structures of injustice and to traditional concepts of sin." *Cf.* Burghardt, 188–189.

[37] Milton Rokeach, *The Nature of Human Values* (New York: The Free Press, 1973) 189, concludes that "two values alone, equality and freedom, underlie similarities and differences in major ideological differences." For this reason, women's experience of inequality is to be taken seriously.

[38] As O'Hanlon says: "A *diakonia* which is not flexible enough to serve the basic purposes for which it exists, namely, the unity, the *communio* of all Christians and their unified witness and service to all men, simply ceases to be truly diakonia." *Cf. Reconsiderations . . . ,* 152.

[39] The *Declaration* seems oriented in a different direction, especially in its warning: "The priestly office cannot become the goal of social advancement; no merely human progress of society or of the individual can of itself give access to it; it is of another order," Sec. 6, par. 38. I have taken a different position in this chapter, especially on the basis of the continuum of experience between the religious and secular spheres. Elisabeth Schüssler Fiorenza pleads for a truly all-inclusive, Catholic community called church, that, in line with Paul's observation in Galatians 3:28, proves capable of transcending ideological sexist forms. *Cf.*, Burghardt, 43.

Notes to
Chapter Ten, pages 133–141

[1] Sigmund Freud, *New Introductory Lectures on Psychoanalysis*, trans, James Strachey (New York: W. W. Norton & Co., 1965) esp. 124–127, and 135.

[2] Erik Erikson, "Inner and Outer Space: Reflections on Womanhood," *The Women in America*, ed. Robert Jay Lifton (Boston: Houghton Mifflin, Co., 1965) 13.

[3] For Karen Horney, *cf.* especially, *Feminine Psychology* (New York: W. W. Norton & Co., 1967), *passim.* For Margaret Mead, *cf. Male and Female: a Study of the Sexes in a Changing World* (New York: W. Morrow, 1949).

[4] As a single reference which brings together the Jungian material on the feminine

in a readable and competently critical way, I suggest the book by Ann Belford Ulanov, *The Feminine in Jungian Psychology and in Christian Theology* (Evanston: Northwestern University Press, 1971).

⁵ *Cf.*, C. G. Jung, *Psychology and Alchemy* (CW, XII, 1967) 144. See likewise the excursus in Jung, *Mysterium Conjunctionis* (CW, XIV, 1963) 89ff.

⁶ *Cf.*, C. G. Jung's essay, "Woman in Europe," in *Civilization in Transition* (CW, X, 1964) *passim*; and see also the fine chapter by Ruth Tiffany Barnhouse, M.D., "An Examination of the Ordination of Women to the Priesthood in terms of the Symbolism of the Eucharist," *Women and Orders*, ed. Robert J. Heyer (New York: Paulist Press, 1974) 26–29.

⁷ June Singer, "The Age of Androgony," in *Quadrant*, 8 (No. 2; Winter 1975) 80.

⁸ June Singer, *Androgony* (New York: Anchor Press/Doubleday, 1976) preface, viii.

⁹ Carolyn G. Heilbrun, *Towards Androgony: Aspects of Male and Female in Literature* (London: Victor Gollancz, 1973) *passim*.

¹⁰ Treatment of this important issue is not within the scope of this chapter but the issue is addressed at length by Gilbert Ostdiek in ch 6 of this book.

¹¹ *Cf.*, Section 5, par. 25–33.

¹² *Cf.*, the study by Mary Douglas, *Natural Symbols* (New York: Division Books, 1970) *passim*.

¹³ *Cf.*, Mary Douglas, *op. cit.*, preface; and see also chapter 10. Likewise, A. N. Whitehead, *Symbolism* (New York: Macmillan Co., Capricorn Books, 1959) chapters 1, 5 and 10. Also, Louis Dupre, *The Other Dimension* (New York: Doubleday & Co., 1972) ch 4. In ch 2, sec III of this book Carroll Stuhlmueller pointed out how a single Old Testament symbol could contain clashing components and how dramatic developments took place in the long history of a single period.

¹⁴ C. G. Jung, *Psychology and Alchemy* (CW, XII, 1967) Par 12. And, for a fuller study of Jung's meaning, *cf.* Charles B. Hanna, *The Face of the Deep* (Philadelphia: Westminster Press, 1967) esp. chapters 2 and 5.

¹⁵ *Declaration*, Sec. 5, par. 27–32.

¹⁶ *Cf.*, *The Christian Century* (March 16, 1977) 256–258.

¹⁷ See the *Declaration*'s introductory statement, par. 1–5.

¹⁸ *Declaration*, Sec. 6, par. 36–38.

¹⁹ Ann Belford Ulanov, *op. cit.*, 109.

²⁰ Quoted from an unpublished presentation given by Rev. Nathan Mitchell, O.S.B., Assistant Professor of Theology in the St. Meinrad School of Theology, at the 5th Annual Presbyteral Meeting sponsored by the Presbyteral Senate of the Archdiocese of Chicago, Dec. 1, 1976.

²¹ Quoted in Ann Belford Ulanov, *op. cit.*, 137.

Notes to
Chapter Eleven, pages 143–155

¹ Address to the Religious Newswriters Association in Chicago, May 17, 1977.

² The American Institute of Public Opinion in an August 7, 1977, release shows that the proportion who agree that it would be a good thing if women were allowed to be ordained as priests has grown from 29 percent in 1974 to 36 percent.

³ While I am in agreement with the *Declaration* that the ordination of women should be consistent with our tradition, the argumentation and conclusion of the *Declaration* need to be refined and corrected. The theological aspects of tradition have been handled in ch 6 of this volume by Gilbert Ostdiek.

⁴ Private correspondence.

⁵ Names and minor details have been changed to protect the identity of these women.

⁶ From another perspective I have heard highly educated sisters with a theological background talk about ordination for themselves. They seemed to be responding to an injustice rather than to a call to ministry from a local community. This would be supporting the present model for male seminaries who are presently being "called" by the seminary faulty or religious order rather than by the local community. The politics of the ordination of women

needs to be addressed. It seems to this writer that some of the enthusiasm for the ordination of women is a way of focusing the larger issue of women's rights. Therefore, in particular cases, the woman asking for ordination may be asking for openness to ordination for all women rather than expressing her unique call to ministry flowing from both religious experience and affirmation in ministry. Likewise much of the opposition to the ordination of women stems from both men and women who are opposed to the general thrust to equality of sexes and therefore is emotional rather than theological.

[7] *the Catholic Connection*, Vol 2, No 1, 1.

APPENDICES

CHURCH DOCUMENTATION

APPENDIX: I

SACRED CONGREGATION FOR
THE DOCTRINE OF THE FAITH

DECLARATION
ON THE QUESTION OF THE ADMISSION OF WOMEN
TO THE MINISTERIAL PRIESTHOOD

Introduction

The Role of Women in Modern Society and the Church

1. Among the characteristics that mark our present age, Pope John XXIII indicated, in his Encyclical *Pacem in Terris* of April 11, 1963, "the part that women are now taking in public life. . . . This is a development that is perhaps of swifter growth among Christian nations that are heirs to different traditions and imbued with a different culture."[1] Along the same lines, the Second Vatican Council, enumerating in its Pastoral Constitution *Gaudium et Spes* the forms of discrimination touching upon the basic rights of the person which must be overcome and eliminated as being contrary to God's plan, gives first place to discrimination based upon sex.[2] The resulting equality will secure the building up of a world that is not levelled out and uniform but harmonious and unified, if men and women contribute to it their own resources and dynamism, as Pope Paul VI recently stated.[3]

2. In the life of the Church herself, as history shows us, women have played a decisive role and accomplished tasks of outstanding value. One has only to think of the foundresses of the great religious families, such as

212

Saint Claire and Saint Teresa of Avila. The latter, moreover, and Saint Catherine of Siena, have left writings so rich in spiritual doctrine that Pope Paul VI has included them among the Doctors of the Church. Nor could one forget the great number of women who have consecrated themselves to the Lord for the exercise of charity or for the missions, and the Christian wives who have had a profound influence on their families, particularly for the passing on of the faith to their children.

3.   But our age gives rise to increased demands. "Since in our time women have an ever more active share in the whole life of society, it is very important that they participate more widely also in the various sectors of the Church's apostolate." [4] This charge of the Second Vatican Council has already set in motion the whole process of change now taking place: these various experiences of course need to come to maturity. But as Pope Paul VI also remarked,[5] a very large number of Christian communities are already benefitting from the apostolic commitment of women. Some of these women are called to take part in councils set up for pastoral reflection, at the diocesan or parish level; and the Apostolic See has brought women into some of its working bodies.

4.   For some years now various Christian communities stemming from the sixteenth-century Reformation or of later origin have been admitting women to the pastoral office on a par with men. This initiative has led to petitions and writings by members of these communities and similar groups, directed towards making this admission a general thing; it has also led to contrary reactions. This therefore constitutes an ecumenical problem, and the Catholic Church must make her thinking known on it, all the more because in various sectors of opinion the question has been asked whether she too could not modify her discipline and admit women to priestly ordination. A number of Catholic theologians have even posed this question publicly, evoking studies not only in the sphere of exegesis, patrology and Church history but also in the field of the history of institutions and customs, of sociology and of psychology. The various arguments capable of clarifying this important problem have been submitted to a critical examination. As we are dealing with a debate which classical theology scarcely touched upon, the current argumentation runs the risk of neglecting essential elements.

5.   For these reasons, in execution of a mandate received from the Holy Father and echoing the declaration which he himself made in his letter of November 30, 1976,[6] the Sacred Congregation for the Doctrine of the Faith judges it necessary to recall that the Church, in fidelity to the example of the Lord, does not consider herself authorized to admit women to priestly ordination. The Sacred Congregation deems it opportune at the present juncture to explain this position of the Church. It is a position which will perhaps cause pain but whose positive value will become

apparent in the long run, since it can be of help in deepening understanding of the respective roles of men and of women.

1
THE CHURCH'S CONSTANT TRADITION

6.   The Catholic Church has never felt that priestly or episcopal ordination can be validly conferred on women. A few heretical sects in the first centuries, especially Gnostic ones, entrusted the exercise of the priestly ministry to women: this innovation was immediately noted and condemned by the Fathers, who considered it as unacceptable in the Church.[7] It is true that in the writings of the Fathers one will find the undeniable influence of prejudices unfavorable to women, but nevertheless, it should be noted that these prejudices had hardly any influence on their pastoral activity, and still less on their spiritual direction. But over and above considerations inspired by the spirit of the times, one finds expressed — especially in the canonical documents of the Antiochian and Egyptian traditions — this essential reason, namely, that by calling only men to the priestly Order and ministry in its true sense, the Church intends to remain faithful to the type of ordained ministry willed by the Lord Jesus Christ and carefully maintained by the Apostles.[8]

7.   The same conviction animates medieval theology,[9] even if the Scholastic doctors, in their desire to clarify by reason the data of faith, often present arguments on this point that modern thought would have difficulty in admitting or would even rightly reject. Since that period and up to our own time, it can be said that the question has not been raised again, for the practice has enjoyed peaceful and universal acceptance.

8.   The Church's tradition in the matter has thus been so firm in the course of the centuries that the Magisterium has not felt the need to intervene in order to formulate a principle which was not atatcked, or to defend a law which was not challenged. But each time that this tradition had the occasion to manifest itself, it witnessed to the Church's desire to conform to the model left to her by the Lord.

9.   The same tradition has been faithfully safeguarded by the Churches of the East. Their unanimity on this point is all the more remarkable since in many other questions their discipline admits of a great diversity. At the present time these same Churches refuse to associate themselves with requests directed towards securing the accession of women to priestly ordination.

2
THE ATTITUDE OF CHRIST

10.   Jesus Christ did not call any woman to become part of the Twelve. If he acted in this way, it was not in order to conform to the customs of his

time, for his attitude towards women was quite different from that of his milieu, and he deliberately and courageously broke with it.

11.   For example, to the great astonishment of his own disciples Jesus converses publicly with the Samaritan woman (cf. Jn 4:27); he takes no notice of the state of legal impurity of the woman who had suffered from haemorrhages (cf. Mt 9:20-22), he allows a sinful woman to approach him in the house of Simon the Pharisee (cf. Lk 7:37 ff.); and by pardoning the woman taken in adultery, he means to show that one must not be more severe towards the fault of a woman than towards that of a man (cf. Jn 8:11). He does not hesitate to depart from the Mosaic Law in order to affirm the equality of the rights and duties of men and women with regard to the marriage bond (cf. Mk 10:2-11; Mt 19:3-9)

12.   In his itinerant ministry Jesus was accompanied not only by the Twelve but also by a group of women: "Mary, surnamed the Magdalene, from whom seven demons had gone out, Joanna the wife of Herod's steward Chuza, Susanna, and several others who provided for them out of their own resources" (Lk 8:2-3). Contrary to the Jewish mentality, which did not accord great value to the testimony of women, as Jewish law attests, it was nevertheless women who were the first to have the privilege of seeing the risen Lord, and it was they who were charged by Jesus to take the first paschal message to the Apostles themselves (cf. Mt 28:7-10; Lk 24:9-10; Jn 20:11-18), in order to prepare the latter to become the official witnesses to the Resurrection.

13.   It is true that these facts do not make the matter immediately obvious. This is no surprise, for the questions that the Word of God brings before us go beyond the obvious. In order to reach the ultimate meaning of the mission of Jesus and the ultimate meaning of Scripture, a purely historical exegesis of the texts cannot suffice. But it must be recognized that we have here a number of convergent indications that make all the more remarkable the fact that Jesus did not entrust the apostolic charge[10] to women. Even his Mother, who was so closely associated with the mystery of her Son, and whose incomparable role is emphasized by the Gospels of Luke and John, was not invested with the apostolic ministry. This fact was to lead the Fathers to present her as the example of Christ's will in this domain; as Pope Innocent III repeated later, at the beginning of the thirteenth century, "Although the Blessed Virgin Mary surpassed in dignity and in excellence all the Apostles, nevertheless it was not to her but to them that the Lord entrusted the keys of the Kingdom of Heaven."[11]

3
THE PRACTICE OF THE APOSTLES

14.   The apostolic community remained faithful to the attitude of Jesus towards women. Although Mary occupied a privileged place in the little

circle of those gathered in the Upper Room after the Lord's Ascension (cf. Acts 1:14), it was not she who was called to enter the College of the Twelve at the time of the election that resulted in the choice of Matthias: those who were put forward were two disciples whom the Gospels do not even mention.

15.   On the day of Pentecost, the Holy Spirit filled them all, men and women (cf. Acts 2:1; 1:14), yet the proclamation of the fulfillment of the prophecies in Jesus was made only by "Peter and the Eleven" (Acts 2:14).

16.   When they and Paul went beyond the confines of the Jewish world, the preaching of the Gospel and the Christian life in the Greco-Roman civilization impelled them to break with Mosaic practices, sometimes regretfully. They could therefore have envisaged conferring ordination on women, if they had not been convinced of their duty of fidelity to the Lord on this point. In the Hellenistic world, the cult of a number of pagan divinities was entrustsed to priestesses. In fact the Greeks did not share the ideas of the Jews: although their philosophers taught the inferiority of women, historians nevertheless emphasize the existence of a certain movement for the advancement of women during the Imperial period. In fact we know from the book of the Acts and from the Letters of Saint Paul that certain women worked with the Apostle for the Gospel (cf. Rom 16:3-12; Phil 4:3). Saint Paul lists their names with gratitude in the final salutations of the Letters. Some of them often exercised an important influence on conversions: Priscilla, Lydia and others; especially Priscilla, who took it on herself to complete the instruction of Apollos (cf. Acts 18:26); Phoebe, in the service of the Church of Cenchreae (cf. Rom 16:1). All these facts manifest within the Apostolic Church a considerable evolution vis-a-vis the customs of Judaism. Nevertheless at no time was there a question of conferring ordination on these women.

17.   In the Pauline Letters, exegetes of authority have noted a difference between two formulas used by the Apostle: he writes indiscriminately "my fellow workers" (Rom 16:3; Phil 4:2-3) when referring to men and women helping him in his apostolate in one way or another; but he reserves the title "God's fellow workers" (1 Cor 3:9; cf. 1 Thess 3:1) to Apollos, Timothy and himself, thus designated because they are directly set apart for the apostolic ministry and the preaching of the Word of God. In spite of the so important role played by women on the day of the Resurrection, their collaboration was not extended by Saint Paul to the official and public proclamation of the message, since this proclamation belongs exclusively to the apostolic mission.

4

PERMANENT VALUE OF THE ATTITUDE OF JESUS
AND THE APOSTLES

18.   Could the Church today depart from this attitude of Jesus and the Apostles, which has been considered as normative by the whole of tradition up to our own day? Various arguments have been put forward in favor of a positive reply to this question, and these must now be examined.

19.   It has been claimed in particular that the attitude of Jesus and the Apostles is explained by the influence of their milieu and their times. It is said that, if Jesus did not entrust to women and not even to his Mother a ministry assimilating them to the Twelve, this was because historical circumstances did not permit him to do so. No one however has ever proved — and it is clearly impossible to prove — that this attitude is inspired only by social and cultural reasons. As we have seen, an examination of the Gospels shows on the contrary that Jesus broke with the prejudices of his time, by widely contravening the discriminations practiced with regard to women. One therefore cannot maintain that, by not calling women to enter the group of Apostles, Jesus was simply letting himself be guided by reasons of expediency. For all the more reason, social and cultural conditioning did not hold back the Apostles working in the Greek milieu, where the same forms of discrimination did not exist.

20.   Another objection is based upon the transitory character that one claims to see today in some of the prescriptions of Saint Paul concerning women, and upon the difficulties that some aspects of his teaching raise in this regard. But it must be noted that these ordinances, probably inspired by the customs of the period, concern scarcely more than disciplinary practices of minor importance, such as the obligation imposed upon women to wear a veil on the head (1 Cor 11:2-16); such requirements no longer have a normative value. However, the Apostle's forbidding of women "to speak" in the assemblies (cf. 1 Cor 14:34-35; 1 Tim 2:12) is of a different nature, and exegetes define its meaning in this way: Paul in no way opposes the right, which he elsewhere recognizes as possessed by women, to prophesy in the assembly (cf. 1 Cor 11:5); the prohibition solely concerns the official function of teaching in the Christian assembly. For Saint Paul this prescription is bound up with the divine plan of creation (cf. 1 Cor 11:7; Gen 2:18-24): it would be difficult to see in it the expression of a cultural fact. Nor should it be forgotten that we owe to Saint Paul one of the most vigorous texts in the New Testament on the fundamental equality of men and women, as children of God in Christ (cf. Gal 3:28). Therefore there is no reason for accusing him of prejudices against women, when we note the trust that he shows towards them and the collaboration that he asks of them in his apostolate.

21.   But over and above these objections taken from the history of apostolic times, those who support the legitimacy of change in the matter turn to the Church's practice in her sacramental discipline. It has been noted, in our day especially, to what extent the Church is conscious of possessing a certain power over the sacraments, even though they were instituted by Christ. She has used this power down through the centuries in order to determine their signs and the conditions of their administration: recent decisions of Popes Pius XII and Paul VI are proof of this.[12] However, it must be emphasized that this power, which is a real one, has definite limits. As Pope Pius XII recalled: "The Church has no power over the substance of the sacraments, that is to say, over what Christ the Lord, as the sources of Revelation bear witness, determined should be maintained in the sacramental sign."[13] This was already the teaching of the Council of Trent, which declared: "In the Church there has always existed this power, that in the administration of the sacraments, provided that their substance remains unaltered, she can lay down or modify what she considers more fitting either for the benefit of those who receive them or for respect towards those same sacraments, according to varying circumstances, times or places."[14]

22.   Moreover, it must not be forgotten that the sacramental signs are not conventional ones. Not only is it true that, in many respects, they are natural signs because they respond to the deep symbolism of actions and things, but they are more than this: they are principally meant to link the person of every period to the supreme Event of the history of salvation, in order to enable that person to understand, through all the Bible's wealth of pedagogy and symbolism, what grace they signify and produce. For example, the sacrament of the Eucharist is not only a fraternal meal, but at the same time the memorial which makes present and actual Christ's sacrifice and his offering by the Church. Again, the priestly ministry is not just a pastoral service; it ensures the continuity of the functions entrusted by Christ to the Apostles and the continuity of the powers related to those functions. Adaptation to civilizations and times therefore cannot abolish, on essential points, the sacramental reference to constitutive events of Christianity and to Christ himself.

23.   In the final analysis it is the Church, through the voice of her Magisterium, that in these various domains, decides what can change and what must remain immutable. When she judges that she cannot accept certain changes, it is because she knows that she is bound by Christ's manner of acting. Her attitude, despite appearances, is therefore not one of archaism but of fidelity: it can be truly understood only in this light. The Church makes pronouncements in virtue of the Lord's promise and the presence of the Holy Spirit, in order to proclaim better the mystery of Christ and to safeguard and manifest the whole of its rich content.

24.   This practice of the Church therefore has a normative character: in the fact of conferring priestly ordination only on men, it is a question of an unbroken tradition throughout the history of the Church, universal in the East and in the West, and alert to repress abuses immediately. This norm, based on Christ's example, has been and is still observed because it is considered to conform to God's plan for his Church.

5

THE MINISTERIAL PRIESTHOOD
IN THE LIGHT OF THE MYSTERY OF CHRIST

25.   Having recalled the Church's norm and the basis thereof, it seems useful and opportune to illustrate this norm by showing the profound fittingness that theological reflection discovers between the proper nature of the sacrament of Order, with its specific reference to the mystery of Christ, and the fact that only men have been called to receive priestly ordination. It is not a question here of bringing forward a demonstrative argument, but of clarifying this teaching by the analogy of faith.

26.   The Church's constant teaching, repeated and clarified by the Second Vatican Council and again recalled by the 1971 Synod of Bishops and by the Sacred Congregation for the Doctrine of the Faith in its Declaration of June 24, 1973, declares that the bishop or the priest, in the exercise of his ministry, does not act in his own name, in persona propria: he represents Christ, who acts through him: "the priest truly acts in the place of Christ," as Saint Cyprian already wrote in the third century.[15] It is this ability to represent Christ that Saint Paul considered as characteristic of his apostolic function (cf. 2 Cor 5:20; Gal 4:14). The supreme expression of this representation is found in the altogether special form it assumes in the celebration of the Eucharist, which is the source and center of the Church's unity, the sacrificial meal in which the People of God are associated in the sacrifice of Christ: the priest, who alone has the power to perform it, then acts not only through the effective power conferred on him by Christ, but in *persona Christi*,[16] taking the role of Christ, to the point of being his very image, when he pronounces the words of consecration.[17]

27.   The Christian priesthood is therefore of a sacramental nature: the priest is a sign, the supernatural effectiveness of which comes from the ordination received, but a sign that must be perceptible[18] and which the faithful must be able to recognize with ease. The whole sacramental economy is in fact based upon natural signs, on symbols imprinted upon the human psychology: "Sacramental signs," says Saint Thomas, "represent what they signify by natural resemblance."[19] The same natural resemblance is required for persons as for things: when Christ's role in

the Eucharist is to be expressed sacramentally, there would not be this "natural resemblance" which must exist between Christ and his minister if the role of Christ were not taken by a man: in such a case it would be difficult to see in the minister the image of Christ. For Christ himself was and remains a man.

28. Christ is of course the firstborn of all humanity, of women as well as men: the unity which he re-established after sins is such that there are no more distinctions between Jew and Greek, slave and free, male and female, but all are one in Christ Jesus (cf. Gal 3:28). Nevertheless, the Incarnation of the Word took place according to the male sex: this is indeed a question of fact, and this fact, while not implying an alleged natural superiority of man over woman, cannot be disassociated from the economy of salvation: it is, indeed, in harmony with the entirety of God's plan as God himself has revealed it, and of which the mystery of the Covenant is the nucleus.

29. For the salvation offered by God to men and women, the union with him to which they are called — in short, the Covenant — took on, from the Old Testament Prophets onwards, the privileged form of a nuptial mystery: for God the Chosen People is seen as his ardently loved spouse. Both Jewish and Christian tradition has discovered the depth of this intimacy of love by reading and rereading the Song of Songs; the divine Bridegroom will remain faithful even when the Bride betrays his love, when Israel is unfaithful to God (cf. Hos 1–3; Jer 2). When the "fullness of time" (Gal 4:4) comes, the Word, the Son of God, takes on flesh in order to establish and seal the new and eternal Covenant in his blood, which will be shed for many so that sins may be forgiven. His death will gather together again the scattered children of God; from his pierced side will be born the Church, as Eve was born from Adam's side. At that time there is fully and eternally accomplished the nuptial mystery proclaimed and hymned in the Old Testament: Christ is the Bridegroom; the Church is his Bride, whom he loves because he has gained her by his blood and made her glorious, holy and without blemish, and henceforth he is inseparable from her. This nuptial theme, which is developed from the Letters of Saint Paul onwards (cf. 2 Cor 11:2; Eph 5:22-23) to the writings of Saint John (cf. especially in Jn 3:29; Rev 19:7, 9) is present also in the Synoptic Gospels: the Bridegroom's friends must not fast as long as he is with them (cf. Mk 2:19); the Kingdom of Heaven is like a king who gave a feast for his son's wedding (cf. Mt 22:1-14). It is through this Scriptural language, all interwoven with symbols, and which expresses and affects man and woman in their profound identity, that there is revealed to us the mystery of God and Christ, a mystery which of itself is unfathomable.

30. That is why we can never ignore the fact that Christ is a man. And therefore, unless one is to disregard the importance of this symbolism for the economy of Revelation, it must be admitted that, in actions which demand the character of ordination and in which Christ himself, the author of the Covenant, the Bridegroom and Head of the Church, is represented, exercising his ministry of salvation — which is in the highest degree the case of the Eucharist — his role (this is the original sense of the word persona) must be taken by a man. This does not stem from any personal superiority of the latter in the order of values, but only from a difference of fact on the level of functions and service.

31. Could one say that, since Christ is now in the heavenly condition, from now on it is a matter of indifference whether he be represented by a man or by a woman, since "at the resurrection men and women do not marry" (Mt 22:30)? But this text does not mean that the distinction between man and woman, insofar as it determines the identity proper to the person, is suppressed in the glorified state; what holds for us holds also for Christ. It is indeed evident that in human beings the difference of sex exercises an important influence, much deeper than, for example, ethnic differences: the latter do not affect the human person as intimately as the difference of sex, which is directly ordained both for the communion of persons and for the generation of human beings. In Biblical Revelation this difference is the effect of God's will from the beginning: "male and female he created them" (Gen 1:27).

32. However, it will perhaps be further objected that the priest, especially when he presides at the liturgical and sacramental functions, equally represents the Church: he acts in her name with "the intention of doing what she does." In this sense the theologians of the Middle Ages said that the minister also acts *in persona Ecclesiae*, that is to say, in the name of the whole Church and in order to represent her. And in fact, leaving aside the question of the participation of the faithful in a liturgical action, it is indeed in the name of the whole Church that the action is celebrated by the priest: he prays in the name of all, and in the Mass he offers the sacrifice of the whole Church. In the new Passover, the Church, under visible signs, immolates Christ through the ministry of the priest.[20] And so, it is asserted, since the priest also represents the Church, would it not be possible to think that this representation could be carried out by a woman, according to the symbolism already explained? It is true that the priest represents the Church, which is the Body of Christ. But if he does so, it is precisely because he first represents Christ himself, who is the Head and Shepherd of the Church. The Second Vatican Council[21] used this phrase to make more precise and to complete the expression *in persona Christi*. It is in this quality that the

priest presides over the Christian assembly and celebrates the Eucharistic sacrifice "in which the whole Church offers and is herself wholly offered." [22]

33.   If one does justice to these reflections, one will better understand how well-founded is the basis of the Church's practice; and one will conclude that the controversies raised in our days over the ordination of women are for all Christians a pressing invitation to meditate on the mystery of the Church, to study in greater detail the meaning of the episcopate and the priesthood, and to rediscover the real and pre-eminent place of the priest in the community of the baptized, of which he indeed forms part but from which he is distinguished because, in the actions that call for the character of ordination, for the community he is — with all the effectiveness proper to the sacraments — the image and symbol of Christ himself who calls, forgives, and accomplishes the sacrifice of the Covenant.

6

THE MINISTERIAL PRIESTHOOD ILLUSTRATED BY
THE MYSTERY OF THE CHURCH

34.   It is opportune to recall that problems of sacramental theology, especially when they concern the ministerial priesthood, as is the case here, cannot be solved except in the light of Revelation. The human sciences, however valuable their contribution in their own domain, cannot suffice here, for they cannot grasp the realities of faith: the properly supernatural content of these realities is beyond their competence.

35.   Thus one must note the extent to which the Church is a society different from other societies, original in her nature and in her structures. The pastoral charge in the Church is normally linked to the sacrament of Order: it is not a simple government, comparable to the modes of authority found in States. It is not granted by people's spontaneous choice: even when it involves designation through election, it is the laying on of hands and the prayer of the successors of the Apostles which guarantee God's choice: and it is the Holy Spirit, given by ordination, who grants participation in the ruling power of the Supreme Pastor, Christ (cf. Acts 20:28). It is a charge of service and love: "If you love me, feed my sheep" (cf. Jn 21:15-17).

36.   For this reason one cannot see how it is possible to propose the admission of women to the priesthood in virtue of the equality of rights of the human person, an equality which holds good also for Christians. To this end use is sometimes made of the text quoted above, from the Letter to the Galatians (3:28), which says that in Christ there is no longer any distinction between men and women. But this passage does not con-

cern ministries: it only affirms the universal calling to divine filiation, which is the same for all. Moreover, and above all, to consider the ministerial priesthood as a human right would be to misjudge its nature completely: baptism does not confer any personal title to public ministry in the Church. The priesthood is not conferred for the honor or advantage of the recipient, but for the service of God and the Church; it is the object of a specific and totally gratuitous vocation: "You did not choose me, no, I chose you; and I commissioned you . . ." (Jn 15:16; cf. Heb 5:4).

37.   It is sometimes said and written in books and periodicals that some women feel that they have a vocation to the priesthood. Such an attraction, however noble and understandable, still does not suffice for a genuine vocation. In fact a vocation cannot be reduced to a mere personal attraction, which can remain purely subjective. Since the priesthood is a particular ministry of which the Church has received the charge and the control, authentication by the Church is indispensable here and is a constitutive part of the vocation: Christ chose "those he wanted" (Mk 3:13). On the other hand, there is a universal vocation of all the baptized to the exercise of the royal priesthood by offering their lives to God and by giving witness for his praise.

38.   Women who express a desire for the ministerial priesthood are doubtless motivated by the desire to serve Christ and the Church. And it is not surprising that, at a time when they are becoming more aware of the discriminations to which they have been subject, they should desire the ministerial priesthood itself. But it must not be forgotten that the priesthood does not form part of the rights of the individual, but stems from the economy of the mystery of Christ and the Church. The priestly office cannot become the goal of social advancement; no merely human progress of society or of the individual can of itself give access to it: it is of another order.

39.   It therefore remains for us to meditate more deeply on the nature of the real equality of the baptized which is one of the great affirmations of Christianity: equality is in no way identity, for the Church is a differentiated body, in which each individual has his or her role. The roles are distinct, and must not be confused; they do not favor the superiority of some vis-á-vis the others, nor do they provide an excuse for jealousy; the only better gift, which can and must be desired, is love (cf. 1 Cor 12:13). The greatest in the Kingdom of Heaven are not the ministers but the saints.

40.   The Church desires that Christian women should become fully aware of the greatness of their mission: today their role is of capital importance, both for the renewal and humanization of society and for the rediscovery by believers of the true face of the Church.

41.   *His Holiness Pope Paul VI, during the audience granted to the undersigned Prefect of the Sacred Congregation on October 15, 1976 approved this Declaration, confirmed it and ordered its publication.*

Given in Rome, at the Sacred Congregation for the Doctrine of the Faith, on October 15, 1976, the feast of Saint Teresa of Avila.

FRANJO CARDINAL SEPER
Prefect
✝Fr. Jerome Hamer, O.P.
Titular Archbishop of Lorium
Secretary

NOTES

[1] *Acta Apostolicae Sedis* 55 (1963) pp. 267–268.

[2] Cf. Second Vatican Council, Pastoral Constitution *Gaudium et Spes*, 29 (December 7, 1965): *AAS* 58 (1966) pp. 1048–1049.

[3] Cf. Pope Paul VI, Address to the members of the Study Commission on the Role of Women in Society and in the Church and to the members of the Committee for International Women's Year, April 18, 1975: *AAS* 67 (1975) p. 265.

[4] Second Vatican Council, Decree *Apostolicam Actuositatem*, 9 (November 18, 1965): *AAS* 58 (1966) p. 846.

[5] Cf. Pope Paul VI, Address to the members of the Study Commission on the Role of Women in Society and in the Church and to the members of the Committee for International Women's Year, April 18, 1975: *AAS* 67 (1975) p. 266.

[6] Cf. *AAS* 68 (1976) pp. 599–600; cf. *ibid.*, pp. 600–601.

[7] Saint Irenaeus, *Adversus Haereses*, 1, 13, 2: PG 7, 580–581; ed. Harvey, 1, 114–122; Tertullian, *De Praescrip. Haeretic.* 41, 5: CCL 1, p. 221; Firmilian of Caesarea, in Saint Cyprian, *Epist.*, 75: CSEL 3, pp. 817–818; Origen, *Fragmentum* in 1 Cor. 74, in *Journal of Theological Studies* 10 (1909), pp. 41–42; Saint Epiphanius, *Panarion* 49, 2–3; 78, 23; 79, 2–4: vol. 2, GCS 31, pp. 243–244; vol. 3, GCS 37, pp. 473, 477–479.

[8] *Didascalia Apostolorum*, ch. 15, ed. R.H. Connolly, pp. 133 and 142; *Constitutiones Apostolicae*, bk. 3, ch. 6, nos. 1–2; ch. 9, nos. 3–4; ed F.H. Funk, pp. 191, 201; Saint John Chrysostom, *De Sacerdotio* 2, 2: PG 48, 633.

[9] Saint Bonaventure, *In IV Sent.*, Dist. 25, art, 2, ql, ed. Quaracchi, vol. 4, p. 649; Richard of Middleton, *In IV Sent.*, Dist. 25, art. 4, n. 1, ed. Venice, 1499, f 177ʳ; John Duns Scotus, *In IV Sent.*, Dist. 25: Opus Oxoniense, ed. Vives, vol. 19, p. 140; *Reportata Parisiensia*, vol. 24, pp. 369–371; Durandus of Saint-Pourcain, *In IV Sent.*, Dist. 25, q. 2, ed. Venice, 1571, f 364ᵛ.

[10] Some have also wished to explain this fact by a symbolic intention of Jesus: the Twelve were to represent the ancestors of the twelve tribes of Israel (cf. Mt 19–28; Lk 22:30). But in these texts it is only a question of their participation in the eschatological judgment. The essential meaning of the choice of the Twelve should rather be sought in the totality of their mission (cf. Mk 3:14): they are to represent Jesus to the people and carry on his work.

[11] Pope Innocent III, *Epist.* (December 11, 1210) to the Bishops of Palencia and Burgos, included in *Corpus Juris, Decret.* Lib 5, tit. 38, *De Paenit*, ch. 10 Nova: ed. A. Friedberg, vol. 2, col. 886–887; cf. *Glossa in Decretal.* Lib. 1, tit. 33, ch. 12 *Dilecta*, v *Iurisdictioni*. Cf. Saint Thomas, *Summa Theologiae*, III, q. 27, a. 5 and 3; Pseudo-Albert the Great, *Mariale*, quaest. 42, ed. Borgnet 37, 81.

[12] Pope Pius XII, Apostolic Constitution *Sacramentum Ordinis*, November 30, 1947: *AAS* 40 (1948) pp. 5–7; Pope Paul VI, Apostolic Constitution *Divinae Consortium Naturae*, August 15, 1971: *AAS* 63 (1971) pp. 657–664; Apostolic Constitution *Sacram Unctionem*, November 30, 1972: *AAS* 65 (1973) pp. 5–9.

[13] Pope Pius XII, Apostolic Constitution *Sacramentum Ordinis: loc. cit.*, p. 5

[14] Session 21, chap. 2: Denzinger-Schonmetzer, *Enchiridion Symbolorum*, 1728.

[15] Saint Cyprian, *Epist*, 63, 14: PL 4, 397 B; ed. Hartel, vol. 3, p. 713.

[16] Second Vatican Council, Constitution *Sacrosanctum Concilium* 33 (December 4, 1963): ". . . by the priest who presides over the assembly in the person of Christ . . ."; Dogmatic Constitution *Lumen Gentium*, 10 (November 21, 1964): "The ministerial priest; by the sacred power he enjoys, molds and rules the priestly people. Acting in the person of Christ, he brings about the Eucharistic Sacrifice, and offers it to God in the name of all the people . . ."; 28. "By the powers of the sacrament of Order, and in the image of Christ the eternal High Priest . . . they exercise this sacred function of Christ above all in the Eucharistic liturgy or synaxis. There, acting in the person of Christ . . ."; Decree *Presbyterorum Ordinis*, 2 (December 7, 1965): ". . . priests, by the anointing of the Holy Spirit, are marked with a special character and are so configured to Christ the priest that they can act in the person of Christ the Head"; 13: "As ministers of sacred realities, especially in the Sacrifice of the Mass, priests represent the person of Christ in a special way": cf. 1971 Synod of Bishops, *De Sacerdotio Ministeriali* 1, 4; Sacred Congregation for the Doctrine of the Faith, *Declaratio circa catholicam doctrinam de Ecclesia*, 6 (June 24, 1973).

[17] Saint Thomas, *Summa Theologiae*, III, q. 83, art. 1, ad 3: "It is to be said that [just as the celebration of this sacrament is the representative image of Christ's Cross: *ibid.* ad 2], for the same reason the priest also enacts the image of Christ, in whose person and by whose power he pronounces the words of consecration."

[18] "For since a sacrament is a sign, there is required in the things that are done in the sacraments not only the '*res*' but the signification of the '*res*'", recalls Saint Thomas, precisely in order to reject the ordination of women: *In IV Sent.*, dist. 25, q. 2, art. I, quaestiuncula 1^a, corp.

[19] Saint Thomas, *In IV Sent.*, dist. 25, q. 2, quaestiuncula 1^a ad 4um.

[20] Cf. Council of Trent, Session 22, chap. 1: DS 1741.

[21] Second Vatican Council, Dogmatic Constitution *Lumen Gentium*, 28: "Exercising within the limits of their authority the function of Christ as Shepherd and Head"; Decree *Presbyterorum Ordinis*, 2; "that they can act in the person of Christ the Head"; 6: "the office of Christ the Head and the Shepherd". Cf. Pope Pius XII, Encyclical Letter *Mediator Dei:* "the minister of the altar represents the person of Christ as the Head, offering in the name of all his members": *AAS* 39 (1947) p. 556; 1971 Synod of Bishops, *De Sacerdotio Ministeriali*, 1, 4; "[The priestly ministry] . . . makes Christ, the Head of the community, present . . .".

[22] Pope Paul VI, Encyclical Letter *Mysterium Fidei*, September 3, 1965: *AAS* 57 (1965) p. 761.

APPENDIX: II

REPORT OF PONTIFICAL BIBLICAL COMMISSION*

The Pontifical Biblical Commission was asked to study the role of women in the Bible in the course of research being carried out to determine the place that can be given to women today in the church.

The question for which an answer is especially sought is whether or not women can be ordained to the priestly ministry (especially as ministers of the eucharist and as leaders of the Christian community). In making this biblical inquiry, one must keep in mind the limits of such a study.

1. In general the role of women does not constitute the principal subject of biblical texts. One has to rely often on information given here and there. The situation of women in the biblical era was probably more or less favorable judging from the limited data that we have at our disposal.

2. The question asked touches on the priesthood, the celebrant of the eucharist and the leader of the local community. This is a way of looking at things which is somewhat foreign to the Bible.

A) Surely the New Testament speaks of the Christian people as a priestly people (1 Peter 2, 5.9; Apoc. 1,6; 5, 10). It describes that certain members of this people accomplish a priestly and sacrificial ministry (1 Peter 2,5.12; Rom 12,1; 15,16; Phil 2,17). However it never uses the technical term *hiereus* for the Christian ministry. *A fortiori* it never places *hiereus* in relationship with the eucharist.

B) The New Testament says very little on the subject of the ministry of the eucharist, Luke 22,19 orders the apostles to celebrate the eucharist in memory of Jesus (cf. 1 Cor 11,24). Acts 20,11 shows also that Paul broke the bread (see also Acts 27,35).

C) The pastoral epistles which give us the most detailed picture of the leaders of the local community (episkopos and presbyteroi), never attribute to them a eucharistic function.

3. Beyond these difficulties resulting from a study of the biblical data from the perspective of a later conception of the eucharistic priesthood, it is necessary to keep in mind that this conception itself is now placed in question as one can see in the more recent declarations of the magisterium which broaden the concept of priesthood beyond that of eucharistic ministry.

(*) reprint from *Origins* 6 (July 1, 1976) 92–96.

PART I

Woman's Place in the Family

1. "In the Beginning."

In Genesis, the "beginning" serves less to present the beginning of history than the fundamental plan of God for mankind. In Genesis 1, man and woman are called together to be the image of God (Gen 1,26f) on equal terms and in a community of life. It is in common that they receive rule over the world. Their vocation gives a new meaning to the sexuality that man possesses as the animals do.

In Gen. 2, man and woman are placed on equal terms: woman is for man a "helper who is his partner" (2,18), and by community in love they become "the two of them one body" (2,24). This union includes the vocation of the couple to fruitfulness but it is not reduced to that.

Between this ideal and the historical reality of the human race, sin has introduced a considerable gap. The couple's existence is wounded in its very foundations: love is degraded by covetousness and domination (3,16). The woman endures pains in her condition as mother which nevertheless put her closely in contact with the mystery of life. The social degradation of her condition is also related to this wound, manifested by polygamy (cf. Gen 4), divorce, slavery, etc. She is nevertheless the depository of a promise of salvation made to her descendants.

It is noteworthy that the ideal of Gen. 1 and 2 remained present in the thought of Israel like a horizon of hope: it is found again explicitly in the book of Tobias.

2. The Symbolism of the Sexes in the Old Testament

The Old Testament excluded the sexual symbolism used in Eastern mythologies, in relation to the fertility cults: there is no sexuality in the God of Israel. But very early, the biblical tradition borrowed traits from the family structure to trace pictures of God the Father. Then also it had recourse to the image of the spouse to work out a very lofty concept of the God of the covenant.

In correlation with these two fundamental images, the prophets gave value to the dignity of women by representing the people of God with the help of feminine symbols of the wife (in relation to God) and of the mother (in relation to the human partners of the covenant, men and women). These symbols were used particularly to evoke in advance the eschatological covenant in which God is to realize his plan in its fullness.

3. The Teachings of Jesus

Considering the social and cultural milieu in which Jesus lived, his teaching and behavior with regard to women are striking in their newness. We leave aside here his behavior (cf. the following reports). Questioned about divorce by the Pharisees (Mk. 10, 1-12), Jesus moves away from the rabbinic casuistry that, on the basis of Deut. 24,1, discriminated between the respective rights of men and women.

Reminding the Pharisees of the original plan of God (Gen. 1,27 and 2,24), he shows his intention of establishing here below a state of things that realizes the plan fully: the reign of God, inaugurated by his preaching and his presence, brings with it a full restoration of feminine dignity. But it brings also a surpassing of the ancient juridical structures in which repudiation showed the failure of marriage "by reason of the hardness of hearts." It is in this perspective that the practice of celibacy "for the sake of the kingdom of God" (Matt. 19,12), for himself and for those "to whom it is given" (19,11) is understood. His attitude toward women should be examined from that point of departure.

Thus Jesus inaugurates in the framework of the present world the order of things that constitutes the final horizon of the kingdom of God: that order will result, in "a new heaven and a new earth," in a state in which the risen will no longer need to exercise their sexuality (Matt. 21,31). Consequently, to represent the joy of the kingdom of heaven, Jesus can properly use the image of the virgins called to the wedding feast of the bridegroom (Matt. 25,1-10).

4. From the Mother of Jesus to the Church.

Considering the historical existence of Jesus, son of God sent into the world (Gal. 4,4 etc.), one might take a look at his beginnings.

The evangelists, Matthew and especially Luke, have made clear the irreplaceable role of his mother Mary. The value proper to femininity that the Old Testament presented are recapitulated in her, so that she accomplishes her unique role in the plan of God. But in the very accomplishment of this maternal role, she anticipates the reality of the new covenant of which her son will be the mediator. In fact she is the first one called to a faith that concerns her son (Luke 1,42) and to an obedience in which she "listens to the word of God and puts it into practice" (Luke 11,28, cf. 1,38).

Moreover, the Spirit who brings about in her the conception of Jesus (Luke 1,35, Matt. 1,18) will make a new people spring up in history on the day of Pentecost (Acts 2). Her historic role is therefore linked to a resumption of the feminine symbolism used to evoke the new people: from then on, the church is "our mother" (Gal. 4,20). At the end of time, it will be the "spouse of the Lamb" (Apoc. 21). It is by reason of this relationship between Mary, concrete woman, and the church, symbolic woman, that in Apoc. 12 the new humanity rescued from the power of sin and death can be presented as giving birth to Christ, her first born (Apoc. 12,4-15), expecting to have as posterity "those who keep the word of God and have the testimony of Jesus."

5. Woman in the Church

Nuptial symbolism is specifically taken up again by St. Paul to evoke the mystery of Christ and his church (Eph. 5,22-23). But it is first of all the relationship between Christ and the church, his body, which casts light on the reality forming the basis for Paul's approach.

Despite an institutional framework which implies the submission of women to their husbands (cf. Eph. 5,22; Col. 3,18; 1 Pt. 3,1), Paul reverses the perspective to emphasize their mutual submission (Eph. 5,21) and love (5,25.33) for which Christ's love is the source and model: charity (cf. 1 Cor. 13) becomes the measure of conjugal love. It is through it that the "original perfection" (that is to say the fullness of the plan of God for the human couple) can be attained (cf. Eph. 5,31 citing Gen. 2,24). That supposes only an equality of rights and duties explicitly affirmed (1 Cor. 7,3-4), but also an equality in adoptive sonship (Gal. 3,28, II Cor. 6,18) and in the reception of the Spirit who brings about participation in the life of the church (cf. Acts 2,17-18).

Marriage, having thus received its full meaning, thanks to its symbolic relationship with the mystery of Christ and the church (Eph. 5,32), can regain also its indissoluble solidity (1 Cor. 7,10-12; cf. Luke 16,18.).

At the heart of a sinful world, maternity has a saving value (1 Tim. 2,15). Outside conjugal life, the church grants a place of honor to consecrated widowhood (1 Tim. 5,3) and it recognizes in virginity the possible meaning of eschatological witness (1 Cor. 7,25-26) and of a more complete freedom to consecrate oneself to "the business of the Lord" (1 Cor. 7,32ff.). Such is the background against which theological reflection on the place and function of women in society and in the church takes place.

PART II

The Social Condition of Woman According to Biblical Revelation

I. The Bible, especially the New Testament, teaches very clearly the equality of man and woman in the spiritual domain (relationships with God) and in the moral area (relationships with other human beings). But the problem of the social condition of woman is a sociological problem that must be treated as such:

1. In terms of the laws of sociology: physical and psychosomatic data of feminine behavior in an earthly society;

2. In terms of the history of the societies in which the people of God lived during and after the composition of the Bible;

3. In terms of the laws of the church of Christ, his body, whose members live an ecclesial life under the direction of a magisterium instituted by Christ, while belonging to other societies and states.

II. The biblical experience shows that the social condition of woman has varied, but not in a linear manner as if there were continual progress. Ancient Egypt experienced a real flourishing of woman before the existence of Israel. The Israelite woman experienced a certain flourishing under the monarchy, then her condition became subordinate once more. In the time of Christ the status of woman appears, in Jewish society, inferior to what it is in Greco-Roman society where their lack of legal status is in the process of disappearing and in which "women handle their business themselves" (Gaius).

In relation to his contemporaries, Christ has a very original attitude with regard to woman which gives renewed value to her situation.

III. Christian society is established on a basis other than that of Jewish society. It is founded on the cornerstone of the risen Christ and is built upon Peter in collegiality with the twelve. According to the witness of the New Testament, especially the Pauline epistles, women are associated with the different charismatic ministries (diaconies) of the church (1 Cor. 12,4; 1 Tim. 3,11, cf. 8): prophecy, service, probably even apostolate . . . without, nevertheless, being of the twelve. They have a place in the liturgy at least as prophetèsses. (1 Cor. 11,4). But according to the Pauline corpus (1 Cor. 14,33-35; cf. 1 Tim. 2,6-15) an apostle such as Paul can withdraw the word from them.

This Christian society lives not only on the government of the twelve who are called apostles in Luke and elsewhere in the New Testament, but also on the liturgical sacramental life in which Christ communicates his spirit as high priest no longer according to Aaron but according to Melchisedech, king and priest (Heb. 8; cf. Ps. 110).

Sociologically speaking, in Jewish society, therefore for Christians until the break, the consecrated priesthood of Aaron (Lev. 9) assured an authentic liturgical and sacrificial life in the temple of stone. But Christ is the true high priest and the true temple (John 2,21). He was consecrated and sent (hagiazein, apostellein) by the Father (Jn. 10,26), and he consecrates himself in order to consecrate the apostles in the truth that he himself is (Jn. 17,17.19). It is a fundamental characteristic of the society that is the church in the midst of other societies, that it dispenses eternal life through its own liturgy.

IV. The problem is to know whether in Christian society ruled by the apostles — the twelve, Paul, Titus, Timothy — and by their successors (bishops, presbyters, higoumenes) women can be called to participate in this liturgical ministry and in the direction of local communities, as the queens of the Old Testament, especially widows, were called to participate in the royal functions of anointed kings. In fact in the New Testament no text formally supports this hypothesis, even though one may note the role of widows in the pastoral epistles (1 Tim. 5) and what Luke says of Anna in the Temple (latreuein). This study is no longer a matter of sociology, but of the labors of our third section (condition of woman in cult).

PART III

Ecclesial Condition of Woman

Old Testament

In the Old Testament, the Yahwist religion was not reserved to men alone, as is said elsewhere. Women as well as men could have sacrifices offered, participate in worship. Nevertheless, contrary to the customs of the contemporary pagan peoples, the worship of the second temple was exclusively reserved to men of the tribe of Levi (not only the function of priests, but also that of cantor, porter, etc.).

Moreover, there are women who bore the name of prophetess (Miriam, Deborah, Huldah, Noadiah), while not playing the role of the great prophets. Other women exercised an important function for the salvation of the people of God at critical moments of this people's history (for example, Judith, Esther) (cf. section 2).

(Amendment of Father Wambacq:) "In the Old Testament, the Yahwist religion was not a religion in which women were excluded, as is sometimes held. Women as well as men could participate in worship. Contrary to the usages of the contemporary pagan peoples, the official exercise of the temple worship was reserved to men, in the second temple to those of the tribe of Levi."

The Gospels

In striking contrast to the contemporary usages of the Jewish world, we see Jesus surrounding himself with women who follow him and serve him (Luke 8,2-3). Mary of Bethany is even described as the exemplary disciple "listening to the word" (Luke 10,38-42). It is the women who are charged with announcing the resurrection "to the apostles and to Peter." (Mark 16,7).

The fourth gospel stresses this role of witness attributed to women: the Samaritan woman, whose mere conversation with Jesus had astonished the apostles, goes carrying her witness to Jesus to her fellow citizens. After the resurrection, the evangelist emphasizes the role of Mary Magdalene whom tradition will call "the apostle of the apostles."

Acts and Paul

As Christianity spread, women took a notable part. That again distinguished the new religion sharply from contemporary Judaism.

Some women collaborated in the properly apostolic work. This is shown at numerous points in the Acts and the epistles. We shall limit ourselves to a few of them.

In the establishment of local communities, they are not content with offering their houses for meetings, as Lydia (Acts 16,14-15), the mother of Mark (Acts 12,12), Prisca (Rom. 16,5), but, according to Phil. 4,2, for example, Evodia and Syntyche are explicitly associated with "Clement and the other collaborators of Paul" in the community. Of the 27 persons thanked or greeted by Paul in the last chapter of the Epistle to the Romans, nine or perhaps 10 are women. In the case of several of them, Paul insists on specifying that they have tied themselves for the community, using a Greek verb (kopian) most often used for the work of evangelization properly so called.

The case of Prisca and her husband Aquila whom Paul calls "his collaborators in Christ" and of whom he says that "to them are indebted not only himself but all the churches of the Gentiles" (Rom. 16,3-4), shows us concretely an example of this "collaboration": their role in the story of Appollos is well known (Acts 18,24-28).

Paul mentions explicitly a woman as "deacon" (diaconos) of the church of Cenchrees, who "was also," he says, "for many Christians and for himself a protectress' (Rom. 16,1-2). In the pastoral epistles, the women indicated after the bishops and the deacons probably had a status of diaconos (1 Tim. 3,11). Also notable is the case of Junias or Junio, placed in the rank of the apostles (Rom. 16,7), with regard to whom one or another raises the question of whether it is a man.

PART IV

Reply to the Question about the Eventual Ordination of Women to the Priesthood

1. The Ministry of Leadership According to Jesus and the Apostolic Church

In establishing the kingdom of God, Jesus, during his ministry, chose a group of 12 men who, after the fashion of the 12 patriarchs of the Old Testament, would be the leaders of the renewed people of God (Mk. 3:14-19). These men whom he destined to "sit upon twelve thrones judging the twelve tribes of Israel (Mt. 19:28) were first sent to "proclaim that the kingdom of heaven is at hand." (Mt. 10:7).

After his death and resurrection, Christ confided to his apostles the mission of evangelizing all nations (Mt. 28:19, Mk. 16:5). These men would become his witnesses, beginning at Jerusalem and reaching to the ends of the earth (Acts 1:8, Lk. 24:47). "As my Father sent me," he told them, "I also send you" (Jn. 20:21).

Upon leaving the earth to return to his Father, he also delegated to a group of men whom he had chosen the responsibility to develop the kingdom of God and the authority to govern the church. The apostolic group thus established by the Lord appeared thus, by the testimony of the New Testament, as the basis of a community which has continued the work of Christ, charged to communicate to humanity the fruits of his salvation.

As a matter of fact, we see in the Acts of the Apostles and the epistles that the first communities were always directed by men exercising the apostolic power.

The Acts of the Apostles show that the first Christian community of Jerusalem knew only one ministry of leadership, which was that of the apostles: this was the urministerioum from which all the others derived. It seems that, very early, the Greek community received its own structure, presided over by the college of seven (Acts 6:5). A little later there was a question for the Jewish group about a college of presbyters (*ibid.* 11:30). The church at Antioch was presided over by a group of "five prophets and teachers" (*ibid.* 13:1). At the end of their first missionary journey, Paul and Barnabas installed presbyters in the newly founded churches (*ibid.* 14:23).

There were also presbyters at Ephesus (*ibid.*, 20:17), to whom were given the name of bishop (*ibid.* 20:28).

The epistles confirm the same picture: There are proistamenoi in 1 Thess, 5:12 (cf. 1 Tim. 5:17 "hoi kalos proestotes presbyteroi"), of Christian presbyteroi (1 Tim 5:1,2,17,19; Titus 1,5; James 5,4; 1 Pet. 5:1,5), of episkopoi, of hegoumenoi (Heb. 13:7,13,24; cf. Lk. 22:26).

1 Cor 16:16 recommends "submission" to Christians regarding those of the "house of Stephanas" who were sent for the service of the saints.

Whatever this last designation may be, (verse 17 speaks of Stephanus, Fortunatus and Achaikos), all that we can know of those who held a role of leadership in the communities leads to the conclusion that this role was always held by men (in conformity with the Jewish custom). (N.B. The "presbytides" mentioned in Titus 2:3 were elderly women, and not priestesses.)

The masculine character of the hierarchical order which has structured the church since its beginning thus seems attested to by scripture in an undeniable way. Must we conclude that this rule must be valid forever in the church?

We must however recall that according to the gospels, the Acts and St. Paul, certain women made a positive collaboration in service to the Christian communities.

Yet one question must still always be asked: What is the normative value which should be accorded to the practice of the Christian communities of the first centuries?

2. The Ministry of Leadership and the Sacramental Economy.

One of the essential elements of the church's life is the sacramental economy which gives the life of Christ to the faithful. The administration of this economy has been entrusted to the church for which the hierarchy is responsible.

Thus the question is raised about the relationship between the sacramental economy and the hierarchy.

In the New Testament the primordial role of the leaders of the communities seems always to lie in the field of preaching and teaching. These are the people who have the responsibility of keeping the communities in line with the faith of the apostles.

No text defines their charge in terms of a special power permitting them to carry out the eucharistic rite or to reconcile sinners.

But given the relationship between the sacramental economy and the hierarchy, the administration of the sacraments should not be exercised independently of this hierarchy. It is therefore within the duties of the leadership of the community that we must consider the issue of eucharistic and penitential ministry.

In fact there is no proof that these ministries were entrusted to women at the time of the New Testament. Two texts (1 Cor. 14:33-35 and 1 Tm. 2:11-15) forbid women to speak and to teach in assemblies. However, without mentioning doubts raised by some about their Pauline authenticity, it is possible that they refer only to certain concrete situations and abuses. It is possible that certain other situations call on the church to assign to women the role of teaching which these two passages deny them and which constitute a function belonging to the leaders.

Is it possible that certain circumstances can come about which call on the church to entrust in the same way to certain women some sacramental ministries?

This has been the case with baptism which, though entrusted to the apostles (Mt. 28:19 and Mk. 16:15f.) can be administered by others as well. We know that at least later, it will be entrusted also to women.

Is it possible that we will come to this even with the ministry of eucharist and reconciliation which manifest eminently the service of the priesthood of Christ carried out by the leaders of the community?

It does not seem that the New Testament by itself alone will permit us to settle in a clear way and once and for all the problem of the possible accession of women to the presbyterate.

However, some think that in the scriptures there are sufficient indications to exclude this possibility, considering that the sacraments of eucharist and reconciliation have a special link with the person of Christ and therefore with the male hierarchy, as borne out by the New Testament.

Others, on the contrary, wonder if the church hierarchy, entrusted with the sacramental economy, would be able to entrust the ministries of eucharist and reconciliation to women in light of circumstances, without going against Christ's original intention.

NOTE: Seventeen members present at the plenary session of the Pontifical Biblical Commission, voted on various aspects of the report. They agreed unanimously that the New Testament by itself does not seem able to settle in a clear way and once and for all whether women can be ordained priests. The members voted 12–5 that scriptural grounds alone are not enough to exclude the possibility of ordaining women.

Contributors

This book shares with a wide audience the dialog which certain faculty members of the CATHOLIC THEOLOGICAL UNION AT CHICAGO conducted with one another about priesthood and the ministerial role of women within the Roman Catholic Church. The vigorous interaction within these chapters displays a key idea of this school, *union* on a theological and pastoral level.

Established in 1967, the Catholic Theological Union brought together within the framework of a single, accredited institution the faculties, student bodies, libraries and other resources of formerly independent seminaries. The school endeavors to reflect and nurture the variety and richness of theological and religious traditions entrusted to a number of religious communities within the Roman Catholic Church, and to carry on the work of theological education in an ecumenical, university and urban setting.

Catholic Theological Union serves as a theological center for seventeen religious communities engaged in stateside and overseas ministries. It welcomes all men and women seeking theological education for ministry within the Roman Catholic Church.

DISMAS BONNER, O.F.M., holds the doctorate in Church Law from the Catholic University of America. He is Professor of Church Law at Catholic Theological Union. He has done extensive work with religious communities of both men and women, conducting retreats, workshops and study days, and has served as adviser to many communities in the work of revising their Constitutions. For over fourteen years he has served as canonical assistant to a federation of contemplative women.

ALCUIN COYLE, O.F.M., President of the Catholic Theological Union, received the Licentiate in Sacred Theology and the Doctorate in Church Law from the Antonianum, Rome. He was Vice Rector, Christ the King Seminary, St. Bonaventure University (1964–70), and on the faculty of the Washington Theological Union (1970–75). He is a consultant for the Conference of Major Superiors of Men, for the U.S. Bishops' Committee on the Permanent Diaconate, and a charter member and Trustee of the House of Affirmation.

DENNIS J. GEANEY, O.S.A., Director of Field Education at the Catholic Theological Union, summer school faculty of Immaculate Conception Seminary, Darlington, New Jersey, and St. Mary's Seminary, Orchard Lake, Michigan. He currently contributes to *U.S. Catholic* and *National Catholic Reporter* and is author of many books. He has recently completed an Association of Theological Schools project on non-ordained ministry.

CAROL FRANCES JEGEN, B.V.M., holds a doctorate in Religious Studies from Marquette University and is Director of the Graduate Program in Religious Studies at Mundelein College for women. She served on the National Advisory Council to the U.S. Conference of Catholic Bishops from 1969 to 1974. St. Mary of the Woods,Indiana, bestowed an Honorary Doctorate on her, 1977, as a "leader for justice in the theological order." She is a member of the Board of Trustees at Catholic Theological Union.

ROBERT J. KARRIS, O.F.M., Associate Professor of New Testament Studies, obtained his doctorate from Harvard Divinity School. Besides his editing and publishing commitments, he is deeply committed to the continuing education of clergy and religious women and men. He has been actively involved in the summer M.A. Program in Sacred Science at St. Bonaventure University, heavily subscribed to by religious women.

RALPH A KEIFER, Associate Professor of Liturgy at Catholic Theological Union and in Notre Dame University's Summer Graduate Program in Liturgical Studies. M.A. and Ph.D. in Theology from Notre Dame University. Also taught at Duquesne University, St. Mary's College, Notre Dame, Indiana, Catholic University, St. Mary's Seminary in Baltimore. General Editor for the International Committee on English in the Liturgy, 1971–73. Author of numerous articles and co-author of several books. Married and father of three children.

SEBASTIAN MAC DONALD, C.P., Professor of Moral Theology, received his doctorate from the University of St. Thomas (the former Angelicum) in Rome. He has published on moral issues and has lectured across the country. He has directed many workshops for religious women. He has held administrative positions within his religious congregation and has been actively involved in community organizations in the city of Chicago.

THOMAS MORE NEWBOLD, C.P., Emeritus Professor in Pastoral Theology and Psychology. He did his doctoral work in theology and psychology at L'Institut d'Etudes Médiévales d'Albert le Grand, and the University of Montreal. He has conducted workshops, retreats and special programs for religious communities of men and women in the U.S., Europe and Asia, and has served as consultant for several religious communities during the post-Vatican II period.

CAROLYN OSIEK, R.S.C.J., Assistant Professor of New Testament, is completing a doctorate in New Testament and Christian Origins at Harvard Divinity School. She has collaborated on several studies regarding the ministry of women, and has done extensive research on women in the early church. In 1976–77 she was Research/Resource Associate in Women's Studies at Harvard Divinity School.

GILBERT OSTDIEK, O.F.M., Professor of Doctrinal Theology, holds the doctorate from the Pontifical Athenaeum Antonianum, Rome. Work with early leaders in the deaconess movement in the 1960's triggered his interest in the question of women in ministry. Since then, he has actively engaged in workshops and theology programs preparing women for ministry at the Catholic Theological Union, where he served as dean for six years, and at St. Bonaventure University.

HAYIM G. PERELMUTER, Chautauqua Professor of Jewish Studies at the
Catholic Theological Union, where he offers courses in Rabbinic Judaism and
the Early Church, the liturgy of the synagogue, Jewish Mysticism and Mes-
sianism. His degrees include M.H.L., Jewish Institute of Religion, New York;
D.D., Hebrew Union College, Cincinnati; and D.H.L. (Cand.), Hebrew Union
College-Hebrew University, Jerusalem. Rabbi of K.A.M. Isaiah-Israel Congregation; President-elect of the Chicago Board of Rabbis.

CARROLL STUHLMUELLER, C.P., Professor of Old Testament Studies,
completed doctoral work at the Pontifical Biblical Institute, Rome. Besides
publications, he has lectured in the U.S. and abroad, including l'Ecole Biblique, Jerusalem. In 1957 he was teaching in the first graduate school of
theology for women in U.S. (St. Mary's College, Notre Dame, Ind.) and since
then has been researching the topics of religious leadership and the role of
women in the Church.

HYANG SOOK CHUNG YOON received her B.A. in English literature and
M.A. in Educational Administration from Seoul National University in Korea.
She received her M.L.S. from the University of Texas at Austin. Since 1971
she has been assistant professor of bibliography, Catholic Theological Union,
and is librarian in charge of Technical Services. Mrs. Yoon has been active in
library associations, such as the ALA, ATLA, CATLA and CCTS.

INDEX TO BIBLICAL REFERENCES

INDEX TO MODERN AUTHORS

Index to References to the Vatican
Declaration on Women Ordination*

*References follow the paragraph numbers according to the text printed in this book, pages 212–225

GENERAL INDEX

245